5ᵗʰSemester

Renewable Power Generation Systems

Module I: **(15 Hours)**

Introduction: Conventional energy Sources and its Impacts, Non conventional energy–
Seasonal variations and availability, Renewable energy – sources and features, Distributed
energy systems and dispersed generation (DG). Solar Energy: Solar processes and spectral
composition of solar radiation. Solar Thermal system-Solar collectors, Types and
performance characteristics, Applications-Solar water heating systems(active & passive) ,
Solar space heating & cooling systems , Solar desalination systems, Solar cooker. Solar
photovoltaic system-Operating principle, Photovoltaic cell concepts, Cell, module,
array, Losses in Solar Cell, Effects of Shadowing-Partial and Complete Shadowing, Series
and parallel connections, Cell mismatching, Maximum power point tracking, Applications
Battery charging,Pumping,Lighting,Peltier cooling. Modeling of PV cell.

Module II: **(10 Hours)**

Wind Energy: Wind energy, Wind energy conversion; Wind power density, efficiency limit
for wind energy conversion, types of converters, aerodynamics of wind rotors, power ~ speed
and torque speed characteristics of wind turbines, wind turbine control systems; conversion to
electrical power: induction and synchronous generators, grid connected and self excited
induction generator operation, constant voltage and constant frequency generation with power
electronic control single and double output systems, reactive power compensation,
Characteristics of wind power plant, Concept of DFIG.

Module III: **(9 Hours)**

Biomass Power: Principles of biomass conversion, Combustion and fermentation, Anaerobic
digestion, Types of biogas digester, Wood gassifier, Pyrolysis, Applications. Bio gas, Wood
stoves, Bio diesel, Combustion engine, Application.

Module IV: **(6 Hours)**

Hybrid Systems: Need for Hybrid Systems, Range and type of Hybrid systems, Case studies
Of Diesel-PV, Wind-PV, Microhydel-PV, Biomass-Diesel systems, electric and hybrid electric
vehicles.

Text Books:

[1] Godfrey Boyle"Renewable Energy- Power for a Sustainable Future",Oxford
University Press.
[2] B.H.Khan, "Non-Conventional Energy Resources",Tata McGrawHill, 2009.
[3] S. N. Bhadra, D. Kastha, S. Banerjee, "Wind Electrical Systems",Oxford University
Press, 2005.

Reference Books:

[1] S. A. Abbasi, N. Abbasi, "Renewable Energy Sources and Their Environmental
Impact", Prentice Hall of India, New Delhi, 2006

.Digital Learning Resources:

Course Name: Energy Resources and Technology
Course Link: https://nptel.ac.in/courses/108/105/108105058/
Course Instructor: Prof. S Banerjee, IIT Kharagpur

Module-1

Energy Sources:- Energy storage can be defined as means of storing energy in a readily recoverable form when the supply exceeds the demand for use at other times. Storage of primary fuels (e.g. coal, oil and gas) is also a form of energy storage, but the term 'energy storage' generally applies to secondary energy rather than primary energy.

Classification:-
Energy resources can be classified on the basis of following criteria:

1. Based on Usability of Energy

a) Primary resources- Examples of primary energy resources are coal, crude oil, sunlight, wind, running rivers, vegetation and radioactive material like uranium etc.

These resources are generally available in raw forms and are therefore, known as raw energy resources. Generally, this form of energy cannot be used as such. These are located, explored, extracted, processed and are converted to a form as required by the consumer.

$$\text{Energy Yield Ratio} = \frac{\text{Energy received from raw energy source}}{\text{Energy spent to obtain raw energy source}}$$

(b) Secondary Resources The energy resources supplied directly to consumer for utilization after one or more steps of transformation are known as secondary or usable energy, e.g. electrical energy, thermal energy (in the form of steam or hot water), refined fuels or synthetic fuels such as hydrogen fuels, etc.

2. Based on Traditional Use

(a) Conventional Energy resources, which are being traditionally used, for many decades and were in common use around oil crisis of 1973, are called conventional energy resources, e.g. fossil fuels, nuclear and hydro resources.

(b) Non-conventional Energy resources, which are considered for large-scale use after the oil crisis of 1973, are called non-conventional energy sources, e.g. solar,wind, biomass, etc.

3. Based on Long-Term Availability

(a) Non-renewable Resources, which are finite and do not get replenished after their consumption, are called non-renewable e.g. fossil fuels, uranium, etc. They are likely to deplete with time.

(b) Renewable Renewable energy is energy obtained from sources that are essentially inexhaustible. Examples of renewable resources include wind power, solar power, geothermal energy, tidal power and hydroelectric power. The most important feature of renewable energy is that it can be harnessed without the release of harmful pollutants.

4. Based on Commercial Application

(a) Commercial Energy Resource-The energy sources that are available in the market for a definite price are known as commercial energy. Most important forms of commercial energy are electricity, coal and refined petroleum products. Applications of solar energy, wind energy, hydro energy for electricity and lifting water from the ground require technology are termed as commercial energy sources.

(b) Non-commercial Energy The energy sources that are not available in the commercial market for a price are classified as non-commercial energy. All energy sources which are available in nature like wind, sun, hydro etc. are non-commercial energy sources. Non-commercial energy sources include fuels such as firewood, cattle dung and agricultural wastes, which are traditionally gathered, and not bought at a price, used especially in rural households.

5. Based on origin

(a) Fossil fuels energy
(b) Nuclear energy

(c) Hydro energy
(d) Solar energy
(e) Wind energy
(f) Biomass energy
(g) Geothermal energy
(h) Tidal energy
(i) Ocean thermal energy
(j) Ocean wave energy

Consumption trend of Primary Energy resources

The global average consumption trend of various primary energy resources of the world is indicated in Fig. 1.

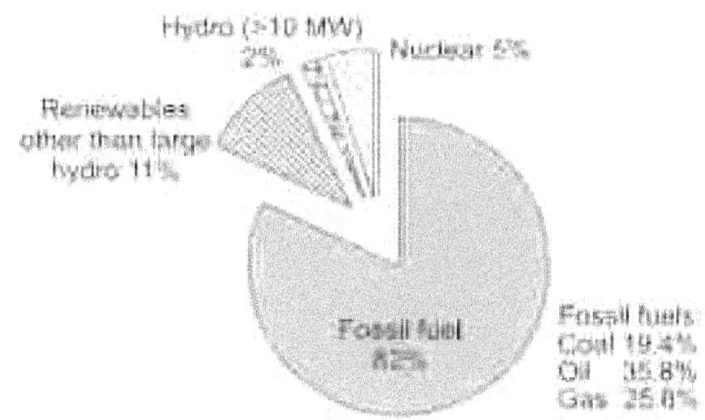

Fig .1

Importance of non-conventional energy sources

The concern for environment due to ever-increasing use of fossil fuels and rapid depletion of these resources has led to development of alternative sources of energy, **which are** renewable and environment friendly. **Following points may be mentioned in this connection:**

1. Conventional sources (except hydro) are non-renewable and finite **assets. With present rate of consumption** their availability is rapidly declining.
 2. **The** demand of energy is increasing exponentially **due to rapid industrialization and population growth,** the conventional sources of energy alone will not be sufficient in the long run, to meet the growing demand.
 3. Conventional sources (fossil fuels, nuclear) **also** cause pollution **leading to degradation of the environment. Ultimately,** their use has to be restricted **within acceptable limits.**
 4. **Large hydro resources affect wild life, cause** deforestation **and pose** various social problems.

Due to these reasons it has become important to explore and develop nonconventional energy resources **to reduce too much dependence on conventional resources. However, the present trend of developments of non-conventional sources indicate that these** will serve as supplement rather than substitute for conventional sources **for some more time to come.**
Realizing the importance of non-conventional energy sources, in March 1981 **the government of India established a** Commission for Additional Sources of Energy (CASE) **in the Department of Science and Technology, on the lines of the Space and Atomic Energy Commissions.**

Energy Chain

The energy available from primary energy source is known as raw energy. This energy undergoes one or more transformation stages before supplying to consumer. The sequence of energy transformations between primary and secondary energy (usable energy) is known as energy chain or energy route.

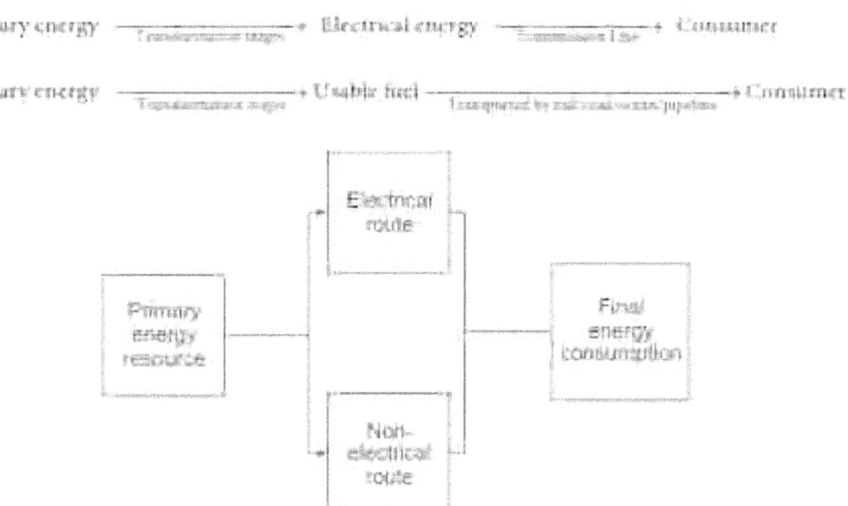

Figure 1.3 Energy routes

Common forms of Energy
1. Electrical Energy
2. Mechanical Energy
3. Thermal Energy
4. Chemical Energy

Advantages and disadvantages of Conventional Energy Sources

Advantages
1. Cost : At present these are cheaper than non-conventional sources.
2. Security : As storage is easy and convenient, by storing certain quantity, the energy availability can be ensured for certain period.
3. Convenience: These sources are very convenient to use as technology for their conversion and use is universally available.

Disadvantages
1. Fossil fuels generate pollutants. Main pollutants generated in the use of these sources are CO, CO_2, NO_x, SO_2, particulate matter and heat. These pollutants degrade the environment, pose health hazards and cause various other problems. CO_x is mainly responsible for global warming also.
2. Coal is also a valuable petro-chemical and is used as raw material for various chemical, pharmaceuticals and paints, etc. industries. From long-term point of view it is desirable to conserve coal for future needs.
3. There are safety and technical issues with nuclear energy. Major problems associated with nuclear energy are as follows:
(a) The waste material generated in nuclear plants has radioactivity of dangerous level; it remains above safe limit for a long period of time and thus is a health hazard. Its safe disposal, which is essential to prevent radioactive pollution, is a challenging task. Also the disposed radioactive waste is required to be guarded for a long period (till its radioactivity level comes down to a safe limit) in order to prevent against going in wrong hands.
(b) Possibility of accidental leakage of radioactive material from reactor (as happened in Chernobyl, former USSR in April 1986)
(c) Uranium resource, for which the technology presently exists, has limited availability.
(d) Sophisticated technology is required for using nuclear resources. Only few countries possess the required expertise to use nuclear energy.
4. Hydroelectric plants are cleanest but large hydro-reservoirs cause following problems:
(a) As large land area submerges into water, it leads to deforestation
(b) Causes ecological disturbances such as earthquakes

(c) Affects wild life

(d) Causes dislocation of large population and their rehabilitation problems

Salient Features of Non-Conventional Energy Sources

Merits

1. Non-conventional sources are available in nature free of cost.
2. They produce no or very little pollution. Thus by and large they are environment friendly.
3. They are inexhaustible(unlimited).

Demerits

1. In general the energy is available in dilute form from these sources.
2. Though available freely in nature the cost of harnessing energy from non-conventional sources is generally high.
3. Uncertainty of availability: the energy flow depends on various natural phenomena beyond human control.
4. Difficulty in transporting this form of energy.
5. Difficulty in storage.

Environmental Aspect of Energy

Greenhouse effect:- Carbon dioxide (CO_2) envelope present around the globe in the atmosphere behaves similar to a glass pane and forms a big global green house. This tends to prevent the escape of heat from earth, which leads to global warming. This phenomenon is known as greenhouse effect.

Apart from CO_2, other gases behaving similar to CO_2 include methane, nitrous oxide (NO),hydro fluorocarbons (HFCs), chlorofluorocarbons (CFCs), hydro chlorofluorocarbons (HCFC), sulphur hexafluoride, ozone and water vapor. These gases are known as greenhouse gases (GHG). Their average concentrations in atmosphere along with Global Warming Potentials (GWPs) relative to CO_2 and atmospheric lifetimes are listed in Table 1.3.

S. N.	Name of the Gas	Concentration in ppm	GWP (100 yr time horizon)	Atmospheric lifetime (yrs)
1.	Carbon dioxide (CO_2)	400	1	100-300
2.	Methane (CH_4)	1.853	28	12
3.	Nitrous oxide (N_2O), commonly known as laughing gas	0.326	265	121
4.	Sulfur hexafluoride (SF_6)	negligible	23,500	3,200

Ex-

A chemical industry produces 5 Tg (teragrams) of NO per day. How much pollution is added into the atmosphere per day in terms of carbon equivalent?

Solution:-The Global Warming Potential (GWP) of NO is 265.

The daily pollution of NO = 5 Tg

The daily pollution in terms of equivalent CO_2 (ref. Table 1.3) = 5 × 265 = 1,325 Tg = 1,325 Million Tons of CO_2

As (12/44) is the carbon to CO_2 molecular weight ratio, the pollution in terms of Million Metric Tons of Carbon Equivalent (MMTCE) = 1,325 × (12/44)= 361.36 MMTCE

Global Warming:- 'Global warming is the continuing rise in the average temperature of the earth's atmosphere and ocean's surface due to greenhouse effect'.

World total primary energy consumption by fuel in 2018

Coal (27%)

Natural Gas (24%)

Hydro (renewables) (7%)

Nuclear (4%)

Oil (34%)

Others (renewables) (4%)

World energy consumption is the total energy produced and used by the entire human civilization.

Closely related to energy consumption is the concept of total primary energy supply (TPES), which – on a global level – is the sum of energy production minus storage changes.

Energy supply, consumption and electricity

Key figures (TWh)

Year	Primary energy supply (TPES) (MTOE)	Final energy consumption (MTOE)	Electricity generation (TWH)
1973	71,013 (Mtoe 6,106)	54,335 (Mtoe 4,672)	6,129
1990	102,569	–	11,821
2000	117,687	–	15,395
2010	147,899 (Mtoe 12,717)	100,914 (Mtoe 8,677)	21,431
2011	152,504 (Mtoe 13,113)	103,716 (Mtoe 8,918)	22,126
2012	155,505 (Mtoe 13,371)	104,426 (Mtoe 8,979)	22,668
2013	157,482 (Mtoe 13,541)	108,171 (Mtoe 9,301)	23,322
2014	155,481 (Mtoe 13,369)	109,613 (Mtoe 9,425)	23,816
2015	158,715 (Mtoe 13,647)	109,136 (Mtoe 9,384)	
2017	162,494 (Mtoe 13,972)	113,009 (Mtoe 9,717)	25,606

[1] converted from Mtoe into TWh (1 Mtoe = 11.63 TWh) and from Quad BTU into TWh (1 Quad BTU = 293.07 TWh)

World total primary energy supply (TPES), or "primary energy" differs from the world final energy consumption because much of the energy that is acquired by humans is lost as other forms of energy during the process of its refinement into usable forms of energy and its transport from its initial place of supply to consumers. For instance, when oil is extracted from the ground it must be refined into gasoline, so that it can be used in a car, and transported over long distances to gas stations where it can be used by consumers. World final energy consumption refers to the fraction of the world's primary energy that is used in its final form by humanity.

In 2014, world primary energy supply amounted to 155,481 terawatt-hour (TWh) or 13,541 million tonne of oil equivalent (Mtoe), while the world final energy consumption was 109,613 TWh or about 29.5% less than the total supply.[11] World final energy consumption includes products as lubricants, asphalt and petrochemicals which have chemical energy content but are not used as fuel. This non-energy use amounted to 9,723 TWh (836 Mtoe) in 2015.[12]

2018 World electricity generation (26,700 TWh) by source (IEA, 2019)[

Coal (38%)
Gas (23%)
Hydro and other (19%)
Nuclear (10%)
Solar PV and wind (7%)
Oil (3%)

Electricity Consumption

The total amount of electricity consumed worldwide was 19,504 TWh in 2013, 16,503 TWh in 2008, 15,105 TWh in 2005, and 12,116 TWh in 2000. By the end of 2014, the total installed electricity generating capacity worldwide was nearly 6.14 TW (million MW) which only includes generation connected to local electricity grids.[16] In addition there is an unknown amount of heat and electricity consumed off-grid by isolated villages and industries. In 2014, the share of world energy consumption for electricity generation by source was coal at 41%, natural gas at 22%, nuclear at 11%, hydro at 16%, other sources (solar, wind, geothermal, biomass, etc.) at 6% and oil at 4%. Coal and natural gas were the most used energy fuels for generating electricity. The world's electricity consumption was 18,608 TWh in 2012.[citation needed] This figure is about 18% smaller than the generated electricity, due to grid losses, storage losses, and self-consumption from power plants (gross generation). Cogeneration (CHP) power stations use some of the heat that is otherwise wasted for use in buildings or in industrial processes.

In 2016 the total world energy came from 80% fossil fuels, 10% biofuels, 5% nuclear and 5% renewable (hydro, wind, solar, geothermal). Only 18% of that total world energy was in the form of electricity.[17] Most of the other 82% was used for heat and transportation.

World total primary energy consumption by fuel in 2018[2]

Coal (27%)
Natural Gas (24%)
Hydro (renewables) (7%)

Nuclear (4%)
Oil (34%)
Others (renewables) (4%)

By source

Oil (32.0%)
Coal/peat/shale (27.1%)
Natural gas (22.2%)
Biofuels and waste (9.5%)
Hydro electricity (2.5%)
Others (renewables) (1.8%)
Nuclear (4.9%)

Availability of resources and future trend

The energy sources like coal and petroleum products take million years for production. These energy sources are going to be exhausted after few years. These energy sources are termed as *non-renewable energy sources.*

Energy sources like solar, wind, hydro, various forms of biomass and marine energy (wave & tidal) are never exhaustible. These are termed as *renewable energy sources.* Geothermal and ocean thermal energy sources are also renewable energy sources.

* The global primary energy supply and consumption is in table below.

Table: Annual primary energy consumption by fuel (2012) in Mtoe*

Country	Oil	Natural Gas	Coal	Nuclear Energy	Hydro-Electric	Renewable & Waste	Total
USA	884	594	615.7	83.8	28.2	77.3	2,283
Canada	152	83	31	9.4	68.6	NA	344
France	83	45	12.4	43.9	14.8	67.4	266.5
Russian Federation	494	438	153	16.3	35.6	NA	1136.9
United Kingdom	76.8	71.2	39.1	20.1	1.3	NA	208.5
China*	436	98.1	2500	12.3	58.5	103.1	3208
India*	205.5	47.1	352	4.1	11.4	98.4	718.5
Japan	199	93	71.6	25.8	8.3	98.1	495.8
Others	1807.3	1276.6	114.5	501.4	70.0	524.1	4293.9
Total	4337.6	2746	3889.3	717.1	296.7	968.4	12995.1

Mtoe-   Million tons of oil equivalent.

Renewable Energy Sources:-

The capacity addition in renewable energy was about 27,300 MW in 2012.

Technology	Capacity Installed in MW by 2012.
Coal	11,202
Hydro	38,990
Renewable	27,300
Gas	18,381
Nuclear	4,780
Total	201,473

Table: India's Installed power generation capacity.

So, total renewable energy's contribution becomes almost 33% (includes Hydro power), plan wise grid connected renewable energy contribution is given in Table below.

Table: Power densities of *renewable energy sources* and *the conventional energy forms*.

Renewable Energy Sources	In KW/m^2
Wave	< 100
Extra terrestrial solar radiation	< 1.35
Wind	< 3
Solar radiation	0.2
Tidal	0.002
Biomass Production	0.002
Geothermal heat	0.00006

Conventional Energy	In KWh/m^2
Hot Plate	100
Coal	500
Nuclear	650
Power Cable	1000,000

Onshore wind energy potential is estimated to be around 49,130 MW at a height of 50 m. It is estimated that around 17% of wind energy is utilized whereas 25,000 MW Has been connected to the grid. Wind energy is considered to be a viable source to tackle the energy problems.

About 1/4th of energy used in India is in the form of biomass that consists of firewood, cattle dung, agriculture waste etc. This sector is managed by rural people without any technology, management and investment. Indian Govt. is promoting to use biomass to make deficit of energy. Studies have estimated that the biomass has potential of generating 17,000MW from agro and forest residues alone.

Biogas is a three decade old program across India which covers estimated 5 million installations.

India has put a national policy to replace the diesel and petrol by the production of biodiesel from *Jatropha, Karanja* and *Mahua* which has been tried for last two decades; and ethanol was considered to be successful replacement of petrol in transportation sector. The technology has been developed by Brazil in 1976 for successful of petrol and diesel. About 95% of cars sold in Brazil are flexible to run in both ethanol and petrol but this is not successful in India.

* Solar energy is distributed over the entire geographical region at the rate of 5-6 kwh/m^2/day. This can be utilized for the purpose of energy utilization in many thermal applications such as cooking or heating or in photovoltaic cells that convert sunlight to electricity.

India has launched a solar mission with an aim to install 20,000MW grid solar power, 2000MW off grid system, 20 million solar lights and20 million m^2 solar thermal collector by 2020.

Origin of Renewable Energy Sources:-

All available energy sources in the world that come from three different primary energy sources.

(i) Isotropic dissociation in the core of the earth.
(ii) Movements of the planets
(iii) Thermonuclear reactions in the earth.
* The largest energy flow comes from solar radiation, which is also responsible for the development of fossil energy sources, namely oil, coal and gas due to bio conversion which has occurred million years ago. All available natural renewable energy sources are presented in the diagram and their conversion is also shown below.

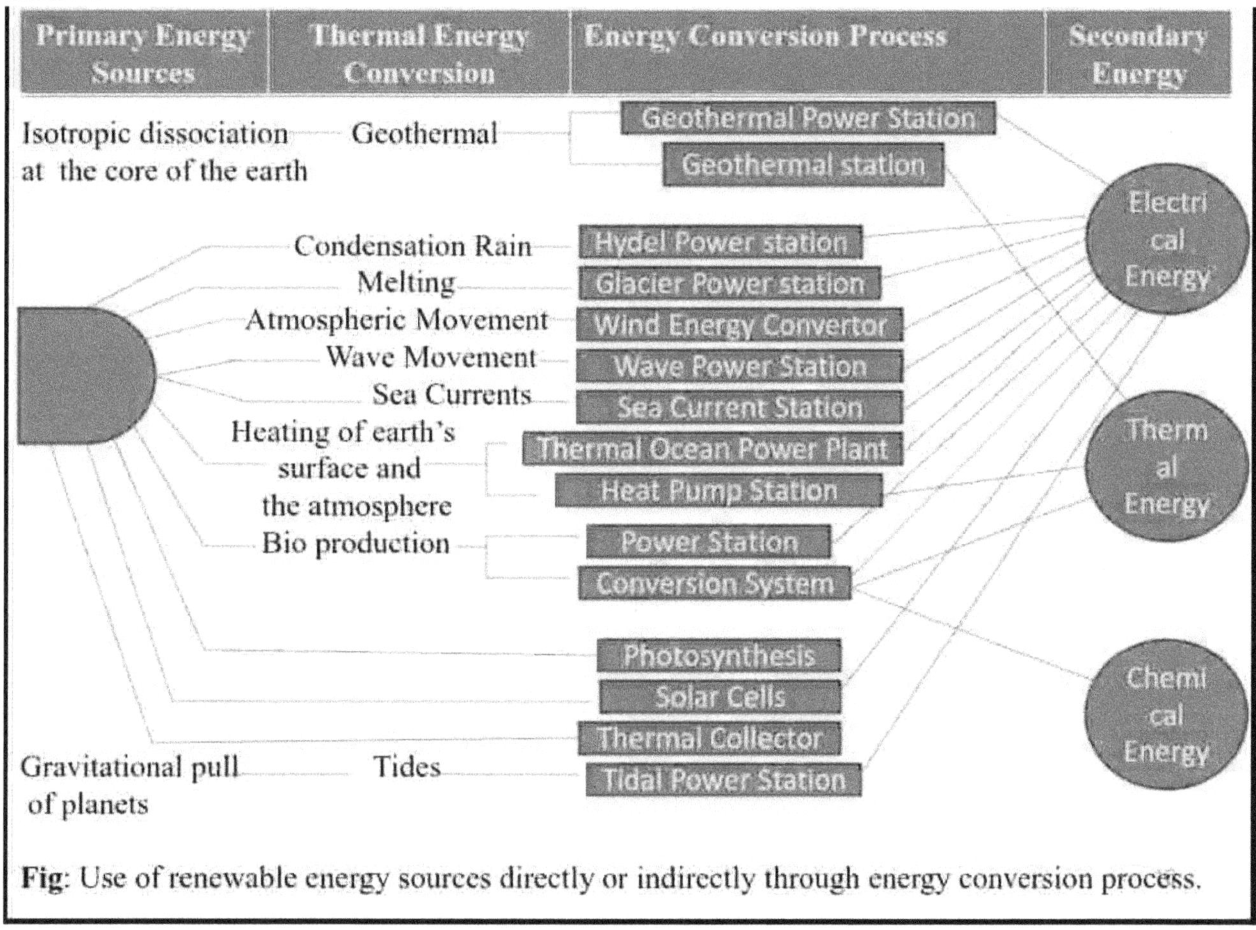

Fig: Use of renewable energy sources directly or indirectly through energy conversion process.

* Another source of energy is the geothermal energy originates from the earth's surface itself . The theoretical potential of geothermal energy is much lesser (less than by an order of 4) than the solar radiation.
* The third source of renewable energy is the movement of the planets . The force of attraction between planets and gravitational pull creates tide in the sea. This energy source magnitude is very less compared to geothermal energy.
Limitations:-
a) The real difficulty with the renewable energy sources are that the power density of those energies are very less in comparison to conventional energy sources.

b) Since the solar and wind energies fluctuate with respect to day and season; the surface area requirement will be large and so also storage device for heat and electricity. The thermal energy storage system (sensible heat storage systems) have low efficiency, while the phase change storage systems suffer density variations in two phases and stability over several cycles. Electrical storage device like batteries are heavy and not environment friendly.

New Delhi: India's renewable capacity installations reached 86 gigawatt (GW) as of 31 December, 2019, according to research firm JMK Research and Analytics. Wind energy became the biggest contributor with 44 per cent share in the total renewable energy mix followed by solar with 39 per cent share. Year wise installation trends in India

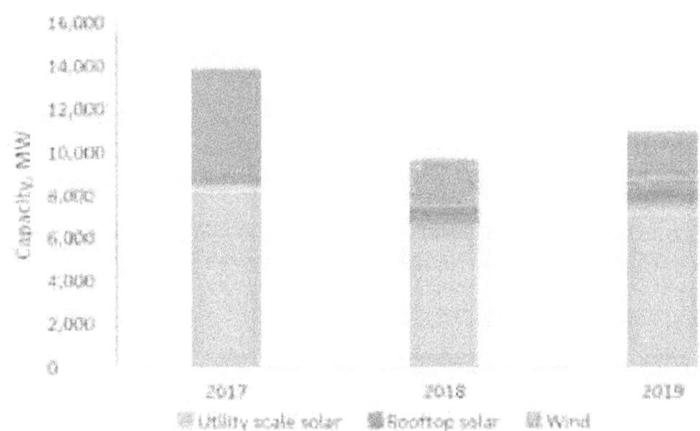

Sources: MNRE, JMK Research

"In 2019, about 7.5 GW of new utility scale solar capacity was added, which is about 14 per cent increase over the previous year. Another one GW was added in rooftop solar installations," it added.

About 2.4 GW of new wind capacity was added in 2019, which was a 10 per cent increase over 2018.

Gujarat led the installations with commissioning of 1.4 GW of new wind projects followed by Tamil Nadu with 650 MW and Maharashtra with 212 MW.

"Most of the wind projects allocated in 2018 and scheduled to commission in 2019 got delayed and are now likely to be commissioned in 2020. This delay in wind projects is primarily attributed to various land availability issues and lack of grid transmission availability," the research firm added.

Karnataka led the market with about 2 GW of new solar capacity additions followed by Rajasthan with 1.7 GW, Tamil Nadu with 1.5 GW, Gujarat with 936 MW, Andhra Pradesh with 917 MW, and Madhya Pradesh with 651 MW.

Distributed and Dispersed Generation

Distributed generation (DG) entails using many small generators, of 2-50 MW output, situated at numerous strategic points throughout cities and towns, so that each provides power to a small number of consumers nearby. While these small generators might be solar or wind turbine units, generating units in this category are most often highly efficient gas turbines in small combined cycle plants, because these are the most economical choices. Although small compared to traditional central station generators, such 2- 500 MW generating units are large, both physically and electrically compared to the needs of individual energy consumers., producing power for between 50 and 400 homes.

Dispersed generation refers to use of still smaller generating units, of less than 500 kW output and often sized to serve individual homes or businesses. These units are small enough to fit into garages or, like central air-conditioners, on a pad behind a house. Micro gas turbines, bel cells, diesel, and small wind and solar PV generators make up this category.

Basics of Distributed generation (DG)

Distributed generators include, but are not limited to synchronous generators, induction generators, reciprocating engines, micro-turbines (combustion turbines that run on high-energy fossil fuels such as oil, propane, natural gas, gasoline or diesel), combustion gas turbines, fuel cells, solar photo-voltaic, and wind turbines.

Applications of Distributed Generating Systems

There are many reasons a customer may choose to install a distributed generator.

- DG can be used to generate a customer's entire electricity supply; for peak shaving (generating a portion of a customer's electricity onsite to reduce the amount of electricity purchased during peak price periods); for standby or emergency generation (as a backup to Wires Owner's power supply); as a green power source (using renewable technology);or for increased reliability.
- In some remote locations, DG can be less costly as it eliminates the need for expensive construction of distribution and/or transmission lines.

Benefits of Distributed Generating Systems

Distributed Generation:

1. Has a lower capital cost because of the small size of the DG (although the investment cost per kVA of a DG can be much higher than that of a large power plant).

2. May reduce the need for large infrastructure construction or upgrades because the DG can be constructed at the load location.

3.If the DG provides power for local use, it may reduce pressure on distribution and transmission lines.

4. With some technologies, produces zero or near-zero pollutant emissions over its useful life (not taking into consideration pollutant emissions over the entire product lifecycle ie. pollution produced during the manufacturing, or after decommissioning of the DG system).

4. With some technologies such as solar or wind, it is a form of renewable energy. Can increase power reliability as back-up or stand-by power to customers. Offers customers a choice in meeting their energy needs.

Challenges associated with Distributed Generating Systems

- There are no uniform national interconnection standards addressing safety, power quality and reliability for small distributed generation systems.
- The current process for interconnection is not standardized among provinces.
- Interconnection may involve communication with several different organizations.
- The environmental regulations and permit process that have been developed for larger distributed generation projects make some DG projects uneconomical.
- Contractual barriers exist such as liability insurance requirements, fees and charges, and extensive paperwork.

Solar Energy: Solar processes and spectral composition of solar radiation.

- Solar energy is an important, clean, cheap and abundantly available renewable energy. It is received on Earth in cyclic, intermittent and dilute form with very low power density 0 to 1 kW/m^2.
- Solar energy received on the ground level is affected by atmospheric clarity, degree of latitude, etc.
- For design purpose, the variation of available solar power, the optimum tilt angle of solar flat plate collectors, the location and orientation of the heliostats should be calculated.

What is Solar Radiation?

Solar radiation is radiant (electromagnetic) energy from the sun. It provides light and heat for the Earth and energy for photosynthesis. This radiant energy is necessary for the metabolism of the environment and its inhabitants . The three relevant bands, or ranges, along the solar radiation spectrum are ultraviolet, visible (PAR), and infrared. Of the light that reaches Earth's surface, infrared radiation makes up 49.4% of while visible light provides 42.3% . Ultraviolet radiation makes up just over 8% of the total solar radiation. Each of these bands has a different impact on the environment.

- Solar radiation provides heat, light, and energy necessary for all living organisms. Infrared radiation supplies heat to all habitats, on land and in the water 24. Without solar radiation, Earth's surface would be about 32°C colder 25

- Solar energy, received in the form of radiation, can be converted directly or indirectly in to other forms of energy, such as heat and electricity. The major draw backs of the extensive application of solar energy of
1. the intermittent and variable manner in which it arrives at the earth's surface and
2. the large area require to collect the energy at a useful rate.

Energy is radiated by the sun as electromagnetic waves of which 99% have wave lengths in the range of 0.2 to 4.0 micro meter (1 micro meter $= 10\text{-}6$ meter)

<u>Solar constant</u>

The sun is a large sphere of very hot gases, the heat being generated by various kinds of fusion reactions. Its diameter is 1.39×10^6 km while that of earth is 1.27×10^4 km. the mean distance between the two is 1.5×10^8 km. although the sun is large, its subtends angle of only 32 min. at the earth's surface.

- The brightness of the sun varies from its center to its edge. However the calculation purpose the brightness all over the solar disc is uniform.

The total radiation from the sun is 5762 degrees K(i.eK=Kelvin)

The rate at which solar energy arise at the top of the atmosphere is called the solar constant I_{sc} . This is the amount of energy received in unit time on a unit area perpendicular to the sun's direction at the mean distance of the earth from the sun.

The solar constant value varies up to 3 % throughout the year, because the distance between the sun and the earth varies little throughout the year.

- The earth is close set of the sun during the summer and farthest during the winter.
- This variation in distance produces sinusoidal variation in the intensity of solar radiation I that reaches the earth.

$$I_{sc} = 1367 \text{ watts/m}^2$$

$$\frac{I}{I_{sc}} = 1+0.033 \cos\frac{360\,n}{365} \qquad \text{where n is the day of the year.}$$

Spectral distribution of solar radiation intensity at the outer limit of the atmosphere .

  - The luminosity of the Sun is about 3.86×1026 watts. This is the total power radiated out into space by the Sun. Most of this radiation is in the visible and infrared part of the electromagnetic spectrum, with less than 1 % emitted in the radio, UV and X-ray spectral bands.

- The sun's energy is radiated uniformly in all directions. Because the Sun is about 150 million kilometres from the Earth, and because the Earth is about 6300 km in radius, only 0.000000045% of this power is intercepted by our planet.

➤ The power of the sun at the earth, per square metre is called the solar constant and is approximately 1370 watts per square metre (W m-2).

➤ The solar constant actually varies by +/- 3% because of the Earth's slightly elliptical orbit around the Sun. The sun-earth distance is smaller when the Earth is at perihelion (first week in January) and larger when the Earth is at aphelion (first week in July). Some people, when talking about the solar constant, correct for this distance variation, and refer to the solar constant as the power per unit area received at the average Earth-solar distance of one "Astronomical Unit" or AU which is 149.59787066 million kilometres. There is also another small variation in the solar constant which is due to a variation in the total luminosity of the Sun itself. This variation has been measured by radiometers aboard several satellites since the late 1970's.

<u>Solar Radiation Measuring Instruments (Radiometers)</u>

A radiometer absorbs solar radiation at its sensor, transforms it into heat and measures the resulting amount of heat to ascertain the level of solar radiation. Methods of measuring heat include resulting amount of heat to ascertain the level of solar radiation.

➤ Methods of measuring heat include taking out heatflux as a temperature change (using a water flow pyrheliometer, a silver-disk pyrheliometer or a bimetallic pyranograph) or as a thermoelectromotive force (using a thermoelectric pyrheliometer or a thermo electric pyranometer).
In current operation, types using a thermopile are generally used.

➤ The radiometers used for ordinary observation are pyrheliometers and pyranometers that measure direct solar radiation and global solar radiation, respectively.

Pyrheliometers

A pyrheliometer is used to measure direct solar radiation from the sun and its marginal periphery. To measure direct solar radiation correctly, its receiving surface must be arranged to be normal to the solar direction. For this reason, the instrument is usually mounted on a sun-tracking device called an equatorial mount.

The structure of an Angstrom electrical compensation pyrheliometeris shown in Figure.2

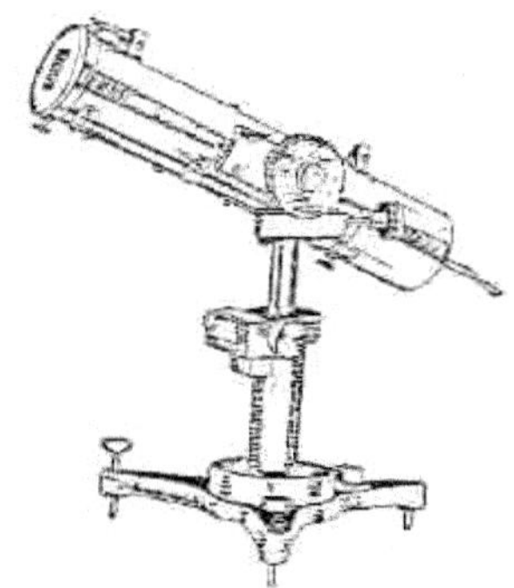

This pyrheliometer has a rectangular aperture, two manganin-strip sensors (20.0 mm × 2.0 mm×0.02 mm) and several diaphragms to let only direct sunlight reach the sensor. The sensor surface is painted optical black and has uniform absorption characteristics for short-wave radiation. A copper constantan thermocouple is attached to the rear of each sensor strip, and the thermocouple is connected to a galvanometer. The sensor strips also work as electric resistors and generate heat when a current flows across them.

Pyranometers:

 A pyranometer is used to measure global solar radiation falling on a horizontal surface. Its sensor has a horizontal radiation-sensing surface that absorbs solar radiation energy from the whole sky (i.e. a solid angle of 2p sr) and transforms this energy into heat. Global solar radiation can be ascertained by measuring thisheat energy. Most pyranometers in general use are now the thermopile type, although bimetallic pyranometers are occasionally found.

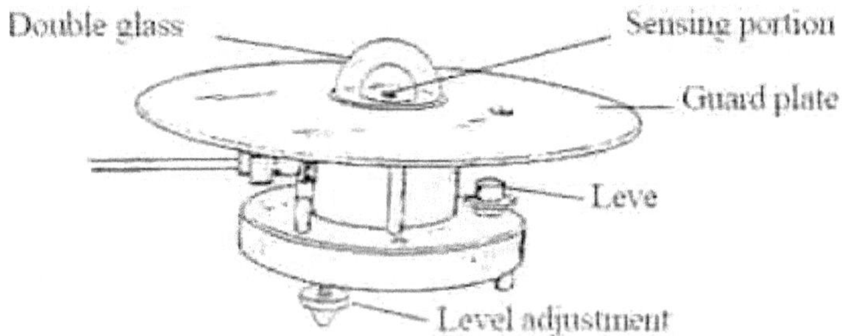

<u>**Sunshine recorder**</u>

 The duration of bright sunshine in a day is measured by means of sun shine recorder. The sun's rays are focused by a glass sphere to a point on a card strip held in a groove in spherical bowl mounted concentrically with the sphere. Whenever there is a bright sun shine the image formed is intensive enough to burn a part on the card strip. through out the day as sun moves across the sky, the image moves along the strip. Thus, a burnt trace whose length is proportional to the duration of sun shine is obtained on the strip.

<u>Solar Radiation Data</u>

 Most radiation data is measured for horizontal surfaces. As shown in figure. It is seen a fairly, smooth variations with the maximum occurring around noon is obtained on a clear day. In contrast an irregular variation with many peaks and valleys may be obtained on a cloudy day.

• Peak values are generally measured in April or may with parts of Rajasthan or Gujarat receiving over 600 Langley's per day.

• During the monsoon and winter months, the daily global radiation decreases to about 300- 400 longley per day.

• Annual average daily diffuse radiation received over the whole country is around 175 longleys per day.

• The maximum value is about 300 langleys in Gujarat in July, while the minimum values between 75 and 100 langleys per day, are measured over many parts of the country during November and December as winter sets in.

<u>Solar radiation on tilted surface:</u>

 The rate of receipt of solar energy on a given surface on the ground depends on the orientation of the surface with reference to the sun. A fully sun – tracking surface that always faces the sun receives the maximum possible solar energy at the particular location.

 A surface of the same area oriented in any other direction will receive a smaller amount of radiation because solar radiation is such a dilute form of energy, it is desirable to capture as much as possible on a ground area. Most of the solar collectors or solar radiation collecting devices are tilted at an angle to horizontal surface with Y=0 facing south for tilted surface.

$$\cos\theta = \sin\delta\,\sin(\phi - s) + \cos\delta\,\cos\omega\,\cos(\phi - s)$$

For horizontal surfaces $\cos\theta_r = \sin\phi\,\sin\delta + \cos\phi\,\cos\delta\,\cos\omega$

Tilt factor for beam radiation

$$\gamma_b = \frac{\cos\theta}{\cos\theta z}$$

$$\gamma_d = \left|\frac{1+\cos s}{2}\right|$$

Solar Radiation through atmosphere:

For estimating efficiencies of the solar systems, one usually takes sky conditions of AM =1.5 i.e. the radiation has to travel 1.5 times more through the atmosphere in comparison to the normal incidence.

Solar radiation without any scattering suffers considerable losses at all wavelength regions while passing through earth's atmosphere. For certain wavelengths, the atmosphere is completely opaque and it is not allowed to reach earth.

The solar radiation received on the earth without any scattering in the atmosphere is known as beam or direct radiation. *The solar radiation received on earth from the sun with multiple scattering is known as diffused or sky radiation.* Summation of both these components yields global solar radiation. The atmosphere also radiates energy to the earth and its intensity is higher than that of global radiation. This radiation is included in the region of long-wavelength radiation to the atmosphere. The earth also radiates back long-wavelength radiation to the atmosphere and part of which gets absorbed.

Table: Radiation balance on a receiving surface on earth.

No.	Incident radiation components	Symbol	No	Reflected radiation components	Symbol
1.	Direct solar radiation	I_D	5.	Reflected direct solar radiation	I_{DR}
2.	Sky radiation	I_d	6.	Reflected diffused sky radiation	I_{dr}
3.	$\sum 1+2$: Global radiation	I_G	7.	$\sum 5+6$: Reflected total radiation	I_{GR}
4.	Atmosphere radiation	I_g	8.	Reflected atmospheric radiation	I_{AR}
			9.	Radiation from the receiving surface	I_E
			10.	$\sum 8+9$: Total re-radiation from the receiving surface	I_R

$$\text{Rate of useful energy, } Q = (I_D) + I_d + I_g - (I_{DR} + I_{dr} + I_{AR} + I_E)$$

The Generalized Transmission Law:

The radiation balance of earth's system fluctuates w.r.t. time and location. The global radiation is affected by the wavelength of the scattering and absorptive radiation phenomena in the atmosphere. These are termed as extinction in meteorology. The radiation reaching the earth's surface can be calculated as:

$$dI_\lambda = -I_{0\lambda} a \, d_s \qquad W/m^2$$

where

dI_λ is the radiation of the remaining wavelength after the incident radiation of the same wavelength $I_{0\lambda}$ has travelled through distance d_s of the atmosphere (w/m²),

d_s is the distance travelled by the solar radiation in the atmosphere (m),

a is extinction coefficient (m⁻¹).

Integrating the above equation over the entire length of the atmosphere (m) yields the general transmission law for radiation passage through the atmosphere, i.e.

$$I = I_0 \exp(-a\,m) \qquad W/m^2$$

Where

I = radiation received on the earth, I_0 = extra-terrestrial radiation, m = air mass.

The transmission factor of the atmosphere

$$\tau_G = \frac{I}{I_G} = \exp(-a\,m)$$

The extinction coefficient (a) depends upon the transmission coefficient which consists of three factors.

$$\tau_G = \tau_{RS}\,\tau_{MS}\,\tau_{AB}$$

Where

τ_{RS} = transmission factor corresponding to Rayleigh scattering.

τ_{MS} = transmission factor due to Mie scattering

τ_{AB} = transmission factor due to absorption.

From the figure given below, the optical path length (m) can be calculated as:

$$m = \frac{H}{\sin \alpha_s} = \frac{H}{\cos Z} \ (m)$$

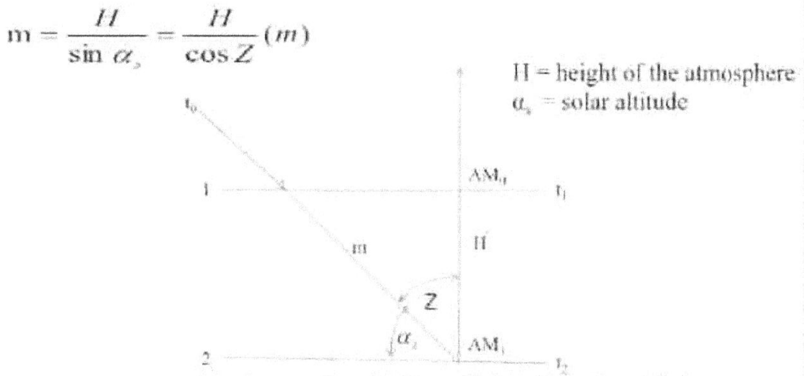

Fig: Penetration of solar radiation through an ideal plane atmosphere of constant density.

Instead of H, one can use only, $m = \dfrac{1}{\sin \alpha_s} = \dfrac{1}{\cos Z}$

<u>**Scattering by the atmosphere:-**</u>

The scattering of radiation by the atmosphere can be divided into two categories:
(i) Rayleigh scattering in molecules (f)
(ii) Mie scattering in aerosols.

The Rayleigh scattering takes place in particles, whose diameter is much smaller than the wavelength of the incident radiation. These particles scatter the *short wavelength of radiation* strongly. The scattered radiation is given by the expression:

$$I_{RS} = \frac{2\pi^2}{N\lambda^4}\left(n^2 - 1\right)^2 \left(\frac{1}{\cos^2 \varphi}\right) I_0 \ \ W/m^3$$

Where

I_{RS} = scattered radiation from a scattering volume (W/m^3).

N = number of molecules in the irradiated volume of air ($1/m^3$).

λ = wavelength (m), φ = angle of scattering (degree), n = refractive index,

I_0 = extra-terrestrial radiation (solar constant).

The solar radiation reaches on the earth surface depends upon the following factors:
(1) Reflection of the extra terrestrial atmosphere and on the earth's surface
(2) Scattering on the earth's atmosphere.
(3) Absorption in the atmosphere.

<u>**Solar Collectors:-**</u>

Solar power has low density ($1kW/m^2$ to $0.1kW/m^2$) per unit area. Hence large amount of solar power collection needs larger area. The solar collector being the first unit in the solar thermal system, collects heat from solar radiation then transfers to the transport fluid efficiently. The transport fluid utilizes the heat for necessary purposes.

Classification:

Classification:

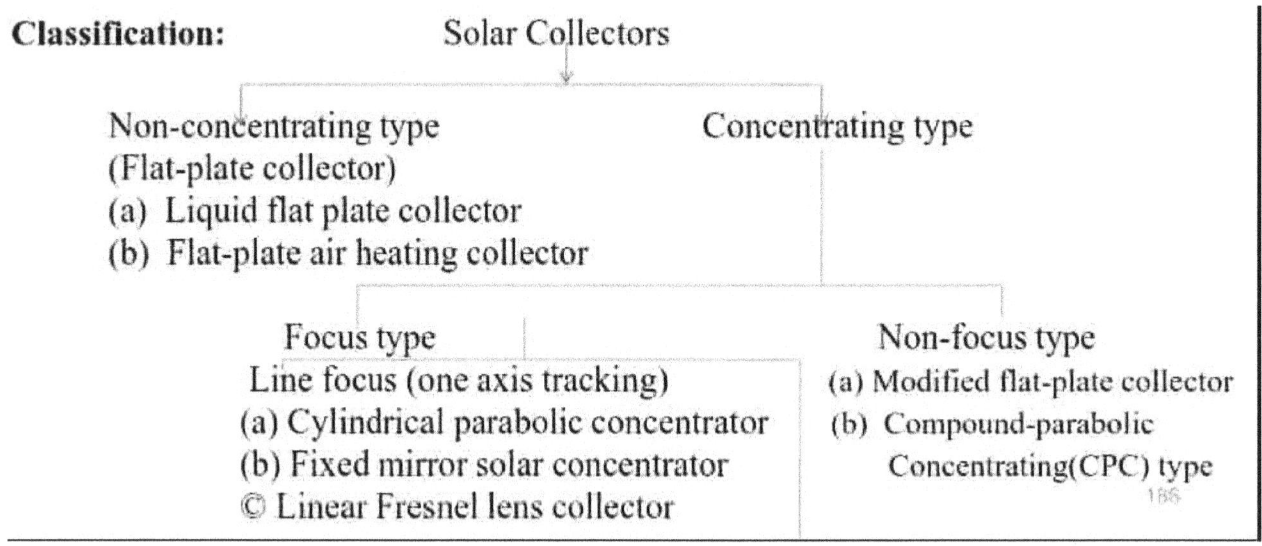

Point focus (two-axis tracking)
(a) Pentaboloidal dish collector.
(b) Hemispherical bowl mirror conc.
(c) Circular Fresnel lens cone.
(d) Central Tower receiver.

(Fig: Types of Solar Collector)

Concentrating type	Non-concentrating type (Flat Plate Type)
(1) In concentrating type solar collectors, solar radiation is converged from a large area into smaller area using optical means. Beam radiation has a unique direction which travels in a straight line, can be converged by reflection or refraction techniques. On the other hand diffused radiation does not have unique direction, can not obey optical principles. Thus diffused radiation does not converge to a single point. Thus concentrating type solar collectors utilizes beam radiation and partly diffused radiation coming directly over the observer.	(1) Non-concentrating (flat plate) type solar collectors absorb both beam type and diffused radiation.
(2) Complex in construction.	(2) The flat plate collector is simple in construction and does not require sun tracking.
(3) It does not sustain harsh atmospheric conditions.	(3) Since it requires outdoor installation, the outside atmospheric harsh conditions are likely to sustain.
(4) It requires high maintenance.	(4) It requires little maintenance.
(5) It attains high temperature due to presence of optical concentration.	(5) Due to absence of optical concentration, the heat loss is more. So it attains low temperature.

Performance Indices: The following performance indices are measured in a Solar collector.

(1) Collector efficiency:- It is defined as the ratio of the energy actually absorbed and transferred to the heat-transport fluid by the collector (useful energy) to the energy incident on the collector.

(2) Concentration ratio:- It is defined as the ratio of the area of the aperture of the system to the area of the receiver. The aperture of the system is the projected area of the collector facing (normal) to the beam.

(3) *Temperature range*: It is the range of temperature to which the heat transport fluid is heated up by the collector.

There are three types of solar collectors based on the temperature ranges.
(i) Low temperature Systems($<150^0$ C):
(ii) Medium-temperature Systems($150-400^0$C):
(iii) High-temperature Systems($400-1000^0$C):

FLAT-PLATE COLLECTORS:

- ❖ Flat-plate collectors are the most common solar collector for solar water-heating systems in homes and solar space heating. A typical flat-plate collector is an insulated metal box with a glass or plastic cover (called the glazing) and a dark-colored absorber plate. These collectors heat liquid or air at temperatures less than 180°F.Flat-plate collectors are used for residential water heating and hydronic space-heating installations.
- ❖ The flat-plate collector is located in a position such that its length is aligned with longitude and is suitably tilted towards south to have maximum collection.
- ❖ Liquid Flat plate collectors:-The schematics of flat plate collectors are shown in the figure (a) and (b). It consists of a black coated plate made of metal or plastic, which absorbs all the solar radiation incident on it and converts into heat. This plate is known as the absorber. Fluid channels are welded below the absorber for carrying a heat transfer fluid generally water. This transport fluid transports the heat from the absorber into the utilisation purposes.
- ❖ Liquid flat plate collectors heat liquid as it flows through tubes in or adjacent to the absorber plate. The simplest liquid systems use potable household water, which is heated as it passes directly through the collector and then flows to the house.

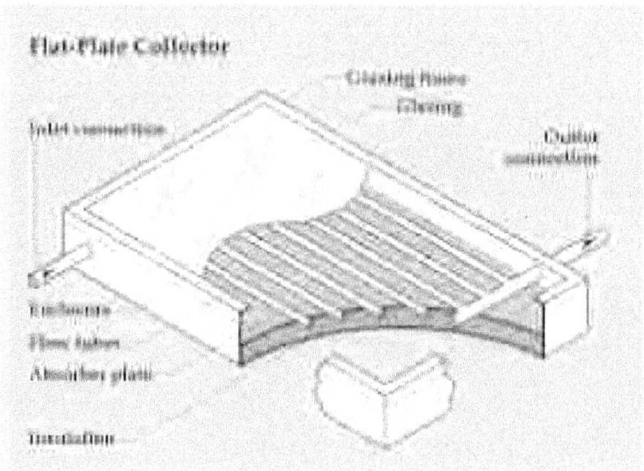

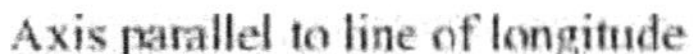

Fig(a): Positioning of flat-plate collector.

To reduce the heat losses, the back side and sides of the collector (below the absorber)are covered with insulation. The front above of the absorber is covered with one or two transparent glass sheets. The whole thing is sealed in a box or some sort of casing. The working of the collector basically depends upon the greenhouse effects. Flat plate collectors can convert solar radiation into heat upto maximum 100^0C.

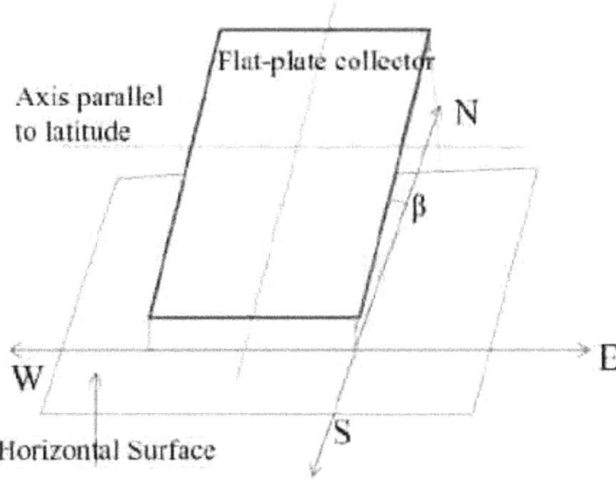

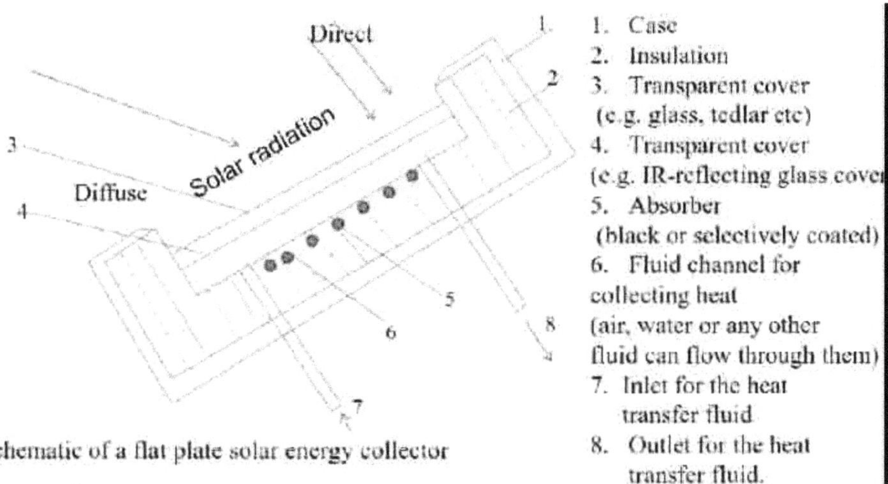

Fig(b): Schematic of a flat plate solar energy collector

1. Case
2. Insulation
3. Transparent cover (e.g. glass, tedlar etc)
4. Transparent cover (e.g. IR-reflecting glass cover)
5. Absorber (black or selectively coated)
6. Fluid channel for collecting heat (air, water or any other fluid can flow through them)
7. Inlet for the heat transfer fluid
8. Outlet for the heat transfer fluid.

- ❖ **Air flat-plate collectors** are used primarily for solar space heating. The absorber plates in air collectors can be metal sheets, layers of screen, or non-metallic materials. The air flows past the absorber by using natural convection or a fan. Because air conducts heat much less readily than liquid does, less heat is transferred from an air collector's absorber than from a liquid collector's absorber, and air collectors are typically less efficient than liquid collectors.
- ❖ Air heating solar collectors are mostly used for agricultural drying and space heating applications. The basic advantages are low sensitivity to leakage, less

corrosion and no need for additional heat exchanger. The main disadvantage is the requirement of larger surface area for heat transfer and higher flow rate.

Flat Plate Collector Efficiency :-

The instantaneous collection efficiency of a flat plate solar collector is defined as :

$$\eta_i = \frac{\text{Useful heat gain}}{\text{Solar Radiation incident on the Collector}} = \frac{Q_u}{I_{G\beta}}$$

Where $I_{G\beta} = Q_u + Q_c + Q_R + Q_e$

If A_c, τ and ρ are the collector area in m^2, transmissivity and reflectivity; the useful

energy is given by: $Q_u = \tau I_{G\beta} (1-\rho) A_c - Q_L$ (W)

For an absorber, $(1-\rho) = \alpha$. So, $Q_u = \tau I_{G\beta} \alpha A_c - Q_L$ (W).

The heat losses Q_L are composed of convection and radiation parts. So Q_L can be

represented as: $Q_L = Q_c + Q_R = U\,A_c\,(t_c - t_s)$ (W)

Where U = Overall heat transfer coefficient of the observer (W/m^2 ^{0}C).

    t_c = Temperature of the collector's absorber (^{0}C).

    t_s = Temperature of the ambient (^{0}C).

The reflected radiation from the absorber is given by: $Q_R = \tau I_{G\beta}\,A_c\,\rho$ (W).

So, $Q_u = \tau I_{G\beta} \alpha A_c - U\,A_c\,(t_c - t_s)$ (W).

Concentrating collectors

- ❖ Unlike solar (photovoltaic) cells, which use light to produce electricity, concentrating solar power systems generate electricity with heat. Concentrating solar collectors use mirrors and lenses to concentrate and focus sunlight onto a thermal receiver, similar to a boiler tube. The receiver absorbs and converts sunlight into heat. The heat is then transported to a steam generator or engine where it is converted into electricity.
- ❖ There are three main types of concentrating solar power systems: parabolic troughs, dish/engine systems, and central receiver systems.
- ❖ These technologies can be used to generate electricity for a variety of applications, ranging from remote power systems as small as a few kilowatts (kW) upto grid-connected applications of 200-350megawatts (MW) or more.
- ❖ A concentrating solar power system that produces 350MW of electricity displaces the energy equivalent of 2.3 million barrels of oil.

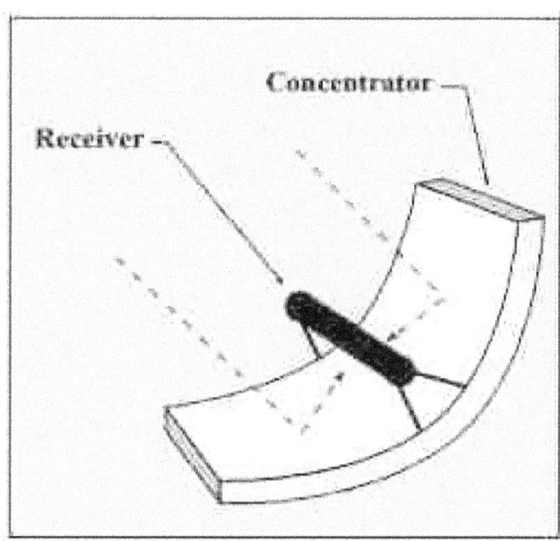

Fig. 1 A parabolic trough

These solar collectors use mirrored parabolic troughs to focus the sun's energy to a fluid-carrying receiver tube located at the focal point of a parabolically curved trough reflector (see Fig.1 above). The energy from the sun sent to the tube heats oil flowing through the tube, and the heat energy is then used to generate electricity in a conventional steam generator. Many troughs placed in parallel rows are called a "collector field." The troughs in the field are all aligned along a north south axis so they can track the sun from east to west during the day, ensuring that the sun is continuously focused on the receiver pipes. Individual trough systems currently can generate about 80 MW of electricity. Trough designs can in corporate thermal storage—setting aside the heat transfer fluid in its hot phase—allowing for electricity generation several hours into the evening. Currently, all parabolic trough plants are "hybrids," meaning they use fossil fuels to supplement the solar output during periods of low solar radiation.

Dish Systems

Each dish produces 5 to 50 kW of electricity and can be used independently or linked together to increase generating capacity.

Central Receiver Systems

Central receivers (or power towers) use thousands of individual sun-tracking mirrors called "heliostats" to reflect solar energy onto a receiver located on top of at all tower. The receiver collects the sun's heat in a heat-transfer fluid (molten salt) that flows through the receiver. The salt's heat energy is then used to make steam to generate electricity in a conventional steam generator, located at the foot of the tower. The molten salt storage system retains heat efficiently, so it can be stored for hours or even days before being used to generate electricity. Therefore, a central receiver system is composed of five main components: heliostats, receiver, heat transport and exchange, thermal storage, and controls (see Fig. 3).

Receiver and generator Concentrator individual dish/engine systems currently can generate about 25 kW of electricity.

Solar Two—a demonstration power tower located in the Mojave Desert—can generate about 10 MW of electricity. In this central receiver system, thousands of sun-tracking mirrors called heliostats reflect sunlight onto the receiver. Molten salt at 554°F (290°C) is pumped from a cold storage tank through the receiver where it is heated to about 1,050°F (565°C). The heated salt then moves on to the hot storage tank. When power is needed from the plant, the hot salt is pumped to a generator that produces steam. The steam activates a turbine/generator system that creates electricity. From the steam generator, the salt is returned to the cold storage tank, where it stored is and can be eventually reheated in the receiver. By using thermal storage, power tower plants can potentially operate for 65percent of the year without the need for a back-up fuel source. Without energy storage, solar technologies like this are limited to annual capacity factors near25 percent. The power tower's ability to operate for extended periods of time on stored solar energy separates it from other renewable energy technologies. Hot salt storage tank Steam generator 1,050°F Cold salt storage tank Condenser cooling tower554°FSystem boundary Substation Steam turbine and electric generator.

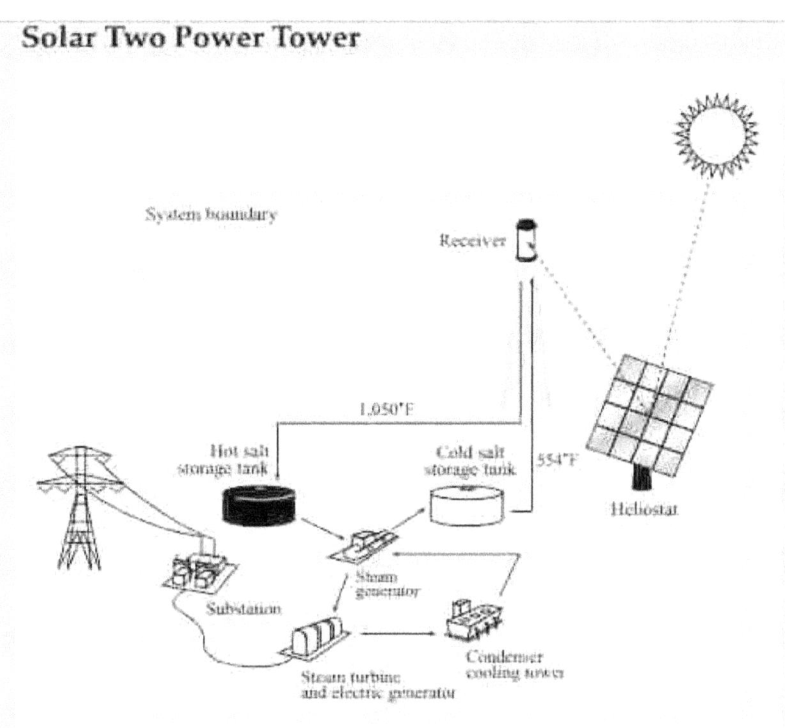

Fig. 3 Solar Two power tower system

Applications of Solar Energy

- Crop And Grain Drying
- Space And Water Heating
- Solar Energy Applications for Agriculture
- Greenhouse Heating
- Remote Electricity Supply (Photovoltaic)
- Water Pumping

Solar Space And Water Heating

- Livestock and diary operations often have substantial air and water heating requirements. Modern pig and poultry farms raise animals in enclosed buildings, where it is necessary to carefully control temperature and air quality to maximize the health and growth of the animals. These facilities need to replace the indoor air regularly to remove moisture, toxic gases odors, and dust. Heating this air, when necessary, requires large amount of energy. With proper planning and design solar air/space heaters can be incorporated into farm buildings to preheat incoming fresh air. These systems can also be used to supplement.

- SOLAR WATER HEATER

The details of most common type of solar water heater are shown in schematic diagram of Fig. 5.17. A tilted flat plate solar collector with water as heat transfer fluid is used. A thermally insulated hot water storage tank is mounted above the collector.The heated water of the collector rises up to the hot water tank and replaces an equal quantity of cold water, which enters the collector. The cycle repeats, resulting in all the water of the hot water tank getting heated up. When hot water is taken out from hot water outlet, the same is replaced by cold water from cold-water make up tank fixed above the hot water tank. The scheme is known as passive heating scheme, as water is circulated in the loop naturally due to thermos-siphon action. When the collector is fixed above the level of hot water tank, a pump is required to induce circulation of water in the loop and the scheme will be known as active (or forced) solar thermal system. An auxiliary electrical emersion heater may be used as back up for use during cloudy periods. In average Indian climatic conditions solar water heater can be used for about 300 days in a year. A typical 100 liters per day (LPD) rooftop, solar water heater costs approximately ` 15,000–21,900 (year 2015) and delivers water at 60–80 °C. It has a life span of 10–12 years and payback period of 2-6 years. Figure 5.18 shows the photograph of an installed and operating solar water heater.

In other schemes the hot water from collector delivers heat to service water through a heat exchanger. In this scheme an anti-freeze solution may be used as heat transport medium to avoid freezing during cold nights.

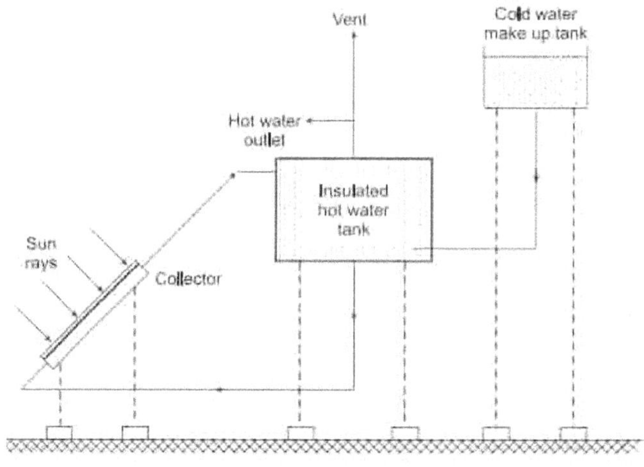

Figure 5.17 Solar water heater

Figure 5.18 Solar water heater

SOLAR PASSIVE SPACE HEATING AND COOLING SYSTEMS
SOLAR PASSIVE SPACE HEATING AND COOLING SYSTEMS

Solar energy is also used for heating or cooling a building to maintain comfortable temperature inside. Passive systems do not require any mechanical device and make use of natural process of convection, radiation and conduction for transport of heat.

Use of passive heating/cooling systems put restrictions on the building design to make possible the flow of heat naturally. Such a specially designed building is called "solar house". The state of the art for passive cooling is much less developed than for passive space heating. Natural passive cooling may not always be sufficient to meet the requirement and at peak load, auxiliary means may also be needed, but it greatly reduces the load on the air conditioner plant.

Active heating/cooling systems employ mechanical devices, e.g. pump, blower, etc.to circulate the working fluid for transportation of heat and therefore special building design is not necessary as required in the case of passive heating. Nevertheless, careful building design and insulation is desirable and will be less expensive than additional heating/cooling load due to poor design.

A solar passive space heating system is shown in Fig. 5.19. The south facing thick wall, called 'Trombe Wall' is made of concrete, adobe, stone or composites of brick blocks and sand, designed for thermal storage. In order to increase the absorption, the outer surface is painted black. The entire south wall is covered by one or two sheets of glass or plastic sheet with some air gap (usually 10–15 cm) between the wall and inner glazing. Solar radiation after penetration through the glazing is absorbed by the thermal storage wall. The air in the air gap between the glazing and the wall thus gets heated, rises up and enters the room through the upper vent

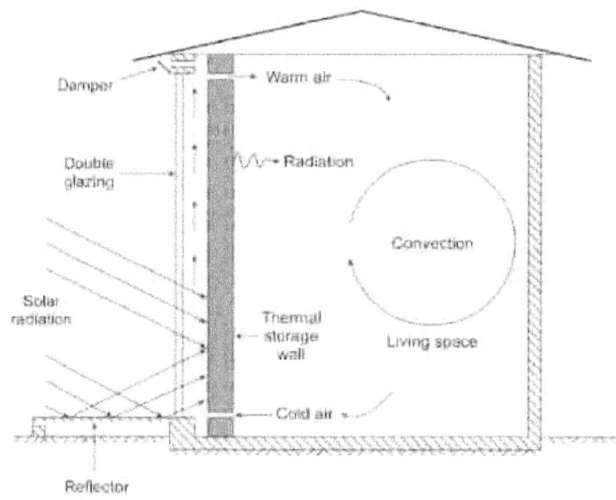

Figure 5.19 Solar space heating

while cool air from the room replaces it from the bottom vent. The circulation of air continues till the wall goes on heating the air. Thus the thermal wall collects stores and transfers the heat to the room. Heating can be adjusted by controlling the airflow through the inlet and outlet vents by shutters. Opening the damper at the top of the glazing allows the excess heat to escape outside, when heating is not required.

Sometimes a reflective horizontal surface is also provided to make available the additional radiation for thermal storage. A movable insulation cover (not shown in figure) also sometimes used to cover the glaze to reduce the heat loss from the storage wall to outside during night. In some models the thermal storage wall is made up of water drums stacked over one another to increase the thermal storage capacity. In another variation the thermal storage mass is provided above a metallic roof of the building instead of a wall.

Solar desalination is a technique to produce water with a low salt concentration from sea-water or brine (i.e Water with salt in it) using solar energy. There are two common methods of solar desalination. Either using the direct heat from the sun or using electricity generated by solar cells to power a membrane process.

- In the direct method, a solar collector is coupled with a distilling mechanism and the process is carried out in one simple cycle.
- Water production by direct method solar distillation is proportional to the area of the solar surface and incidence angle and has an average estimated value of 3–4 litres per square metre (0.074–0.098 US gal/sq ft).

(A solar still distills water with substances dissolved in it by using the heat of the Sun to evaporate water so that it may be cooled and collected, thereby purifying it. They are used in areas where drinking water is unavailable, so that clean water is obtained from dirty water or from plants by exposing them to sunlight.)

(Distillation is the process of separating the components or substances from a liquid mixture by using selective boiling and condensation.)

Indirect solar desalination employs two separate systems; a solar collection array, consisting of photovoltaic and/or fluid-based thermal collectors, and a separate conventional desalination plant. Production by indirect method is dependent on the efficiency of the plant and the cost per unit produced is generally reduced by an increase in scale.

Solar stills

The solar still is one of the oldest and by far the simplest water desalination method. A solar still consists of a structural element called a basin covered with a transparent material to allow the incident solar radiation to pass through to the basin saline water for thermal absorption and evaporation. Solar energy absorption, saline water evaporation, and fresh water condensation occur within a single enclosure for a solar still. Solar stills are inherently direct collection systems. Solar distillation using solar stills is considered to be a mature technology. Because it has a low maintenance requirement, it is used worldwide to produce fresh water. Typically, the basin is colored in dark or black to enhance solar flux absorption. The water is heated by the solar rays absorbed by the basin, which increases the water vapor pressure until some portion of the saline water evaporates as shown in Figure 1. The water vapor moves upward and typically condenses on the cool glass cover and run downs through a guiding channel to the collection reservoir. There exist many types of solar stills, including single slope, double slope, single and double basin, inverted, tubular, spherical, double effect multi wick, and greenhouse integrated solar stills as shown in Figure 2.
Solar stills can be passive or active, depending on whether water circulation is needed.
The main advantages of passive solar stills are that they do not require electrical energy for pumping (passive solar collector), it is simple, and it is easy to operate.
However, the main drawback of the solar still is that it typically has low water production due to the loss of latent heat of condensation through the solar still transparent.

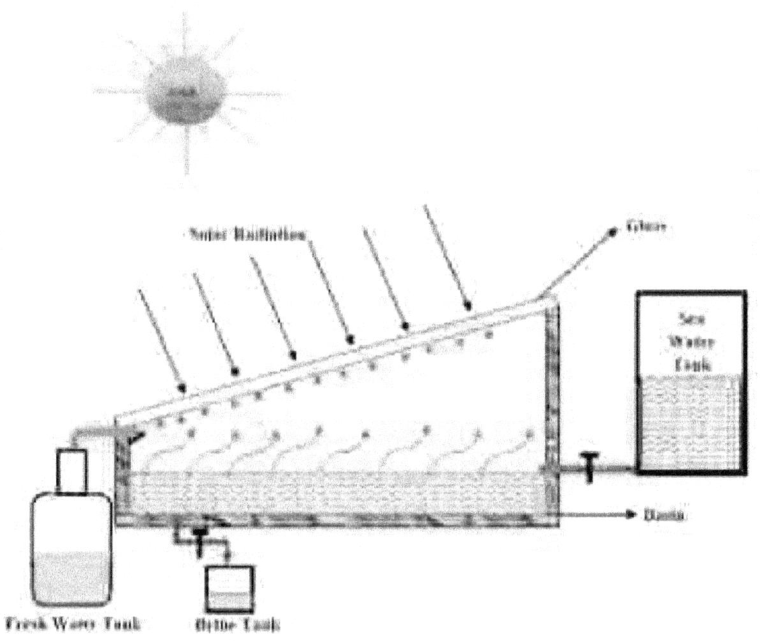

Figure 1. Solar still [47].

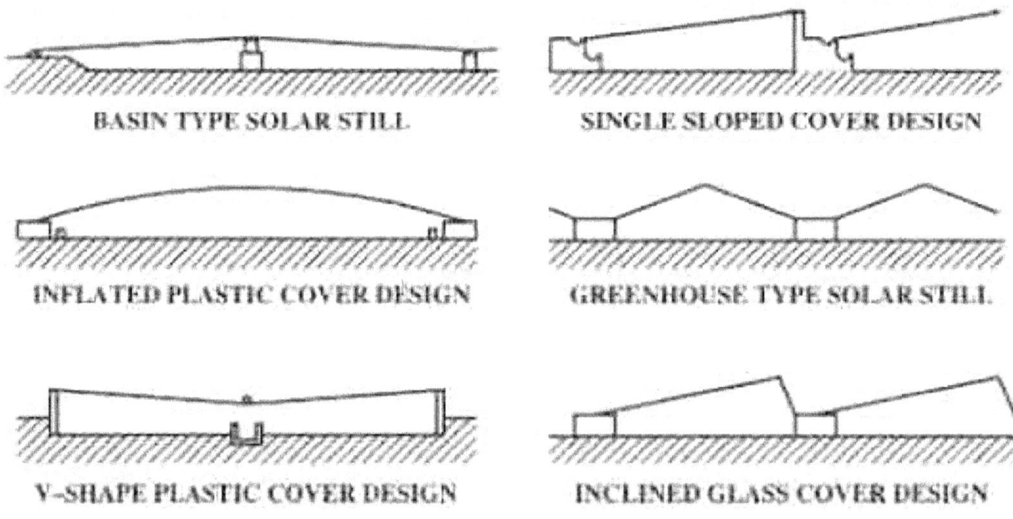

Figure 2. Common designs of solar stills [2].

Transmissivity based on Reflection-Refraction

The direction of incident and refracted beams are related to each other by Snell's law as
follows:

As shown in Fig. 5.43, I_{bn} is the intensity of the incoming beam radiation striking the interface of two medium at an angle of incidence of q. The reflected beam has reduced intensity of Ir1 making an angle of reflection which is equal to angle of incidence. The direction of incident and refracted beams are related to each other by Snell's law as follows:

$$\frac{\sin\theta_1}{\sin\theta_2} = \frac{n_2}{n_1}$$

where, θ_1 = angle of incidence,
   θ_2 = angle of refraction, and
n_1, n_2 = refractive indices of the two media

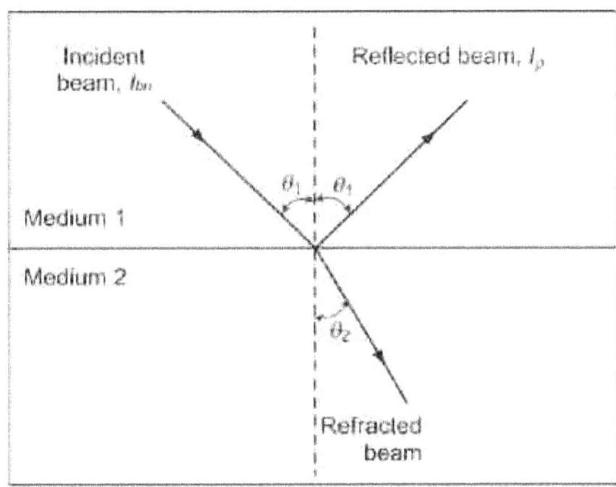

Figure 5.43 Reflection and refraction of the incident beam

The reflectivity ρ ($= I_\rho/I_{bn}$) is related to the angle of incidence and refraction as follows:

$$\rho = \frac{I_\rho}{I_{bn}} = \frac{1}{2}(\rho_I + \rho_{II}) \tag{5.7}$$

SOLAR COOKERS-

-By using Soar cooker, Solar energy can be used for cooking purposes. Thermal energy requirements for cooking purpose forms a major share of total energy consumed, especially in rural areas. Variety of fuels like coal, kerosene, cooking gas, firewood, dung cakes and agricultural wastes are being used to meet the requirement. Fossil fuel is a fast depleting resource and need to be conserved, firewood for cooking causes deforestation and cow dung, agricultural waste, etc., may be better used as a good fertilizer. Harnessing solar energy for cooking purpose is an attractive and relevant option. A variety of solar cookers have been developed, which can be clubbed in four types of basic designs: (i) box type solar cooker, (ii) dish type solar cooker,(iii) community solar cooker, and (iv) advance solar cooker.

1. Box Type Solar Cooker

The construction of a most common, box type solar cooker is schematically shown in Fig. 5.27. The external dimensions of a typical family size (4 dishes) box type cooker are 60 × 60 × 20 cm. This cooker is simple in construction and operation. An insulated box of blackened aluminum contains the utensils with food material. The box receives direct radiation and also reflected radiation from a reflector mirror fixed on inner side of the box cover hinged to one side of the box. The angle of reflector can be adjusted as required. A glass cover consisting of two layers of clear window glass sheets serves as the box door. The glass cover traps heat due to greenhouse effect. Maximum air temperature obtained inside the box is around 140–160 °C. This is enough for cooking the boiling type food slowly in about 2–3 hours. It is capable of cooking 2 kg of food and can save 3–4 LPG cylinder fuel in a year. Electrical backup is also provided in some designs for use during non-sunshine hours. Its cost varies from Rs.5,000 to Rs.6,290 (year 2016) depending on the type, size, quality and electrical backup facility etc. A more affordable, folding type model of solar cooker, made of cardboard material is also developed.

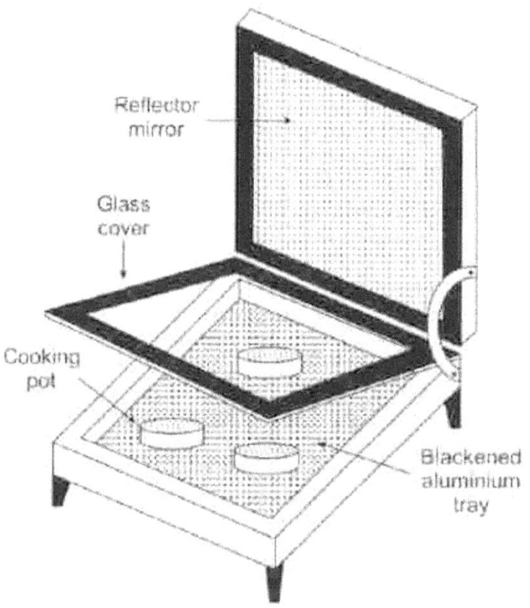

Figure 5.27 Box type solar cooker

2. Paraboloidal Dish Type (Direct Type) Solar Cooker

A specially designed paraboloidal reflector surface concentrates the beam radiation at its focus, where a cylindrical brass vessel containing food material is placed. A commercial dish type solar cooker, SK 14, developed by EG solar, an NGO of Germany, and being manufactured in India is shown in Fig. 5.28. The vessel directly receives the concentrated solar radiation. The reflector is periodically adjusted to track the sun. A fairly high temperature of about 450 °C can be obtained and a variety of food requiring boiling, baking and frying can be cooked for 10–15 persons. It can save on fuel up to 10 LPG cylinders annually on full use. Cooking time is approximately 20–30 minutes. The approximate cost of the cooker is Rs.8,500 (year 2016).

3. Community Solar Cooker

Community solar cooker has been developed for indoor cooking. It has a large automatically tracked paraboloidal reflector standing outside the kitchen. Solar Thermal Systems The reflector reflects the sunrays into the kitchen through an opening in its north wall.

A secondary reflector further concentrates the rays on to the bottom of the cooking pot, which is painted black. It can cook all types of food for about 40–50 people and can save up to 30 LPG cylinders in a year with optimum use.

In another design of community solar cooker, large numbers of automatically tracked paraboloidal reflectors are installed in series and parallel combinations and generate steam for cooking in community kitchen. It can cook food for thousands of people in a short time depending upon its capacity. It is normally installed in conjunction with a boiler that may also use conventional fuel when necessary.

Photovoltaic effect

Conversion of light energy in electrical energy is based on a phenomenon called photovoltaic effect. When semiconductor materials are exposed to light, the some of the photons of light ray are absorbed by the semiconductor crystal which causes a significant number of free electrons in the crystal. This is the basic reason for producing electricity due to photovoltaic effect. **Photovoltaic cell** is the basic unit of the system where the photovoltaic effect is utilised to produce electricity from light energy. Silicon is the most widely used semiconductor material for constructing the photovoltaic cell. The silicon atom has four valence electrons. In a solid crystal, each silicon atom shares each of its four valence electrons with another nearest silicon atom hence creating covalent bonds between them. In this way, silicon crystal gets a tetrahedral lattice structure. While light ray strikes on any materials some portion of the light is reflected, some portion is transmitted through the materials and rest is absorbed by the materials.

The same thing happens when light falls on a silicon crystal. If the intensity of incident light is high enough, sufficient numbers of photons are absorbed by the crystal and these photons, in turn, excite some of the electrons of covalent bonds. These excited electrons then get sufficient energy to migrate from valence band to conduction band. As the energy level of these electrons is in the conduction band, they leave from the covalent bond leaving a hole in the bond behind each removed electron. These are called free electrons move randomly inside the crystal structure of the silicon. These free electrons and holes have a vital role in creating electricity in photovoltaic cell. These electrons and holes are hence called light-generated electrons and holes respectively. These light generated electrons and holes cannot produce electricity in the silicon crystal alone. There should be some additional mechanism to do that.

When a pentavalent impurity such as phosphorus is added to silicon, the four valence electrons of each pentavalent phosphorous atom are shared through covalent bonds with four neighbour silicon atoms, and fifth valence electron does not get any chance to create a covalent bond.

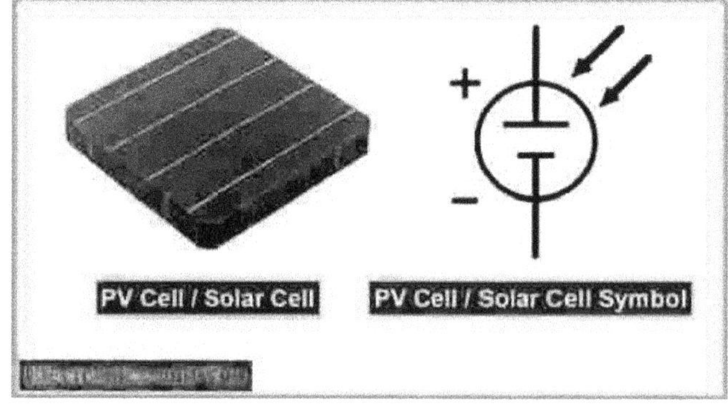

A PV Cell or Solar Cell or Photovoltaic Cell is the smallest and basic building block of a Photovoltaic System (*Solar Module and a Solar Panel*). These cells vary in size ranging from about 0.5 inches to 4 inches. These are made up of

solar photovoltaic material that converts solar radiation into direct current (*DC*)
electricity.

Materials used for photovoltaic include mono crystalline silicon, polycrystalline
silicon, microcrystalline silicon, cadmium telluride, and copper indium selenide
/sulfide.

Different Types of PV Cells

Many new styles of PV cells are being developed today but mainly two distinct
material:

1. Crystalline Silicon PV Cells (Mono crystalline)

These Solar Cells are manufactured from crystalline silicon. Many of you must be
knowing that silicon is the second most common material on Earth and is
abundantly found in sand. To make solar cells out of silicon, manufactured silicon
crystals are sliced to about 300 micrometers thick and coated to work as a
semiconductor to capture solar energy.

2. Thin-film or Polycrystalline PV Cells

Thin-film PV cells use amorphous silicon or an alternative to silicon as
a semiconductor. These solar cells are relatively flexible and can be directly
installed with building materials. They work great even during clouds when there
is low sun light. Here, the disadvantage is that thin-film PV Cells comparatively
generate less electricity than crystalline silicon cells.

Solar PV Module

A bare single cell cannot be used for outdoor energy generation by itself. It is
because (i) the output of a single cell is very small and (ii) it requires protection
(encapsulation) against dust, moisture, mechanical shocks and outdoor harsh
conditions. Workable voltage and reasonable power is obtained by interconnecting
an appropriate number of cells. Cells from same batch are used to make PV
module. This is done to ensure that mismatch losses are minimal in the module.
The electrically connected cells are encapsulated, typically by using two sheets
of ethylene vinyl acetate (EVA) at either side. EVA is a good electrical insulator,
transparent material and has very low water absorption. The encapsulant cannot
provide rigidity to the module, for which glass is provided at the front side of the
module. At the rear side of the module a hard polymer material, typically,
polyvinyl fluoride (PVF, also known as tedlar) is used. Theses layers are arranged
as shown in Fig. 6.29 and hermetically sealed to make it suitable for outside
applications for 20-30 years without environmental degradation. This assembly is
known as solar module a basic building block of a PV system. Most common
commercial modules have a series connection of 32 or 36 silicon cells to make it

capable of charging a 12 V storage battery. However, larger and smaller capacity modules are also available in international market.

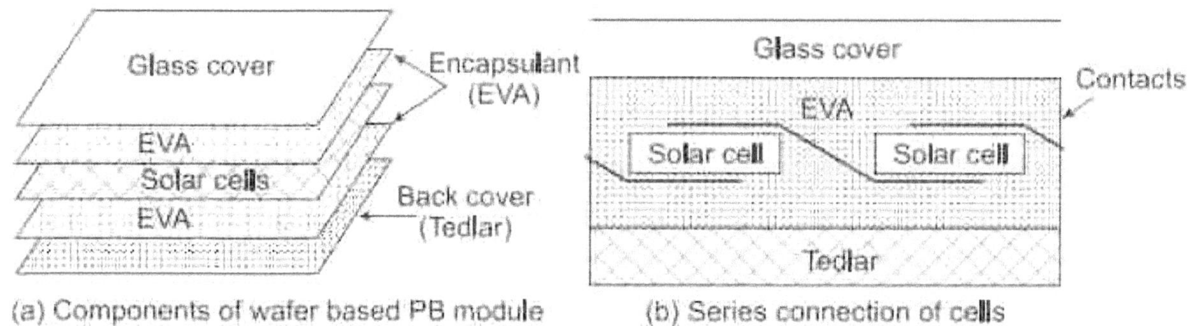

Fig 6.29 PV Module details

Cell Mismatch in a Module

In a module, a number of cells are interconnected, it is very important that these cells should match as closely as possible. That means Voc , Isc, Vm and Im (or fill factor) for all cells must be exactly same. Any mismatch in the characteristics of these cells leads to additional mismatch loss. Therefore, peak power of the combination is always less than the sum of individual peak power of the cells. Only under ideal case when all cells are exactly identical that the resultant peak power would be equal to arithmetic sum of that of its constituents. This is elaborated as follows.

When two cells with mismatched characteristics are connected in series and load is applied, both cells are bound to carry same current.

The composite characteristics of the combination can be obtained by adding the individual output voltage of the cell corresponding to a common current, for all operating points, as shown in Fig. 6.30. At a particular operating point, while one cell may be operating at peak power, the other may not. Thus peak power of the combination is always less than the sum of individual peak power of each cell. This is also clear from the shape of composite characteristics, which has lower fill factor. Also if such a combination is short circuited, equal and opposite voltages V_1', and V_2' are produced by individual cells and therefore, one cell will be generating power while the other will be dissipating it. Had the two cells been perfectly matched no power would be generated or dissipated.

Similar conclusion may be drawn by considering a parallel combination of two mismatched cells. Here the voltages of the cells are bound to be equal, but the currents will be different and hence the maximum power points. The conclusion may be generalized for more than two cells connected in series or in parallel. It can also be shown that larger the number of cells in a module more would be the possibility and quantum of mismatch loss.

To reduce mismatch losses, modules are fabricated from cells belonging to same batch. Also cell sorting is carried out to categorize cells having matched parameters with specified tolerance.

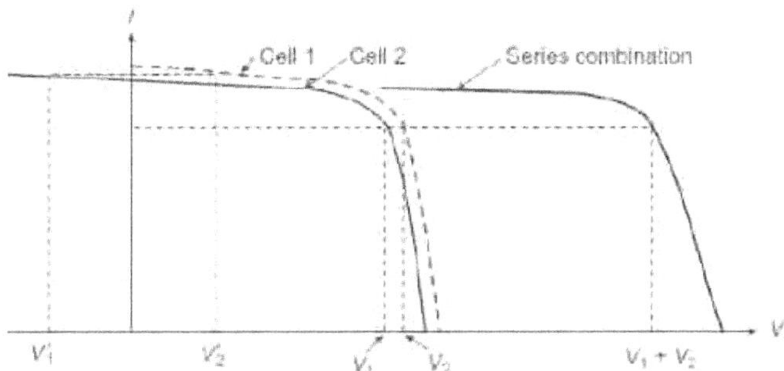

Figure 6.30 Composite characteristic of two cells in series

Effect of Shadowing

Partial shadowing may have serious consequences and may completely damage a module due to creation of hot spot. Let us examine the operation of a module under the conditions of: (i) partial shadowing of a cell in an open circuited, series string of cells and (ii) complete shadowing of one cell in a short circuited, series string of cells.

When a cell is partially shadowed, the shadowed portion will not produce any power but the remaining portion will remain active and produce power. The generated voltage by illuminated portion will forward bias the parallel rectifier corresponding to shadowed portion as shown in Fig. 6.31. If shadowed area is relatively small, the large circulating current through it will result in excessive heating of the shadowed portion. The phenomenon is known as hot spot effect and may completely damage the module for prolonged partial shadowing.

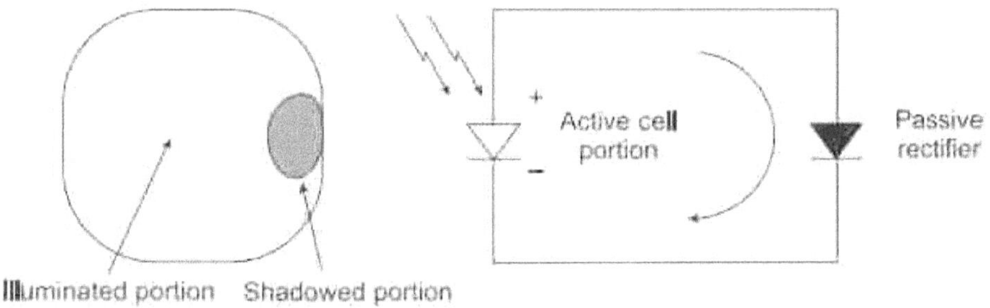

Figure 6.31 Partial shadowing of a cell

A short-circuited, series string of (n + 1) cells with one cell completely shadowed is shown in Fig. 6.32. Here the voltages produced by n illuminated cells add up and appears as reverse bias voltage of nV volts across the shadowed cell. As long as peak inverse voltage (PIV) of the shadowed cell is more than the reverse bias, no current will flow. If, however, the PIV is less than total reverse voltage appearing across the shadowed cell, current will flow through the string, dissipating large power in the shadowed cell, leading to possible damage of the module. The chances of damage to the shadowed cell, due to excessive heating, increase with the number of cells in the string. If the string supplies a load instead of being short-circuited, the chances of damage still persist through to a lesser extent. The damage due to shadowing can be avoided by connecting a bypass diode across the affected cell as shown in Fig. 6.32. This bypass diode would allow an alternative path for the load current. During healthy operation, the bypass diode has no role as the cell voltage would keep it reverse biased. Even so, its use would result some loss because of finite reverse leakage current through it. It is neither practical, nor required to incorporate a bypass diode across each cell in a module. It has been the international practice to provide a bypass diode for every 18 crystalline silicon solar cells in a series string. Thus, the internationally standard module with 34–36 cells would contain two bypass diodes placed inside its terminal box.

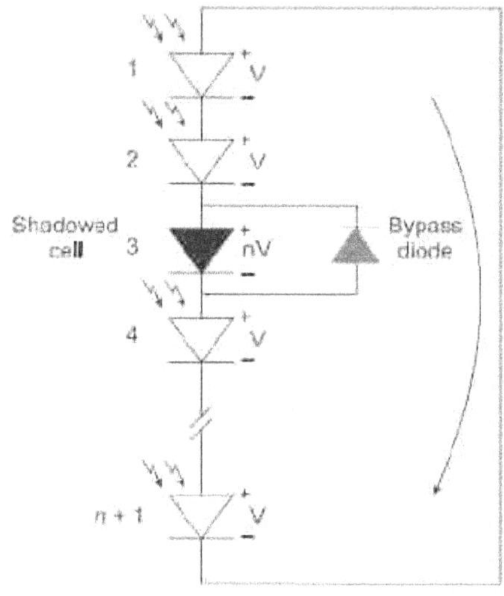

Figure 6.32 Shadowed cell and bypass diode connection

Solar Photovoltaic Panels

An array or Solar PV Cells are electrically connected together to form a PV Module and an Array of such Modules are again electrically connected together to form a Solar Panel. This connection is done by soldering using flux cored solder wire and PV Ribbon.

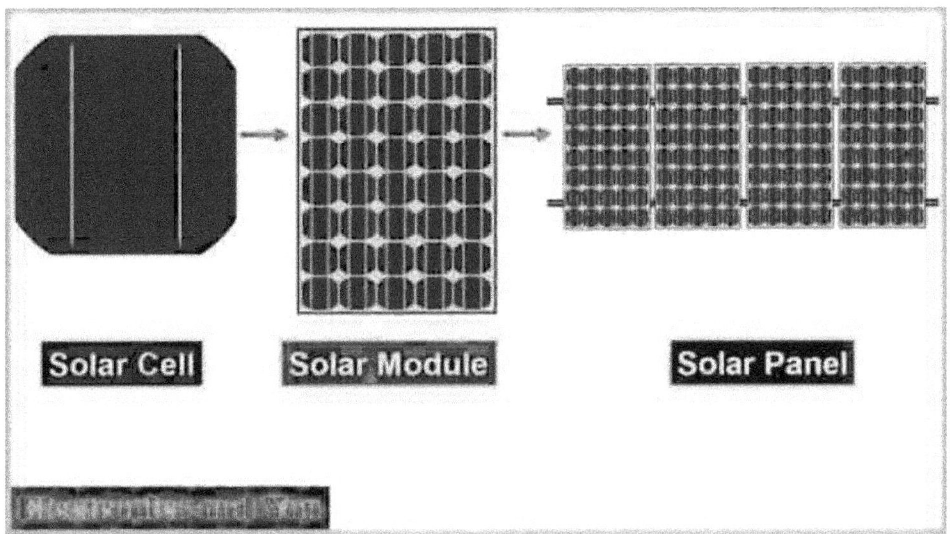

Solar PV Panel

Several solar modules are connected in series/parallel to increase the voltage/current ratings. When modules are connected in series, it is desirable to have each module's maximum power production occur at the same current. When modules are connected in parallel, it is desirable to have each module's maximum power production occur at the same voltage. Thus while interconnecting the modules; the installer should have this information available for each module. Solar panel is a group of several Solar Photovoltaic Systems modules connected in series-parallel combination in a frame that can be mounted on a structure. Fig. 6.33 shows the construction of module and panel.

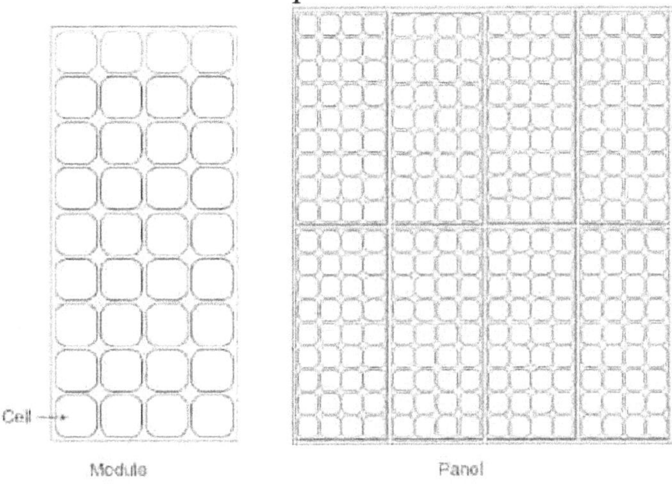

Figure 6.33 Cell, module and panel

Figure 6.34 shows a series-parallel connection of modules in a panel. In parallel connection, blocking diodes are connected in series with each series string of modules, so that if any string should fail, the power output of the remaining series strings will not be absorbed by the failed string. Also bypass diodes are installed across each module, so that if one module should fail, the output of the remaining modules in a string will bypass the failed module. Some modern PV modules come with such internally embedded bypass diodes.

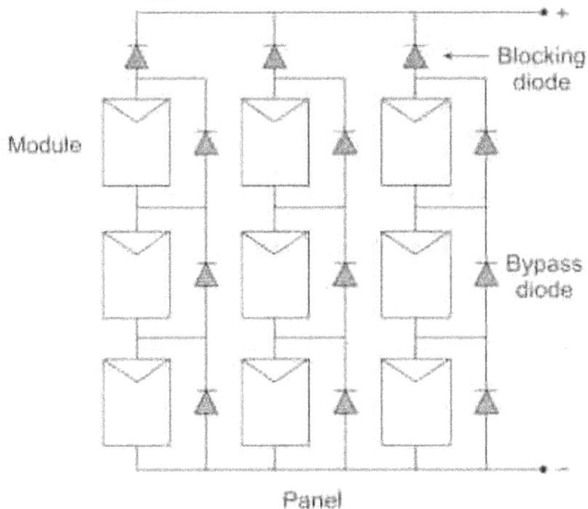

Figure 6.34 A typical panel: Series-parallel connection of modules

Solar PV Array

In general, a large number of interconnected solar panels, known as solar PV array, are installed in an array field. These panels may be installed as stationary or with sun tracking mechanism. It is important to ensure that an installed panel does not cast its shadow on the surface of its neighboring panels during a whole year. The layout and mechanical design of the array such as tilt angle of panels, height of panels, clearance among the panels, etc., are carried out taking into consideration the local climatic conditions, ease of maintenance, etc.

A PV system feeds a dc motor to produce 1 hp power at the shaft. The motor efficiency is 85%. Each module has 36 multicrystalline silicon solar cells arranged in 9×4 matrix. The cell size is 125mm $\times$ 125mm and cell efficiency is 12%. Calculate the number of modules required in the PV array. Assume global radiation incident normally to the panel as 1 kW/m^2.

Solution

Motor output power $= 1$ hp $= 746$ W

Electrical power required by the motor $= 746/0.85 = 877.65$ W

Cell area in one module $= 9 \times 4 \times 125 \times 125 \times 10^{-6} = 0.5625$ m^2

Let n number of modules is required

Solar radiation incident on panel $= 1$ kW/m$^2 = 1000$ kW/m^2

Cell efficiency $= 0.12$

Output of solar array $= 1000 \times 0.5625 \times n \times 0.12 = 67.5 \times n$

The output of solar array is the input to the motor;

$$67.5 \times n = 877.65$$

$$n = 13$$

Therefore 13 modules are required in the panel.

MAXIMISING THE SOLAR PV OUTPUT AND LOAD MATCHING

To make best use of solar PV system, the output is maximized in two ways. The first is mechanically tracking the sun and always orienting the panel in such a direction as to receive maximum solar radiation under changing positions of the sun. That means adjusting the panel such that the sun rays always fall normal to its surface. The second is electrically tracking the operating point by manipulating the load to maximize the power output under changing conditions of insolation and temperature.

The operating point of an electrical system is determined by the intersection of source characteristics (source line) and load characteristics (load line). The operation for a solar PV system connected to a resistive load is shown in Fig. 6.35. For a low value of resistance, R_1 the system operates at Q_1. As the resistance is increased to R_2 and subsequently to R_3 the operating point moves respectively to Q_2 and Q_3. Maximum power is available from the PV system for load resistance of R_2. Such load matching is required for extracting maximum power from PV system.

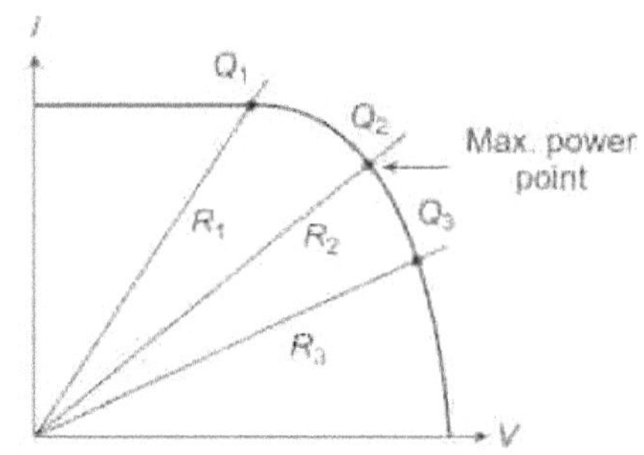

Figure 6.35 Load matching with resistive load

PV Cell or Solar Cell Characteristics

Do you know that the sunlight we receive on Earth particles of solar energy called photons. When these particles hit the semiconductor material (*Silicon*) of a solar cell, the free electrons get loose and move toward the treated front surface of the cell thereby creating holes. This mechanism happens again and again and more and more electrons (*Negative Charge*) flows towards toward the front surface of the cell and creates an imbalance of electrons. Now, when the front (−) and back (+) surface of the photovoltaic cell are joined by a conductor such as a copper wire then electricity is generated.

PV Cell Working Principle to Generate Electricity

Solar cells convert the energy in sunlight to electrical energy. Solar cells contain a material such as silicon that absorbs light energy. The energy knocks electrons loose so they can flow freely and produce a difference in electric potential energy, or voltage. The flow of electrons or negative charge creates electric current.

Solar cells have positive and negative contacts, like the terminals in a Battery. If the contacts are connected with a conductive wire, current flows from the negative to positive contact. The Figure below shows how a PV cell works to generate electricity.

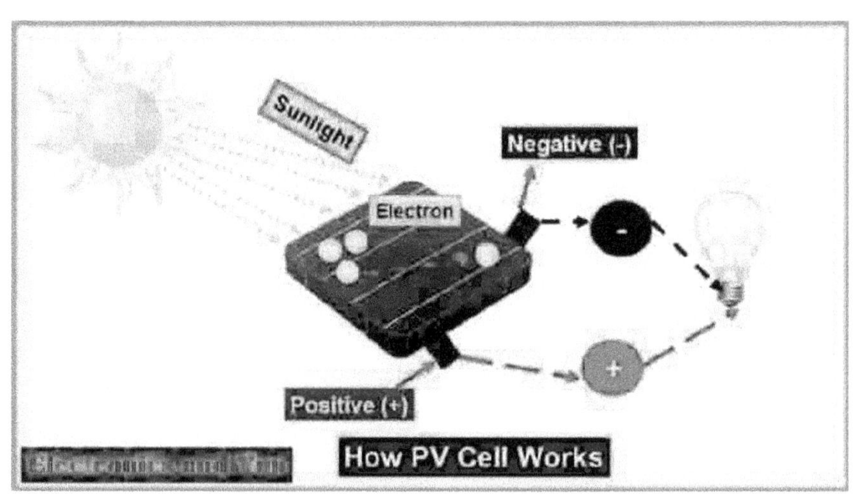

How much Electricity can a PV Cell Generate

A single photovoltaic cell can produce about 1 to 2 watts of electricity. This energy is too less for use in any household or for a commercial purpose.

In order to increase the output of electricity, several photovoltaic cells are electrically connected together to form a photovoltaic module and these modules are further electrically connected to form a photovoltaic panel / photovoltaic array. The number of modules connected to form an array depends on the amount of solar electrical energy needed.

Converting DC to AC Electricity

The PV cells generate DC or direct current. This DC electricity has to be converted to AC or alternating current so that it can be used in a home lighting system or running appliances. An inverter is used to convert DC to AC. This is same as converting DC from a battery to AC.

Storing Electricity Generated by Solar Cells

The electricity generated by solar cells by using solar energy has to be stored so that it can be used later as when required. This is done by running the current into a bank of Solar Batteries.

Solar photovoltaic (PV) systems convert solar energy directly into electrical energy.

Basic conversion device used is known as a solar photovoltaic cell or a solar cell. Solar cells were first produced in 1954 and were rapidly developed to provide power for space satellites based on semiconductor electronics technology. Commercial photocells may have efficiencies in the range of 10–20 per cent and can approximately produce an electrical energy of about 1 kWh per sq. m per day in ordinary sunshine. Typically, it produces a potential difference of about 0.5 V and a current density of about 200 A per sq. m. of cell area in full solar radiation of 1 kW per sq. m. A typical commercial cell of 100 sq-cm area–thus produces a current of 2A. It has a life span in excess of about 20 years. As a PV system has no moving parts it gives almost maintenance free service for long periods and can be used unattended at inaccessible locations.

Major uses of photovoltaics have been in space satellites, remote radio communication booster stations and marine warning lights. These are also increasingly being used for lighting, water pumping and medical refrigeration in remote areas especially in developing countries. Solar powered vehicles and battery charging are some of the recent interesting application of solar PV power. Major advantages of solar PV systems over conventional power systems are:

(i) It converts solar energy directly into electrical energy without going through thermal-mechanical link. It has no moving parts.

(ii) Solar PV systems are reliable, modular, durable and generally maintenance free.

(iii) These systems are quiet, compatible with almost all environments, respond instantaneously to solar radiation and have an expected life span of 20 years or more.

(iv) It can be located at the place of use and hence no or minimum distribution network is required, as it is universally available.

It also suffers from some disadvantages such as:

(i) At present the costs of solar cells are high, making them economically uncompetitive with other conventional power sources.

(ii) The efficiency of solar cells is low. As solar radiation density is also low, large area of solar cell modules are required to generate sufficient useful power.

(iii) As solar energy is intermittent, some kind of electrical energy storage is required, to ensure the availability of power in absence of sun. This makes the whole system more expensive.

Energy Losses and Efficiency

The conversion efficiency of a solar cell is the ratio of electrical power output to incident solar power. The optimum possible theoretical efficiency of 31 per cent for an ideal solar cell under ideal conditions is obtained at band gap of 1.45 eV. In laboratory studies, the highest reported conversion efficiency of a single crystal silicon solar cell is about 24 per cent. Conversion efficiencies of commercially produced single crystal solar cells are in the range 12–18 per cent. Various loss mechanisms lead to limit the conversion efficiency of the cell. Some of these losses are due to inherent nature of internal physical processes and available input. These cannot be influenced by external means. The other category of losses can be influenced by suitable selection of material, processing technology and other parameters of the cell.

1. Loss of Low Energy Photons

The photons having energy, E less than the band gap energy, E do not get absorbed in the material and, therefore, do not contribute to the generation of electron-hole pairs. This is referred as transmission loss, and is almost equal to 23 per cent for a single junction solar cell.

2. Loss Due to Excess Energy Photons

When the photon energy E is higher than the band gap energy EG, the excess energy(E – EGG) is given off as heat to the material. For a single junction solar cell, this is equal to about 33 per cent.

3. Voltage Loss

A fraction of developed voltage is lost due to Auger recombination. The Auger recombination occurs at high level of carrier concentration (>1017). In this process, an electron recombining with hole gives its energy to another electron in the conduction band, pushing it into higher energy level. The second electron then goes through several scattering steps before coming back to conduction band edge.

4. Fill Factor Loss

This type of loss arises due to parasitic resistance (series and shunt resistance) of the cell. In best case FF could be 0.89.

5. Loss by Reflection

There are losses due to reflection from the active surface of the cell. As a result, a fraction of incident photons will not enter the bulk material. To minimize these losses, the active surface must be properly treated, by suitable anti-reflective coating and/or by having a pyramidal or textured structure as shown in Fig. 6.17.

6. Loss Due to Incomplete Absorption

It refers to loss of photons which have enough energy (i.e., $E > E$) to get absorbed in the solar cell, but do not get absorbed due to limited solar cell thickness. As discussed earlier, silicon is an indirect band gap material. Photons of adequate energy require traveling some distance in bulk material in order to get absorbed. If the thickness of the cell is not sufficient (approx. 100 micron) some photons will pass through full thickness of the material without ever getting absorbed. In order to utilize these photons, appropriate light-trapping schemes should be utilized such as; a reflecting G back ohmic contact should be used on the backside, to enhance photon absorption in thinner cells, as shown in Fig. 6.17.

7. Loss Due to Metal Coverage

In wafer-based solar cells, the contact to the front side of the cell is made in the form of finger and bus bar. This metal contact shadows some light which can be up to 10 per cent. Several approaches are adopted to minimize this loss, which include one side contact cell, buried contact solar cell or transparent contacts as used in thin film solar cells.

8. Recombination Losses

Not all the generated electron hole-pairs contribute to photocurrent because some are killed due to recombination. The recombination could occur in the bulk of material or more predominantly at the surface. This type of recombination can be minimized by appropriate surface and bulk passivation techniques in order to obtain high I_L.

MAXIMUM POWER POINT TRACKER

When a solar PV system is deployed for practical applications, the I-V characteristic keeps on changing with insolation and temperature. In order to receive maximum power the load must adjust itself accordingly to track the maximum power point.

The I-V characteristics of PV system, along with some common loads, are shown in Fig. 6.36. An ideal load is one that tracks the maximum power point.

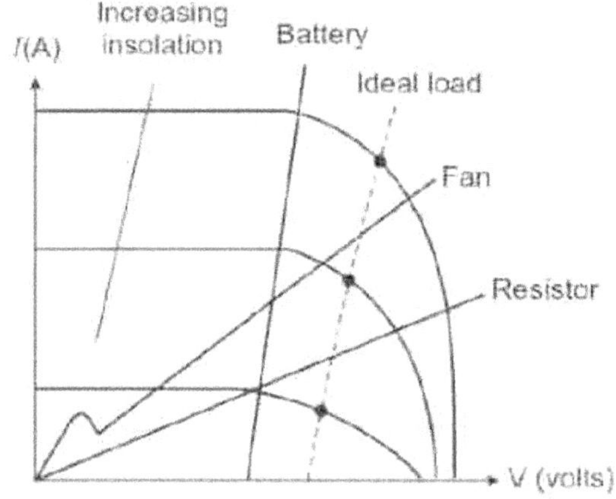

Figure 6.36 Characteristics of PV and some loads

If the operating point departs significantly from maximum power point, it may be desirable to interpose an electronic maximum power point tracker (MPPT) between PV system and load. Generally MPPT is an adaptation of dc-dc switching voltage regulator. Coupling to the load for maximum power transfer may require either providing higher voltage at a lower current or lower voltage for higher current. A buck-boost scheme is commonly used with voltage and current sensors tied into a feedback loop using a controller to vary the switching times. Basic elements of a buck boost converter that may be used in an MPPT are shown in Fig. 6.37. The output voltage of the buck-boost converter is given by:

$$V_{out} = \frac{D}{1-D} V_{in}$$

Where, D is the duty cycle of the MOSFET, expressed as fraction (0 < D < 1). Details of operation and design of the converter may be found in any standard book of power electronics.

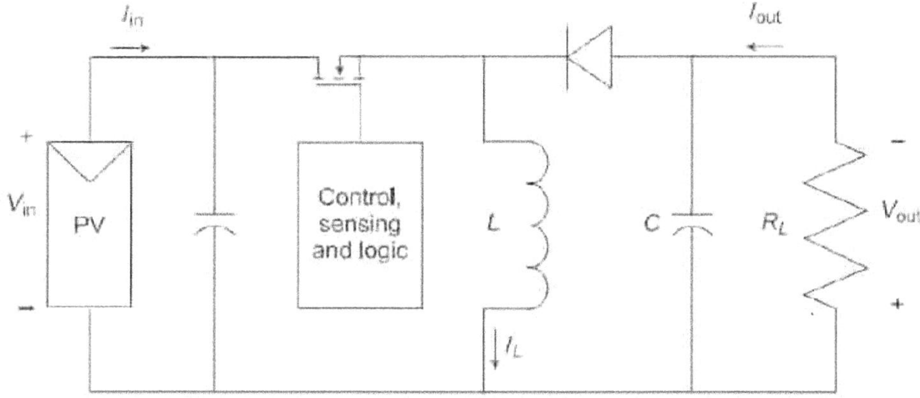

Figure 6.37 Maximum point tracker using buck-boost converter

The power output of a PV system is given by:

$$\Delta P = \Delta V.I + \Delta I.V \qquad (6.41)$$

ΔP must be zero at peak point. Therefore, at peak point the above expression in the limit becomes:

$$\frac{dV}{dI} = -\frac{V}{I} \qquad (6.42)$$

It may be noted here that $\dfrac{dV}{dI}$ is the dynamic impedance of the source, which is required to be equal to negative of static impedance, $\dfrac{V}{I}$.

There are three possible strategies for operation of an MPPT:

(a) By Monitoring Dynamic and Static Impedances A small signal current is being periodically injected into an array bus and the dynamic as well as static bus impedances (Z_d and Z_s respectively) are being measured. The operating voltage is then adjusted until the condition $Z_d = -Z_s$ is achieved.

(b) By Monitoring Power Output From the shape of P-V characteristics given in Fig. 6.14(c) it is clear that the slope, dP/dV is zero at maximum power point. This property is utilized to track the maximum power point. Voltage is adjusted and power output is sensed. The operating voltage is increased as long as dP/dV is positive. That is, voltage is increased as long as we get increased output. If dP/dV is sensed negative, the operating voltage is decreased. The voltage is held unaltered if dP/dV is near zero within a preset dead band.

(c) By Fixing the Output Voltage as a Fraction of V_{oc} This method makes use of the fact that for most PV cells the ratio of the voltage at maximum power point to the open circuit voltage, is approximately constant (say k). This is also evident from Fig. 6.14. For high quality crystalline silicon cell $k = 0.72$. In order to implement this principle, an additional identical unloaded cell is installed on the array to face same environment as the module in use and its open circuit voltage V_{oc} is continuously measured. The operating voltage of the array is then set at $k.V_{oc}$. The implementation of this scheme is simplest among all the available schemes.

Example 6.5

A PV source having IV characteristics as shown in Fig. 6.38 is supplying power to a load whose load line intersects the characteristics at (10 V, 8 A). Determine the additional power gained if an MPPT is interposed between the source and the load. If the cost of the MPPT is Rs. 4000.00, for how long the system needs to operate in order to recover the cost of MPPT. The cost of electricity may be assumed as Rs 7.00 per kWh. The efficiency of MPPT may be assumed as 95%.

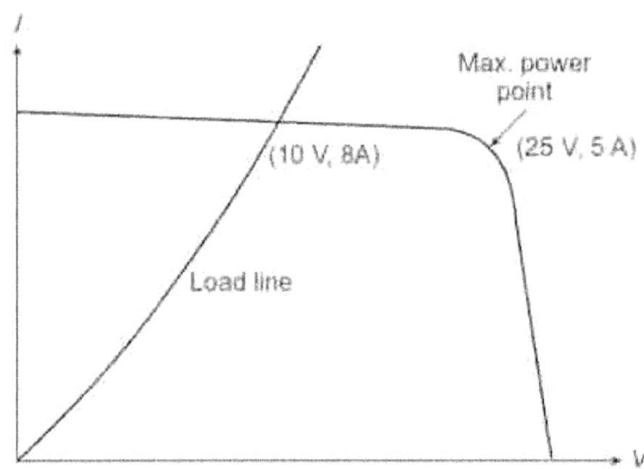

Figure 6.38 PV system – load characteristics

Solution

Power produced without MPPT = $10 \times 8 = 80$ W

Maximum power production capability of the PV module = $25 \times 5 = 125$ W

As the efficiency of the MPPT is 95%, actual power produced with MPPT = $125 \times 0.95 = 118.75$ W

Surplus power produced by use of MPPT = $118.75 - 80 = 38.75$ W

Surplus energy produce in t hours = $\dfrac{38.75 \times t}{1000} = 0.03875 \times t$ kWh

Cost of surplus energy = $7 \times 0.03875 \times t = 0.27125 \times t$

Cost of MPPT = Rs 4000

Time, t (in hours) required to recover the cost of MPPT = $\dfrac{4000}{0.27125} = 14746.54$ hours

Batteries

As solar energy is not available continuously and steadily, some form of energy storage is normally required in most PV systems. Lead acid battery, Nickle cadmium battery and Lithium ion storage batteries are commonly used in PV applications for this purpose. The principles of operation of these batteries are already covered in Section 3.4.2. Some general parameters of batteries are discussed here.

(a) Battery Voltage Three types of voltage available across its terminals are specified: (a) open circuit voltage (maximum voltage); (b) nominal or working voltage (available operating voltage during use), (c) cut-off voltage (minimum voltage after which the battery should be disconnected from the load for recharging). Rechargeable batteries are available with nominal voltages of 3 V, 6 V, 12 V, 24 V, etc.

(b) Battery Capacity It is the maximum charge storage capacity of a battery expressed in Ah. (Ampere-hour). Higher Ah requires more active material. Therefore, as the Ah capacity of a battery increases, the size of the battery also increases. Multiplying Ah with voltage gives energy storage of the battery in Wh (Watt-hours).

(c) Battery Life Cycle It is defined as the number of complete charge/discharge cycles that a battery can perform before its storage capacity falls below 80 per cent of its rated capacity. The aging process (for instance shedding of active material from plates) results in gradual reduction in storage capacity over time. The battery can still be used but its available storage capacity will be lower.

(d) State of Charge (SoC) The SoC at a particular instant indicates the amount of charge available with the battery at that instant. In lead acid battery, the electrolyte's specific gravity provides a convenient indication of the state of charge of the battery.

(e) Depth of Discharge (DoD) This is a measure of energy withdrawn from the battery expressed as percentage of its full capacity. If a battery has a state of charge as 60 per cent, it indicates that its DoD is 40 per cent. The DoD increases as the battery is discharged more and more. Large DoD adversely affects the life cycle of the battery.

(f) Discharge Rate or C-rating C-rating is defined as the charge or discharge current given in terms of capacity of the battery divided by number of hours for full Solar Photovoltaic Systems charge or discharge. For instance a 120 Ah capacity battery with C-rating of C/10(or 0.1C), will have a charge or discharge current of 120/10 = 12 A. Similarly, a 180 Ah capacity battery with C-rating of C/20 (or 0.05C) will have a charge or discharge current of 180/20 = 9 A.

(g) Self-discharge Self-discharge is the loss of stored charge (or energy) when the battery is not in use. It is caused due to internal electrochemical processes and may be considered as equivalent to having a small external load. The self-discharge capacity increases with increase in temperature. Therefore, in order to reduce self-discharge, batteries must be stored at lower temperatures. In SIL batteries some antimony is alloyed with lead to improve mechanical strength. But it also results in increased self-discharge of the battery.

Deep Discharge Batteries

Ordinary batteries are not allowed to discharge beyond 50 per cent DoD. Batteries allowed discharging up to 80 per cent or more are known as deep discharge batteries.

In traction applications where batteries are used to supply the load for longer duration, deep discharge batteries are used. Normal SLI (starting, lighting and ignition) batteries are shallow discharge batteries. They cannot be used in such applications as battery life cycle is significantly reduced due to deep discharge. In deep discharge batteries, the electrode plates are made thicker and stronger to avoid possible wrap of plates. In case of lead acid batteries, tubular batteries are used for such applications.

SLI batteries remain at float charging most of the time. They are normally subjected to only 2–5 per cent depth of discharge during starting of a vehicle. Therefore, these batteries use thin plates with large surface area to supply large current during starting process.

Battery Temperature During Discharge

Both battery capacity and battery voltage decrease, if used at lower temperature. At high temperature also, its capacity may decrease due to deterioration in chemical reaction. Normally, the best battery performance is obtained in temperature range of 20 to 40 °C.

Battery Charging

Different methods of charging are suggested for different type of batteries. A lead acid battery may be charged by constant current, constant voltage or a combination of the two. A typical charging cycle for a lead acid battery is shown in Fig. 6.39. The lead acid battery is charged in three stages: (i) constant-current charge, (ii) topping charge and (iii) float charge (or trickle charge). The battery is first charged with a constant current (specified in data sheet) until its terminal voltage reaches the float potential value, $V_{B, float}$ (typically 2.3 V to 2.45 V per cell). The constant current charge applies the bulk of the charge (about 70 per cent) and takes up roughly half of the required charge time. Thereafter the battery is charged by constant voltage $V_{B, float}$ as the current into the battery tappers off. This phase is known as topping charge phase and continues for few hours to fill the remaining 30 per cent. The battery is fully charged when the Non-Conventional Energy Resources current drops to a set low level. Subsequently the applied voltage across the battery is reduced so that small amount of charge keeps trickling into the battery. The float charge compensates for the loss caused by self-discharge. Lead acid battery charging is sluggish and cannot be charged as quickly as other battery systems. current drops to a set low level. Subsequently the applied voltage across the battery is reduced so that small amount of charge keeps trickling into the battery. The float charge compensates for the loss caused by self-discharge. Lead acid battery charging is sluggish and cannot be charged as quickly as other battery systems.

SOLAR PV APPLICATIONS

Batteries used in PV Applications

The most commonly used batteries in PV applications are the lead acid and nickel cadmium batteries. Lithium-ion and nickel-metal hydride are also used, but to a much lesser extent. Lead acid batteries are most popular. These batteries perform well in deep discharging mode than any other battery.

Grid Interactive PV Power Generation

The first large sized (1 MW $_p$) grid interactive PV plant was installed in Lugo, in California, USA. The second and largest (6.5 MW$_p$) plant was installed in Carissa Plains, California, USA. Also some other large sized plants are operating in various countries and many others are proposed in Italy, Switzerland, Germany, Austria,Spain and Japan. Presently, the biggest solar PV plant of 579 MW capacity, solar star project, is located at Antelope valley, Los Angeles County, California. This is followed by a 550 MW Desert Sunlight Star at Riverside County, and 550 MW Topaz Solar farm at San Louis, Obispo County, California.

In India, a 221 MW solar PV plant at Chankara, Gujarat is the biggest plant.

Another 750 MW plant is underway at Rewa, MP.

A large number of small rooftop grid interactive systems are successfully being operated in various parts of the world.

Water Pumping

Pumping of water for the purpose of drinking or for minor irrigation, during sunshine hours, is very successful application of stand-alone PV system without storage. Water pumping appears to be most suited for Solar PV applications as water demand increases during dry days when plenty of sunshine is available. There would be less need of water during rainy season when the availability of solar energy is also low.

SPV water pumping systems have been successfully used in many parts of the world in the range of few hundred W_p to 5 kW.

An SPV water pumping system is expected to deliver a minimum of 15,000 liters per day for 200 W_p panel and 1, 70,000 liters per day for 2,250 W_p panel from suction of 7 meters and / or a total head of 10 meters on a clear sunny day. Three types of motors have generally been used: (i) permanent magnet dc motor (in low capacity pumping systems), (ii) brush-less dc motors and (iii) variable voltage and variable frequency ac motors, with appropriate electronic control and conversion system. An SPV water pumping system for a fishing farm is shown in Fig. 6.53.

Figure 6.53 An SPV water pumping system for fishing form

Lighting

Next to water pumping, lighting is the second most important and extensive application of stand-alone solar PV system.

As lighting is required when sun is not available battery storage is essential. Energy efficient compact fluorescent lamps (CFL) or low-pressure sodium vapour lamps(LPSVL) are used at 25–35 kHz frequencies, as SPV is an expensive power source. Pole mounted out-door lighting, shown in Fig. 6.54, is designed for 3–6 hours an evening. A typical system has two 35 W modules connected in parallel, an 11W (900 lumens) CFL, a 90 or 120 Ah, 12 V storage battery and associated electronics including inverter, battery charger and timer to switch on and off the light. The approximate cost of one pole mounted streetlight is Rs 30,000.

Figure 6.54 Pole mounted SPV lighting

Medical Refrigeration

In many developing countries where such life-saving vaccines are in great demand, electricity is not available to operate conventional refrigerators. WHO has specified technical details for PV based refrigerators using solar energy for such applications. This has resulted

in success of WHO sponsored immunization program in these countries. The volume
of refrigerator chamber varies from 20-100 liters with freezer volume ranging from
10–35 liters. The PV module size ranges from 100 W_P to over 600 W with 12 V /24 V battery,
of 150 to over 600 Ah capacities. An SPV powered portable medical refrigerator is shown in Fig.
6.56.

Figure 6.56 An SPV powered portable medical refrigerator

Village Power

Solar PV power can be used to meet low energy demands of many remote, small,
isolated and generally unapproachable villages in most developing countries. Two
approaches have generally been used:
 (i) Individual SPV system for every household
 (ii) A centralized SPV plant to meet combined load demand of the whole
village

Telecommunication and Signaling

Solar PV power is ideally suited for telecommunication applications such as, local
telephone exchange, radio and TV broadcasting, microwave and other forms
of electronic communication links. This is because, in most telecommunication
applications, storage batteries are already in use and the electrical systems are basically
dc. An SPV for satellite earth station is shown in Fig. 6.57.

Figure 6.57 SPV for satellite earth station

Link for Solar cell working

https://youtu.be/X0OZ6tpZ3Mc

SOLAR CELL || PRINCIPLE, CONSTRUCTION, WORKING, VI CHARACTERISTICS AND APPLICATIONS OF SOLAR CELL

https://youtu.be/c58uWGY66Z0

Link for SOLAR CELL,Module,Panel,Array

https://youtu.be/FNQzj98x_pA

Theory of solar cells|Solar cell materials|solar cell array|solar cell power plant

https://youtu.be/Moovzsy15aw

Solar cell losses

https://youtu.be/LMoE7uleR18

Solar cell losses, Advantages, Disadvantages and Applications

https://youtu.be/roiNF6_kGFM

Effect of shadowing on Solar PV panels

https://youtu.be/JTDSPjDSrS8

https://youtu.be/Be5eZcLY7FQ

Solar Cell mismatching

https://youtu.be/vj_VyVmCSQU

MPPT

https://youtu.be/61KOruxxxiU

https://youtu.be/5Us5mM87PU8

PV Cell modelling

https://youtu.be/rjLd6eJYMsI

https://youtu.be/RRebGefCFps

Module-II
Wind Energy

Wind power or **wind energy** is the use of <u>wind</u> to provide <u>mechanical power</u> through <u>wind turbines</u> to turn <u>electric generators</u> and traditionally to do other work, like milling or pumping.

- Wind power is a <u>sustainable</u>, <u>renewable energy</u> source that has a much smaller <u>impact on the environment</u> compared to burning <u>fossil fuels</u>.
- Wind turbines convert the kinetic energy in the wind into mechanical power.
- <u>Wind turbines</u> convert the energy in wind to electricity by rotating propeller-like blades around a rotor. The rotor turns the drive shaft, which turns an electric generator. Three key factors affect the amount of energy a turbine can harness from the wind: wind speed, air density, and swept area.

Equation for Wind Power

$$P = \frac{1}{2}\rho A V^3$$

V=Wind speed, ρ = Density of the air, A=Swept area of the turbine

A wind <u>energy</u> conversion system (WECS) is powered by wind energy and generates mechanical energy that sends energy to the electrical generator for making electricity. Fig. 1.3 shows the <u>interconnection</u> of a WECS. The generator of the <u>wind turbine</u> can be a permanent magnet <u>synchronous generator</u> (PMSG), doubly fed induction generator, induction generator, synchronous generator, etc. Wind energy acquired from the wind turbine is sent to the generator. To achieve maximum power from the WECS, the <u>rotational speed</u> of the generator is controlled by a <u>pulse width modulation</u> converter. The output power of the generator is supplied to the grid through a generator-side converter and a grid-side <u>inverter</u>. A <u>wind farm</u> can be distributed in onshore, offshore, seashore, or hilly areas. The WECS might be the most promising DG for future SG.

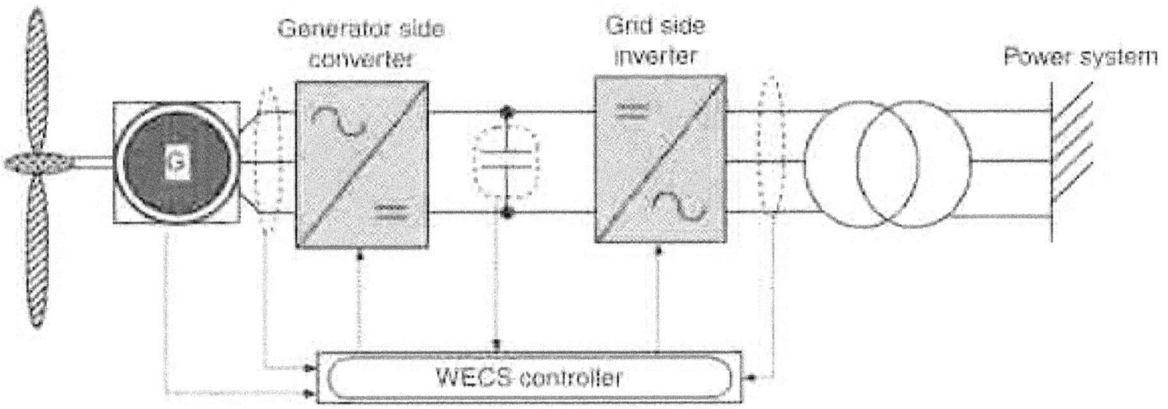

Figure 1.3. Wind energy conversion system.

Wind energy is an alternative to fossil fuels, it is plentiful, renewable, widely distributed, clean, low cost, produces no emissions during operation, and uses a tiny land area [14]. The effects on the environment are generally less problematic than those from other conventional power sources. Due to the variable wind speed, the output power of the WECS fluctuates and may create a frequency deviation of the power grid. To solve this problem, much research has already been conducted.

The world wind energy association (WWEA) published the key statistics of the World Wind Energy Report 2013.

The world wind energy capacity reached 318.5 GW by end of 2013 (this was 282.2 GW in 2012). In total, 103 countries are today using wind power on commercial basis. China was still by far the leading wind market with a new capacity of 16 GW and a total capacity of 91.3 GW. Wind power contributes close to 4% of the global electricity demand. For the year 2020, the WWEA predicts a wind capacity of more than 700 GW [15].

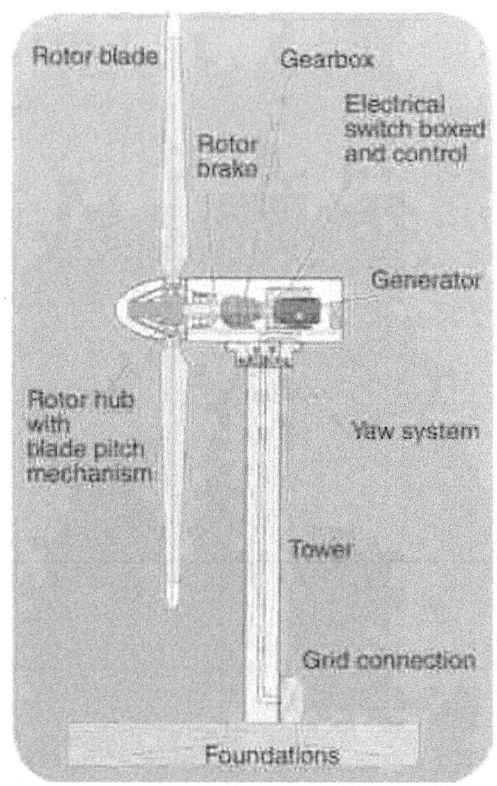

Horizontal-axis wind turbine showing major components.

Two potential wind sites are compared in terms of the specific wind power expressed in watts per square meter of area swept by the rotating blades. It is also referred to as the power density of the site, and is given by the following expression in watts per square meter of the rotor-swept area:

$$\text{specific power of the site} = \frac{1}{2}\rho V^3$$

This is the power in the upstream wind. It varies linearly with the density of the air sweeping the blades and with the cube of the wind speed. The blades cannot extract all of the upstream wind power, as some power is left in the downstream air that continues to move with reduced speed.

History of Wind-Mills:

The wind is a by-product of solar energy. Approximately 2% of the sun's energy reaching the earth is converted into wind energy. The surface of the earth heats and cools unevenly, creating atmospheric pressure zones that make air flow from high- to low pressure areas. The wind has played an important role in the history of human civilization. The first known use of wind dates back 5,000 years to Egypt, where boats used sails to travel from shore to shore. The first true windmill, a machine with vanes attached to an axis to produce circular motion, may have been built as early as 2000 B.C. in ancient Babylon. By the 10th century

A.D., windmills with wind-catching surfaces having 16 feet length and 30 feet height were grinding grain in the areas in eastern Iran and Afghanistan. The earliest written references to working wind machines in western world date from the12th century. These too were used for milling grain. It was not until a few hundred years later that windmills were modified to pump water and reclaim much of Holland from the sea.

A typical modern windmill looks as shown in the following figure. The wind-mill contains three blades about a horizontal axis installed on a tower. A turbine connected to a generator is fixed about the horizontal axis.

Like the weather in general, the wind can be unpredictable. It varies from place to place, and from moment to moment. Because it is invisible, it is not easily measured without special instruments. Wind velocity is affected by the trees, buildings, hills and valleys around us. Wind is a diffuse energy source that cannot be contained or stored for use else where or at another time.

Classification of Wind-mills:

Wind turbines are classified into two general types: Horizontal axis and Vertical axis.

A horizontal axis machine has its blades rotating on an axis parallel to the ground as shown in the above figure. A vertical axis machine has its blades rotating on an axis per pendicular to the ground. There are a number of available designs for both and each type has certain advantages and disadvantages. However, compared with the horizontal axis type, very few vertical axis machines are available commercially.

Horizontal Axis:

This is the most common wind turbine design. In addition to being parallel to the ground, the axis of blade rotation is parallel to the wind flow. Some machines are designed to operate in an upwind mode, with the blades upwind of the tower. In this case, a tail vane is usually used to keep the blades facing into the wind. Other designs operate in a downwind mode so that the wind passes the tower before striking the blades. Without a tail vane, the machine rotor naturally tracks the wind in a downwind mode. Some very large wind turbines use a motor-driven mechanism that turns the machine in response to a wind direction sensor mounted on the tower. Commonly found horizontal axis wind mills are aero-turbine mill with 35% efficiency and farm mills with 15% efficiency.

Vertical Axis:

Although vertical axis wind turbines have existed for centuries, they are not as common as their horizontal counterparts. The main reason for this is that they do not take advantage of the higher wind speeds at higher elevations above the ground as well as horizontal axis turbines.
The basic vertical axis designs are the Darrieus, which has curved blades and efficiency of 35%,the Giromill, which has straight blades, and efficiency of 35%, and the Savonius, which uses Renewable Energy Sources scoops to catch the wind and the efficiency of 30%. A vertical axis machine need not be oriented with respect to wind direction. Because the shaft is vertical, the transmission and generator can be mounted at ground level allowing easier servicing and a lighter weight, lower cost tower. Although vertical axis wind turbines have these advantages, their designs are not as efficient at collecting energy from the wind as are the horizontal machine designs. The following figures show all the above mentioned mills.

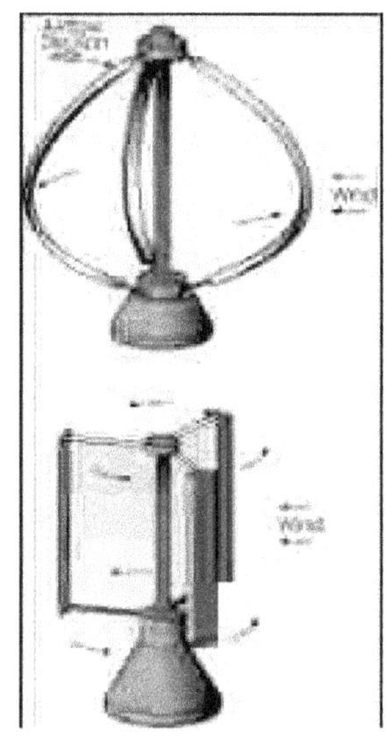

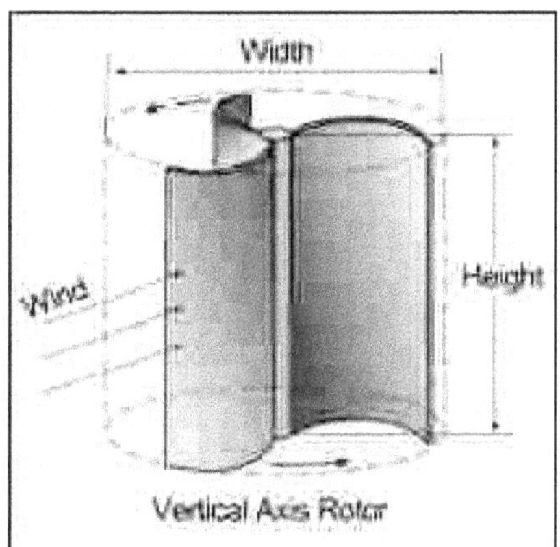

There is one more type of wind-mill called Cyclo-gyro wind-mill with very high efficiency of about 60%. However, it is not very stable and is very sensitive to wind direction. It is also very complex to build.

Link for Videos
Wind Energy
https://youtu.be/vfxX4HMBj6o

https://youtu.be/qSWm_nprfqE
<u>Wind Energy Conversion</u>
https://youtu.be/Q1uedC-1gko
https://youtu.be/Ac8NMoN-vCo
https://youtu.be/eywdMIb2FqE

Main Components of a wind-mill :

Following figure shows typical components of a horizontal axis wind mill.

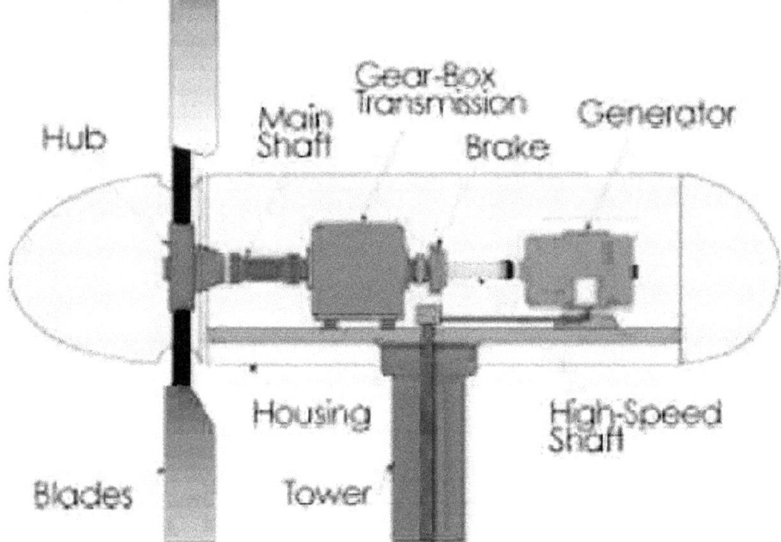

Rotor:

The portion of the wind turbine that collects energy from the wind is called the rotor.

The rotor usually consists of two or more wooden, fiberglass or metal blades which rotate about an axis (horizontal or vertical) at a rate determined by the wind speed and the shape of the blades. The blades are attached to the hub, which in turn is attached to the main shaft.

Drag Design:

Blade designs operate on either the principle of drag or lift. For the drag design, the Wind literally pushes the blades out of the way. Drag powered wind turbines are characterized by slower rotational speeds and high torque capabilities. They are useful for the pumping, sawing or grinding work. For example, a farm-type windmill must develop high torque at start-up in order to pump, or lift, water from a deep well.

Lift Design:

The lift blade design employs the same principle that enables airplanes, kites and birds to fly. The blade is essentially an airfoil, or wing. When air flows past the blade, a wind speed and pressure differential is created between the upper and lower blade surfaces. The pressure at the lower surface is greater and thus acts to "lift" the blade. When blades are attached to a central axis, like a wind turbine rotor, the lift is translated into rotational motion. Lift-powered wind turbines have much higher rotational speeds than drag types and therefore well suited for electricity generation.

Tip Speed Ratio:

The tip-speed is the ratio of the rotational speed of the blade to the wind speed. The Larger this ratio, the faster the rotation of the wind turbine rotor at a given wind speed. Electricity generation requires high rotational speeds. Lift-type wind turbines have maximum tip-speed ratios of around 10, while drag-type ratios are approximately 1.

Given the high rotational speed requirements of electrical generators, it is clear that the lift-type wind turbine is most practical for this application.

The number of blades that make up a rotor and the total area they cover affect wind turbine performance. For a lift-type rotor to function effectively, the wind must flow smoothly over the blades. To avoid turbulence, spacing between blades should be great enough so that one blade will not encounter the disturbed, weaker air flow caused by the blade which passed before it. It is because of this requirement that most wind turbines have only two or three blades on their rotors.

Generator:

The generator is what converts the turning motion of a wind turbine's blades into electricity. Inside this component, coils of wire are rotated in a magnetic field to produce electricity. Different generator designs produce either alternating current (AC) or direct current (DC), and they are available in a large range of output power ratings.

The generator's rating, or size, is dependent on the length of the wind turbine's blades because more energy is captured by longer blades.

It is important to select the right type of generator to match intended use. Most home and office appliances operate on 240 volt, 50 cycles AC. Some appliances can operate on either AC or DC, such as light bulbs and resistance heaters, and many others can be adapted to run on DC. Storage systems using batteries store DC and usually are configured at voltages of between 12 volts and 120 volts.

Generators that produce AC are generally equipped with features to produce the Correct voltage of 240 V and constant frequency 50 cycles of electricity, even when the Wind speed is fluctuating.

DC generators are normally used in battery charging applications and for operating DC appliances and machinery. They also can be used to produce AC electricity with the use of an inverter, which converts DC to AC.

Transmission:

The number of revolutions per minute (rpm) of a wind turbine rotor can range between 40 rpm and 400 rpm, depending on the model and the wind speed. Generators typically require rpm's of 1,200 to 1,800. As a result, most wind turbines require a gear-box transmission to increase the rotation of the generator to the speeds necessary for efficient electricity production. Some DC-type wind turbines do not use transmissions. Instead, they have a direct link between the rotor and generator. These are known as direct drive systems. Without a transmission, wind turbine complexity and maintenance requirements are reduced, but a much larger generator is required to deliver the same power output as the AC-type wind turbines.

Tower:

The tower on which a wind turbine is mounted is not just a support structure. It also raises the wind turbine so that its blades safely clear the ground and so it can reach the stronger winds at higher elevations. Maximum tower height is optional in most cases, except where zoning restrictions apply. The decision of what height tower to use will be based on the cost of taller towers versus the value of the increase in energy production resulting from their use. Studies have shown that the added cost of increasing tower height is often justified by the added power generated from the stronger winds. Larger wind turbines are usually mounted on towers ranging from 40 to 70 meters tall.

Towers for small wind systems are generally "guyed" designs. This means that there are guy wires anchored to the ground on three or four sides of the tower to hold it erect. These towers cost less than freestanding towers, but require more land area to anchor the guy wires.

Some of these guyed towers are erected by tilting them up. This operation can be quickly accomplished using only a winch, with the turbine already mounted to the tower top. This simplifies not only installation, but maintenance as well. Towers can be constructed of a simple tube, a wooden pole or a lattice of tubes, rods, and angle iron. Large wind turbines may be mounted on lattice towers, tube towers or guyed tilt-up towers.

Towers must be strong enough to support the wind turbine and to sustain vibration,wind loading and the overall weather elements for the lifetime of the wind turbine. Their costs will vary widely as a function of design and height.

Wind Energy Conversion
https://youtu.be/Ac8NMoN-vCo

Horizontal and Vertical Axis Turbine
https://youtu.be/NNBFpkNrhbY

https://youtu.be/65k2Nh8YHFI

Vertical Axis Wind Turbine
https://youtu.be/jdtDG0n2MSw

https://youtu.be/QgYYrvAa0Jw

https://youtu.be/qx_M0nvDIGU

Operating Characteristics of wind mills:

All wind machines share certain operating characteristics, such as cut-in, rated and cutout wind speeds.

Cut-in Speed:

Cut-in speed is the minimum wind speed at which the blades will turn and generate usable power. This wind speed is typically between 10 and 16 kmph.

Rated Speed:

The rated speed is the minimum wind speed at which the wind turbine will generate its designated rated power. For example, a "10 kilowatt" wind turbine may not generate 10kilowatts until wind speeds reach 40 kmph. Rated speed for most machines is in the range of 40 to 55 kmph. At wind speeds between cut-in and rated, the power output from a wind turbine increases as the wind increases. The output of most machines levels off above the rated speed.
Most manufacturers provide graphs, called "power curves, "showing how their wind turbine output varies with wind speed.

Cut-out Speed:

At very high wind speeds, typically between 72 and 128 kmph, most wind turbines cease power generation and shut down. The wind speed at which shut down occurs is called the cut out speed. Having a cut-out speed is a safety feature which protects the wind turbine from damage. Shut down may occur in one of several ways. In some machines an automatic brake is activated by a wind speed sensor. Some machines twist or "pitch" the blades to spill the wind.
Still others use "spoilers," drag flaps mounted on the blades or the hub which are automatically activated by high rotor rpm's, or mechanically activated by a spring loaded device which turns the machine sideways to the wind stream. Normal wind turbine operation usually resumes when the wind drops back to a safe level.

Betz Limit:

It is the flow of air over the blades and through the rotor area that makes a wind turbine function. The wind turbine extracts energy by slowing the wind down. The theoretical maximum amount of energy in the wind that can be collected by a wind turbine's rotor is approximately
59%. This value is known as the Betz limit. If the blades were 100%efficient, a wind turbine would not work because the air, having given up all its energy, would entirely stop. In practice, the collection efficiency of a rotor is not as high as 59%.A more typical efficiency is 35% to 45%.
A complete wind energy system, including rotor, transmission, generator, storage and other devices, which all have less than perfect efficiencies, will deliver between 10% and 30% of the original energy available in the wind.

The following plot gives the relationship between wind speed in KMPH and the power density.

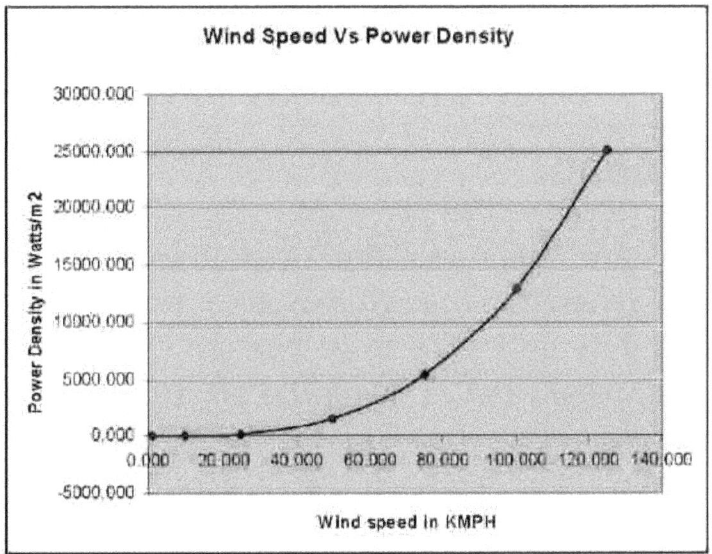

In the last column of the table, we have calculated the output of the turbine assuming that the efficiency of the turbine is 30%. However, we need to remember that the efficiency of the turbine is a function of wind speed. *It varies with wind speed*.

Now, let us try to calculate the wind speed required to generate power equivalent to 1square meter PV panel with 12% efficiency. We know that solar insolation available at the PV panel is 1000 watts/m^{2}at standard condition. Hence the output of the PV panel with 12% efficiency would be 120 watts. Now the speed required to generate this power by the turbine with 30% efficiency can be calculated as follows:

Turbine output required = 120 Watts/m^2

Power Density at the blades = 120/ (0.3) = 400 watts/m^2

Wind Power:-

Wind power is generated on account of flow of wind. The blow of wind takes place due to density difference at two places on the surface of the earth. The density difference occurs when the solar radiation differs on earth's surface. Most of the energy stored in wind is found in high altitudes, over flat areas. But most of the potential is close to the coastal areas, approximately equivalent to

72 TW, or 54,000 Mtoe per year. *The power of the wind is proportional to the cubic power of the velocity.* To assess the frequency of wind speeds at a particular location, a probability distribution function is often fit to the observed data. Different locations will have different wind speed distributions. The worldwide wind generation capacity is 1,94,400 MW. India's present installed capacity is 2,000 MW.

Off-shore Wind Power:-

Offshore wind power refers to the installation of wind power plant in the water. Better wind speeds are obtained if the installation is made in the water than the land. Induction generators are often used for power generation. The power generators behave differently due to fluctuation of wind speed during power generation. So, the installation of advanced electromechanical generators are highly essential.

The capacity factor of wind generator is the ratio of actual productivity in a year to the theoretical maximum. The capacity factor of a wind generator varies from 20-40%. The capacity factor arises due to the variation of wind speed at the site and the generator size. The smaller generator would be cheaper and achieve higher capacity factor. Conversely the larger generator would cost more and produce smaller capacity factor.

* The wind power has low operating cost but it carries high capital cost.

Origin of Wind:

The flow of air starts when there is pressure difference between two places. The region where solar radiation is less the atmospheric air gets low temperature and hence low pressure region. On the contrary where the solar radiation is high the atmospheric air gets heated and pressure is high. These differences in atmospheric air pressure (*pressure gradient*) cause acceleration of the air particles which is called wind.

The rotation of earth about its own axis creates Coriolis force which superimposes on the pressure gradient. The direction of wind motion is affected by this *Coriolis force*. In the Northern hemisphere, the moving object turns towards right due to the effect of the Coriolis force if the observer moves in the direction of wind movement. Similarly, the moving object turns towards left in the southern hemisphere.

* In a friction free, rectilinear and stationary wind movement, the force due to pressure gradient and Coriolis force are of same magnitude but in opposite direction. *The wind motion due to Coriolis force is known as geostropic wind.*

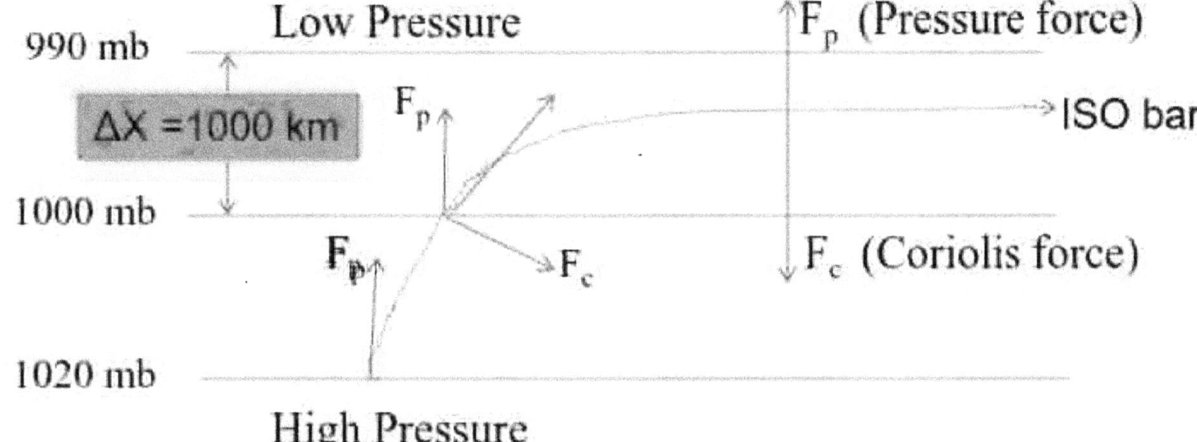

Fig: Geostropic wind on the northern hemisphere

As a result of pressure difference, the air first moves towards low pressure region. It then follows inclined movement towards right due to Coriolis force. This inclination towards right continues till the magnitude of Coriolis force is exactly equal to the pressure gradient force. At this point the wind moves in the direction of isobars whose motion is in the same direction as that of geotropic winds.

Consider a small air element whose Coriolis force is equal to the product of the Coriolis acceleration and mass of the air, i.e. $F_c = 2\omega \sin \phi \times v_g \times (\Delta X \Delta Y \Delta Z) \times \rho_a$

Where

F_c = Coriolis force in newton

$\omega \sin \phi$ = angular velocity of earth at the latitude ϕ (1/sec)

ϕ = latitude

$\Delta X \Delta Y \Delta Z$ = Volume of the considered small air element in (m³)

ρ_a = density of air (m/sec)

v_g = geostropic wind velocity (m/sec)

The pressure force (F_p) on the air element can be written as: $F_p = \Delta p \Delta Y \Delta Z$

Where Δp = pressure difference on the air element (N/m²)

$\Delta Y \Delta Z$ = area of air element (m²).

By equating, $F_c = F_p \Rightarrow 2\omega \sin \phi \, v_g \Delta X \rho_a = \Delta p \Rightarrow v_g = \dfrac{\Delta p}{\Delta X} \dfrac{1}{2\omega (\sin \phi) \rho_a}$

* *It is seen that the pressure gradient is directly proportional to the velocity of the geostropic wind.*

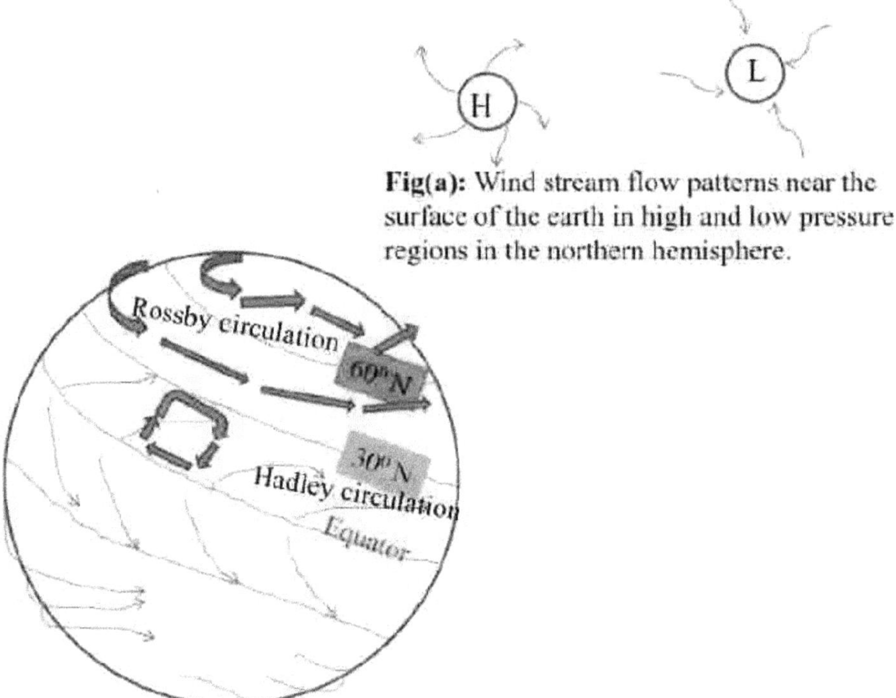

Fig(b): Simplified circulation system of the earth **(WMO 1981)**

If the path of the wind is curved, then the centrifugal force of the wind particle are also affected by the pressure force and Coriolis forces. The air particles close to the earth's surface are affected by the frictional forces. There is a formation of boundary layer over the surface due to these frictional forces. These collective forces creates a mechanism up to the range of heights *300m to 600m*. The wind velocity within this boundary layer is much smaller than that at higher altitudes. The air flow motion in the form of parallel isobars deviate with decreasing altitude.

In figure (a), the wind flow patterns near the surface of the earth at high and low pressure region have been shown in the hemisphere region.

In figure (b), the circulation system of the earth has been shown. It consists of two components: (i) *Hadley circulation* in the equator region and (ii) *Rossby circulation* in the upper and lower region of the earth.

The operating power of Hadley circulation is the strong solar radiation at the equator. The air gets heated, rises high and moves towards north and south, where it is deviated towards east as result of Coriolis force. The air gets cooled and sinks down in the latitude region $\pm30^0$ (+ North, $-$ South) and flows back towards the equator, where it is deviated towards west due to the Coriolis force. These are the regions where local storms overlap and wind-flows are not always predictable. In the northern and southern region around latitudes $\pm60^0$ the westerly winds of Rossby circulation dominate the region. These winds have wave-form character and vary strongly in the flow patterns.

Wind Flow and Wind Direction:-

Wind speed is classified on representative scale of 12. The order of wind classification is in m/sec or knots (1 nautical miles = 1.852km/hr). The direction of wind are normally divided into eight segments: North, North-East, East, South-East, South, South-West, West and North-West.

Power Density of the Wind:-

Power density of the wind is calculated based on the normal area (A) to the direction of flow of wind stream. The kinetic energy (dE) contained within the mass of the element (dM) is:

$$dE = \frac{1}{2}dmv^2 \quad\ldots\ldots\ldots\ldots\ldots(i)$$

Where

dE = Kinetic energy (joule)

dm = Elemental mass (kg)

$v = dx/dt$ = wind velocity (m/sec). (Here dx is the path travelled in the direction of wind in time dt).

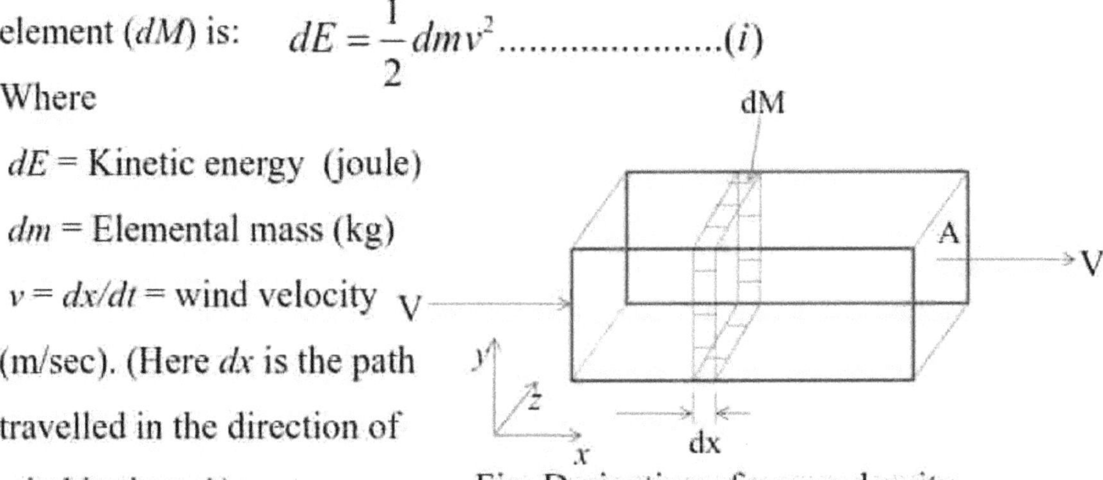

Fig: Derivation of power density

If the density of air is ρ_a and dv is the elemental volume in m³

then $dv = A.dx$ and $dm = \rho_a\, dv$ $\quad\ldots\ldots\ldots\ldots(ii)$

The mass element dm can be expressed as:

$$dm = A\rho_a . v.dt \ (kg)............(iii)$$

So the K.E. is: $dE = (1/2)\,\rho_a A v^3 dt$

The power, P is: $P = \dfrac{dE}{dt}$ and power density in (w/m^2) is: $P = \dfrac{P}{A} = \dfrac{1}{2}\rho_a v^3$

It is seen that the wind power density (Pressure) depends upon the cube of wind velocity.

Wind Measurement: -

Wind pressure Measurement:- $P_t = P_s (\text{Static Pressure}) + (1/2)\rho_a v^2 ....(iv)$

Applying Bernoulli's equation the total pressure (P_t) can be calculated as:

and the velocity can be calculated as: $v = \sqrt{\dfrac{2(P_t - P_s)}{\rho_a}}$ ....(v)

The velocity can be calculated if both the pressures are known. The Prandtl tube is used for pressure measurement.

The Prandtl's pressure tube contains two tubes. Both are concentric tubes. The inner tube converts the dynamic pressure ($(1/2)\rho_a V^2$) to the stagnation condition. This converts the kinetic energy to pressure energy. At the downstream end the inner

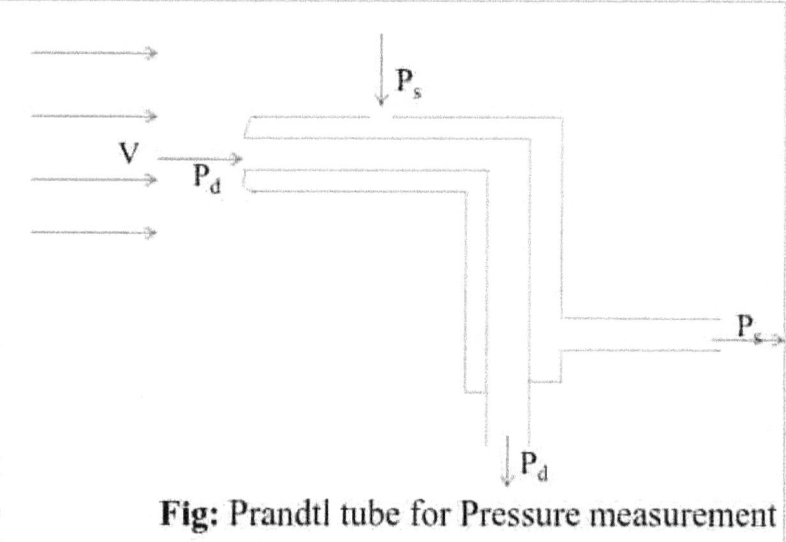

Fig: Prandtl tube for Pressure measurement

tube the pressure head is measured with the manometer. The outer tube measures the static pressure head (P_s) using a manometer.

Annual Average Wind Speed:

The annual average wind velocity at a particular plate can be calculated (in m/sec) by the formula:

$$\bar{v}_i = \frac{\int_{t_1}^{t_2} v\, dt}{t_2 - t_1}$$

Where,

v = Daily average wind velocity (m/sec),

t = time

$t_2 - t_1$ = time duration of one year (sec).

Such annual average values can be obtained for many years by taking average of values for total number of years, i.e.

Where

$$\bar{v} = \frac{1}{n} \sum_{i=1}^{n} \bar{v}_i$$

n = number of years,

$\bar{v}_i$ = annual average value for the year i in m/sec.

Altitude Dependence of Wind Speed:

The maximum velocity of jet stream occurs at a height of 10 km. The velocity there is nearly five times more than its magnitude at a height of 10 m. In the boundary layer the velocity of flow varies linearly on a log-log representation. It indicates the variation of wind velocity is exponential. The wind velocity at a height H is obtained as:

$$\bar{v}_H = \bar{v}_{10}\left[\frac{H}{10}\right]^{g^*} \quad \text{m/sec.}$$

Where

$\bar{v}_H$ = average annual velocity (in m/sec) at a height H (in m).

$\bar{v}_{10}$ = annual average velocity (in m/sec) at a height of 10 m.

H = height (m)

g^* = exponent.

The above equation is accurate up to height of 200m. The values of the exponent are given in table below.

Recording of wind data:

The wind speed is measured by an anemometer and wind direction is measured by a wind vane attached to a direction indicator. Anemometer works on one of the following principles.

(i) The oldest and simplest anemometer is a swinging plate hung vertically and hinged along its top edge. Wind speed is indicated by the angle of deflection of the plate with respect to the vertical.

(ii) A cup anemometer consists of three or four cups mounted symmetrically about a vertical axis. The speed of rotation indicates wind speed.

(iii) A hot-wire anemometer measures the wind speed by recording cooling effect of the wind on a hot-wire. The heat is produced by passing an electric current through the wire.

(iv) An anemometer can also be on sonic effect. Sound travels through still air at a known speed. However, if the air is moving, the speed decreases or increases accordingly.

(v) Wind speed can be recorded by measuring the wind pressure on a flat plate.

(vi) The other methods include the laser drop anemometer, the anemometer and the SODAR Doppler anemometer.

<u>Applications of Wind Power: Mechanical Power:-</u>
(i)   Wind Pumps
(ii)   Heating
(iii)   Sea Transport
Off-grid Electrical Power Source:(i) Machines of lower power with rotor diameter of about 3m to 40-1000 Watt rating can generate sufficient electrical energy for space heating and cooling of homes, water heating, battery charging and for operating domestic appliances
such as fans, lights and small tools.
(ii) Applications of somewhat more powerful turbines of about 50 KW are producing electrical power for navigation signals, remote communication, weather stations and off-shore oil drilling platforms.
(iii) Intermediate power range, roughly 100 to 250 KW aero-generators can power to isolated populations, farm cooperatives, commercial refrigerators and to small industries.
(iii) For lifting water to hill, aero-generator is installed on the top of hill and electrical energy is transmitted to a pump fixed at lower level.
Grid-Connected Electrical Power Source.
(i) Large aero-generators in the range of a few hundred KW to a few MW are planned for supplying power to a utility grid. Large arrays of aero-generators,known as wind farms are being deployed in open plains or off-shore in shallow water for this purpose.
<u>Wind Energy Converters:-</u>
The wind energy converters convert wind energy to electrical and mechanical energies.
<u>Maximum Power Coefficient:</u>*The maximum power coefficient of the wind energy can be defined as the ratio of the convertible power to the theoretically maximum power from the available wind energy.*

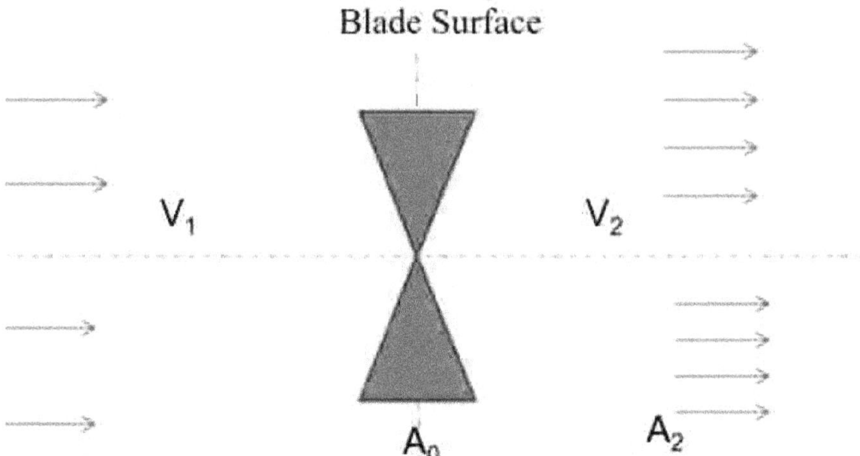

Fig: Wind stream profile in an external wind turbine

The *incompressible, friction free and one dimensional wave* is shown here. The flow is called *Rankine-Froude momentum* theory. The flow velocity (V_1 m/sec) and cross sectional area (A_1 m²) enters into the surface of the wind blade and leaves out with velocity (V_2 m/sec) at a cross sectional area (A_2 m²).

According to the equation of continuity: $\quad m = A_1 v_1 = A_2 v_2$ m³/sec............(vi)

At the surface of the rotor: $\quad m = \rho_a v_0 A_0$ kg/sec.........(vii)

Where ρ_a = air density (kg/m³)

$\qquad v_0$ = Wind velocity at the surface of the rotor (m/sec)

$\qquad A_0$ = rotor disc area (m²)

So v_0 can be written as: $\quad v_0 = \dfrac{1}{2}(v_1 + v_2)$ m/sec...............(viii)

We know that the power density,

$$P_1 = \frac{1}{2}\rho_a v_1^3 A_1 \ (W) \quad \text{and} \quad P_2 = \frac{1}{2}\rho_a v_2^3 A_2 (W)\ldots\ldots(ix)$$

The power of the rotor is:

$$P = P_1 - P_2 \ (W) \quad \text{or} \quad P = \frac{1}{2}\rho_a\left(A_1 v_1^3 - v_2^3 A_2\right)\ (W)\ldots\ldots(x)$$

Or $\quad P = \rho_a v_1 A_1 \dfrac{v_1^2}{2} - \rho_a v_2 A_2 \dfrac{v_2^2}{2}$ (W)

Or $\quad P = \dfrac{1}{2} \dot{m}\left(v_1^2 - v_2^2\right) \qquad \left(\because m = Av\rho\right)$

Or $\quad P = \dfrac{1}{4} \rho_a A_0 \left(v_1 + v_2\right)\left(v_1^2 - v_2^2\right) \qquad \left(\because v_0 = \dfrac{1}{2}\left(v_1 + v_2\right)\right)$

Or $\quad P = \dfrac{1}{4} \rho_a A_0 v_1^3 \left(1 + \dfrac{v_2}{v_1}\right)\left(1 - \dfrac{v_2^2}{v_1^2}\right)$ (W)........................(xi)

The maximum power is obtained when the wind speed (v_2) is zero.

$$P_{max} = \dfrac{1}{4} \rho_a v_1^3 A_0 \text{ (W)}..............(xii)$$

The ideal power coefficient (C_p) of a wind machine is the ratio of the power P of the rotor to the maximum wind power, i.e.

$$C_p = \dfrac{P}{P_{max}} = \dfrac{1}{2}\left(1 + \dfrac{v_2}{v_1}\right)\left(1 - \left(\dfrac{v_2}{v_1}\right)^2\right)....(xiii)$$

The maximum power coefficient (C_p) can be determined by differentiating Eq.(*xiii*) w.r.t. v_2/v_1. So,

$$\frac{\partial C_p}{\partial \left(\dfrac{v_2}{v_1} \right)} = 0 \Rightarrow \frac{v_2}{v_1} = \frac{1}{3} \dots (xiv)$$

From Eq.(xiii) and (xiv), we get

$$C_{pmax} = 0.593 \dots \dots \dots \dots \dots (xv)$$

So, it is clear that the maximum usable power from an ideal wind energy converter is 59.3%.

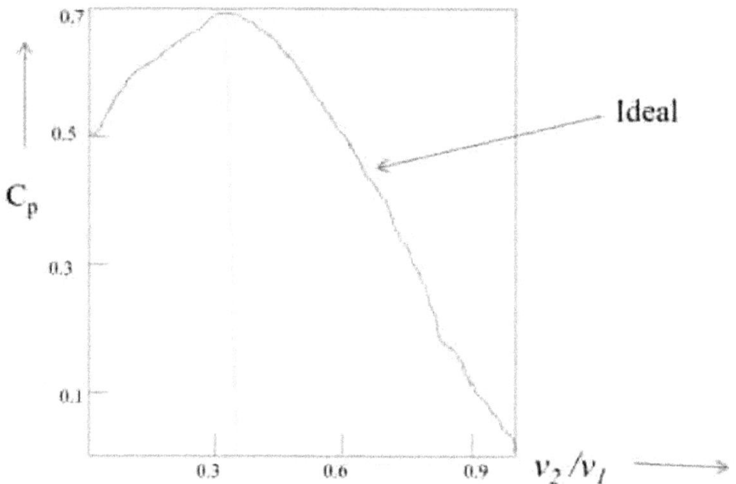

Power Coefficient of a Drag or Resistive type Rotor:-

For an oblique surface, the drag force is:

$$F_R = (1/2)\ C_R\ \rho_a\ v^2 A\ \dots\dots\dots\dots\dots\dots\dots\dots\dots(xvi)$$

Where F_R = Drag force (N),

ρ_a = density of air (kg/m^3)

v = wind velocity (m/sec)

A = area of the resistance rotor (m^2)

C_R = drag coefficient (which depends upon the value of the geometry of the body)

If the motion of the linear speed (u) of the rotor is taken into account, then

$$F_R = \frac{1}{2} C_R \rho_a (v-u)^2 A. \quad \text{newton}\dots\ \dots(xvii)$$

The power produced by the drag is: $\quad P = \dfrac{1}{2}\rho_a C_R (v-u)^2 .u.A\ (W)\dots(xviii)$

The maximum power of the rotor at the surface of the blade is: $P = \dfrac{1}{2}\rho_a v^3 A\ (W)..(xix)$

The power coefficient for the drag type rotor is the ratio of rotor power to the maximum

power.

$$C_{PR} = \frac{P}{P_{max}} = \frac{(1/2)\rho_a C_R (v-u)^2 uA}{(1/2)\rho_a v^3 A} = C_R (1 - \frac{u^2}{v^2})\frac{u}{v} \ldots\ldots(xx)$$

The maximum C_{PR} is obtained by setting $\dfrac{\partial C_{PR}}{\partial \left(\dfrac{u}{v}\right)} = 0$ ....(xxi)

By solving we will get $u/v = 1/3$.

So the maximum value: C_{PR} max $= (4/27)\, C_R$ ....$(xxii)$

Fig: Comparison of ideal power coefficient with maximum values of power coefficient of resistive rotors.

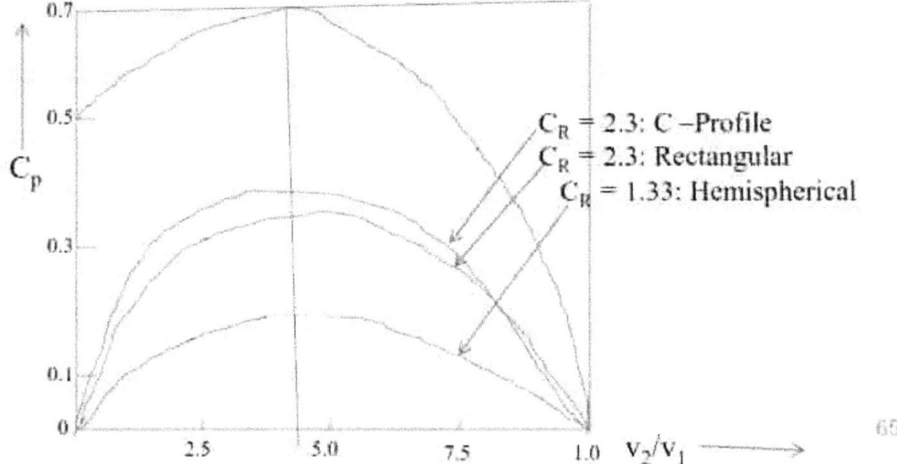

Wind Stream Profiles:-

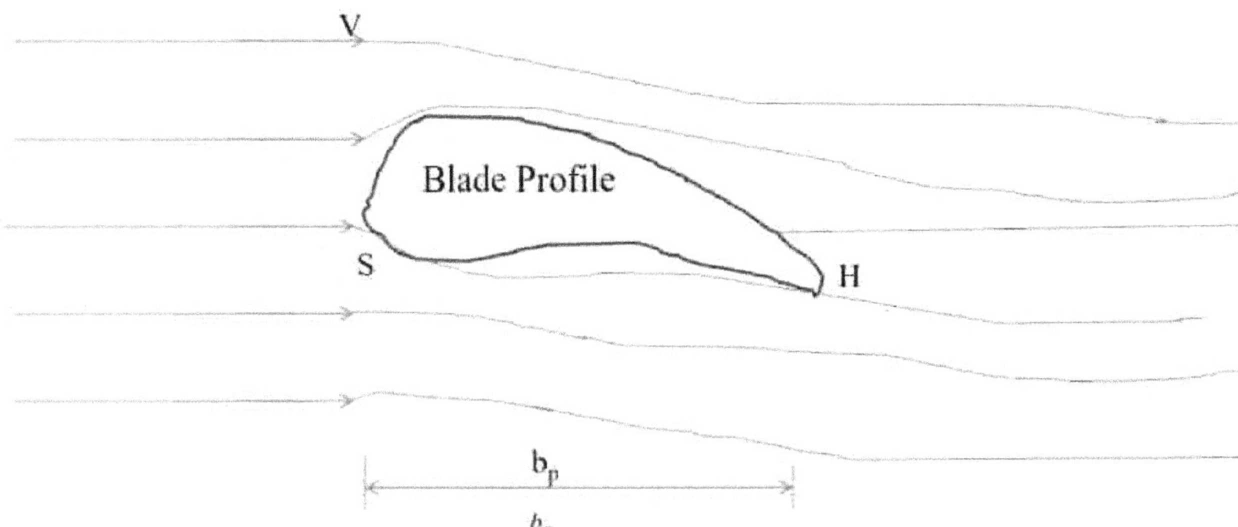

The lift force (F_A) is given by: $F_A = \int_0^{b_p}(P_L - P_u)L dx$............$(xxiii)$

P_L = Pressure at the lower side of the profile (N/m²) , P_u = Pressure at the upper side

of the profile (N/m²), L = Length (m), b_p = width of the profile (m).

* *The pressure is lower on the upper side than the lower side.*

Buoyancy Coefficient and the Drag Coefficient:-

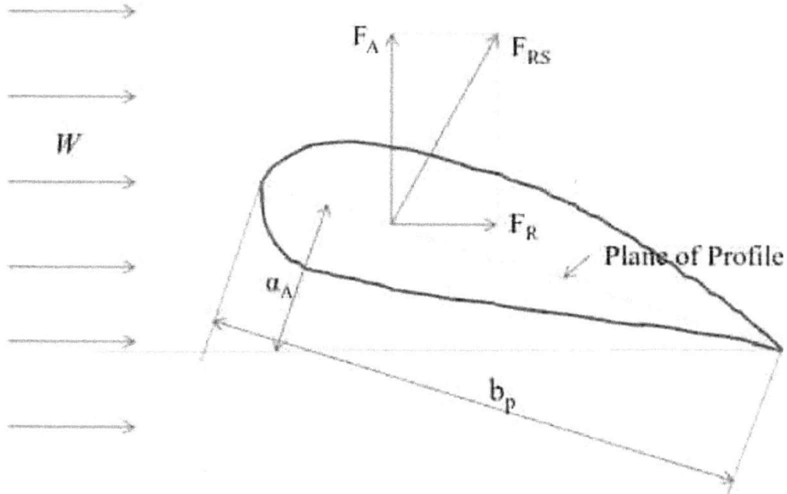

For an asymmetrical profile, there exists two forces:

(1) The lift force (F_A) perpendicular to the direction of flow, and (2) the drag

force (F_R) parallel in the direction of flow.

Let us assume: α_A = incident angle or angle of attack (angle between the profile and

the flow direction).

w = apparent wind velocity (m/sec).

A = profile area (m²) = $b_p L$.

P_a = air density (Kg/m²).

L = length of the profile (m)

b_p = width of the profile (m)

C_R = drag coefficient (dimensionless).

The horizontal drag force (F_R) developed due to friction with the surface of the profile is:

$$F_R = \frac{1}{2}\rho_a C_R w^2 A = \frac{1}{2}\rho_a C_R w^2 b_p L \quad (N)$$

The vertical force lift (F_L) can be calculated as:

$$F_R = \frac{1}{2}\rho_a C_a w^2 A = \frac{1}{2}\rho_a C_a w^2 b_p L \quad (N)$$

The drag coefficient C_R and the lift coefficient C_a are determined experimentally for a particular profile. The values of C_R and C_a are determined from the polar diagram with angle of attack as a parameter which is shown in the next slide.

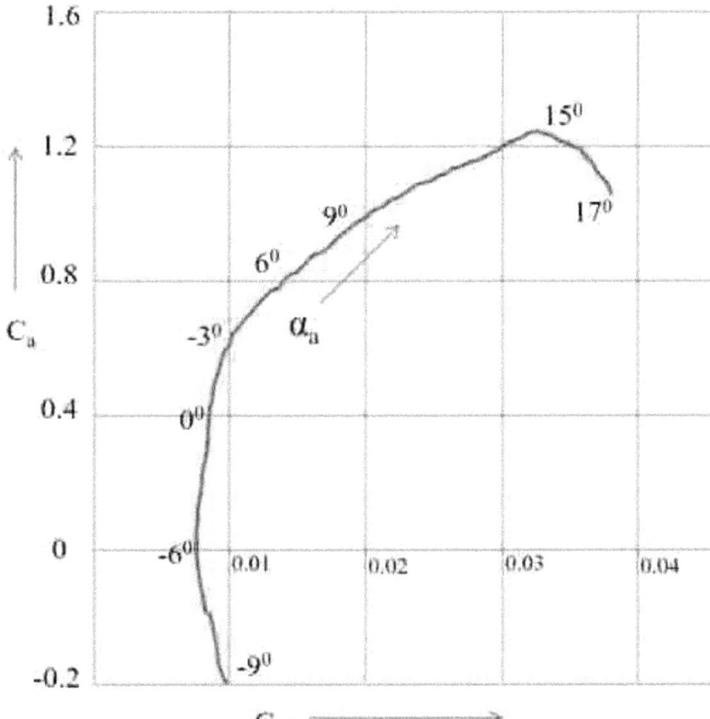

The diagram is shown for the Reynolds number of the flow (Re) as:

$$Re = \frac{w b_p}{v}$$

Where v is the kinematic viscosity (m²/sec)

Fig: A Polar diagram of a simple blade profile (Re = 10^5).

Velocities and Forces at the Rotor Blade:-

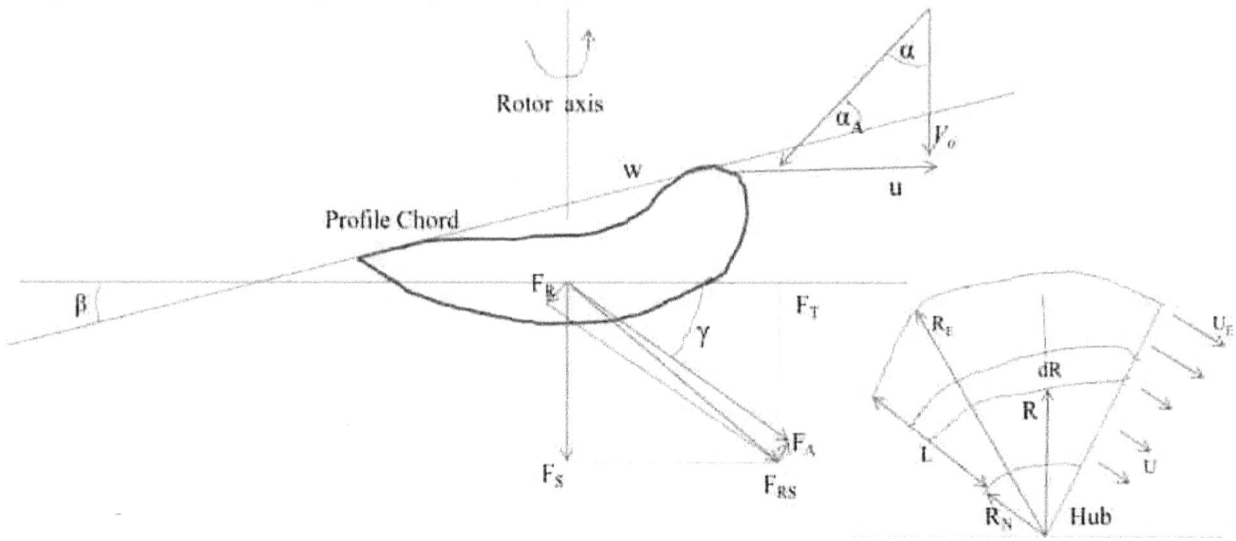

u = Circumferential velocity of rotor blade (m/sec), v_0 = Velocity of wind (m/sec), w = Approach velocity of wind (m/sec), β = Blade angle (Angle between profile plane and rotor plane), F_{RS} = Resultant of the F_A and F_R. F_s = Axial component of F_{RS}, R_E= Outer rotor radius, R_N = radius of the hub, u_E = Peripheral velocity at the edge of the blade, α_A = angle of attack, γ = angle between wind velocity v_0 and relative approach velocity, L = Rotor blade length. For an element which delivered power dP along the length dR of the rotor blade, one can write: $dP = u\, dF_T$ (W)

Where dF_T is an elemental tangential force. It is expressed as:

$$dF_T = dF_A \cos\gamma \quad \text{newton}$$

So the power produced is given by: $dP = u \cos\gamma\, dF_A$ (W)

Using the expression for dF_A we can write:

$$dP = u \cos\gamma\, \frac{C_A}{2}\, \rho_a w^2 dA \ \ (W)$$

$$\text{Again,} \quad \cos\gamma = \frac{v_0}{w} = \frac{v_0}{\sqrt{u^2 + v_0^2}}$$

and for the area element: $dA = b_p N_R dR$

Where N_R is the number of rotor blades and dR is the length of the elemental rotor. By substitution of dA in dP we can get power of an element,

$$dP = \frac{C_A}{2}\, \rho_a w^2 u \left(\frac{v_0}{\sqrt{u^2 + v_0^2}} \right) b_p N_R dR \ \ (W)$$

The total power of the rotor can be calculated by integration of dP from R_N to R_E.

So,

$$P = \int_{R_N}^{R_E} \frac{C_a}{2} \rho_a w^2 u \frac{v_0}{\sqrt{u^2 + v_0^2}} b_p N_R dR \qquad (\text{W})$$

Similarly, thrust force can be calculated on the rotor blades along the vertical axis:

$$dF_s = dF_A \sin \gamma = \frac{C_a}{2} \rho_a w^2 dA \frac{u}{\sqrt{u^2 + v_0^2}} \qquad (\text{N})$$

$$\text{or} \qquad dF_s = \frac{C_a}{2} \rho_a w^2 (b_p N_R dR) \frac{u}{\sqrt{u^2 + v_0^2}} \qquad (\text{N})$$

$$\text{or} \qquad F_s = \int_{R_N}^{R_E} \frac{C_a}{2} \rho_a w^2 (b_p N_R) \frac{u}{\sqrt{u^2 + v_0^2}} dR \qquad (\text{N})$$

Components of a Wind Power Plant:

The different components of a wind converter are described below.

Wind Turbine:-

The wind rotors are various types depending upon number of blades, speed, control system, gear box (or gear less), type of generator etc. All the machines are based upon four basic concepts of rotor dynamics. These are given in the table below.

Table: Classification of selected wind power converters (Hau 2002).

Lift principle horizontal axis	High speed system, one-blade, two-blade or three –blade rotor, Low speed system, Historical wind mill, multiple rotor, Flettner rotor, sail rotor
Lift principle vertical axis	High speed systems, Darrieus rotor, H-rotor, three-blade rotor, low speed systems, Savonius rotor with lift principle.
Concentrating wind mill	Shrouded windmill, tornado type wind mill, delta concentrator wind mill, Berwian windmill.
Drag principle	Savonius windmill, cup anemometer windmill, half shielded windmill

* After extensive field experience, horizontal-axis, three-blade wind rotor has become an established system for field applications.

* In 1980s and 1990s, one and two-blade rotors were also developed because of higher rotational speed. But due to instability experience in operation, these were not used further.
* Gearless rotors are generally low speed converters which requires a special generator.

Tower: -

A component that sustains the whole weight of the rotor and its components is the tower. The tower should have sufficient height to operate the rotor at desired speed. The tower should also be strong enough to sustain the static and dynamic load of the rotor and vibrations during high and gusty winds. Tower are constructed from concrete or steel. Off-shore wind machines are of lower height because the wind speed is larger. So the foundations built in those cases are costly.

Electric Generators:

Electrical generators convert the rotational energy into mechanical energy then to electrical energy. Commercially available generators with slight modification are used for converters with gear box. Specially designed three phase generators are used for gearless converters.

Synchronous Generator:-

These generators are equipped with a fixed stator at the outside and a rotor at the inside located on a pivoting shaft. Normally DC is supplied to the rotor to create a magnetic field. When the shaft drives the voltage is created in the stator whose frequency matches exactly the rotational speed of the rotor. This type of generators are used most of the places but the disadvantage is that it runs with constant speed of the rotor and fixed frequency. It is therefore not suitable for variable speed operations in the wind plants.

Asynchronous Generator:

The asynchronous generator is electromagnetic generator. The stator of this generator is made of numerous coils with three groups and is supplied with three phase current. The three coils are spread around the stator periphery and carry currents, which are not in phase with each other. This combination produces a rotating magnetic field, which is the key feature of the asynchronous generator. The angular speed of the rotating magnetic field is called the synchronous magnetic field and is given by:

$$N_s = 60 \frac{f}{p} \ \text{rpm}$$

Where f = frequency of the stator excitation, p = number of magnetic pole pairs.

The stator coils are embedded in slots of high permeability magnetic core to produce a required magnetic fields intensity with low exciting currents. The rotor in this generator is squirrel cage rotor with conducting bars embedded in the slots of the magnetic core. The bars are connected at ends by a conducting ring. The stator magnetic field rotates at the synchronous speed given above. The relative speed between the stator and the rotor induces a voltage in each rotor turn linking the stator flux $V = (-dF/dt)$, F being the magnetic flux linking the rotor turn.

Foundations:-

The type of foundations required to anchor towers and thus wind energy converters, into the ground depends upon the plant size, meteorological and operational stress and local soil conditions. Erection of wind converters on a coastal line is much more costly. Depending on the soil conditions, there types of foundations namely gravity foundation, monopole foundation and tripod foundations are used . All these foundations are discussed in the beginning.

Turbine Rating:-

The normal rating of a wind turbine has no standard global rating. The power output of a turbine is proportional to the square of the rotor diameter and also to the cube of the wind speed.

* The rotor of a given diameter will generate different power at different wind speed (like 300 KW at 7m/sec and 450 KW at 8 m/sec).
* Many manufacturers mention a combined rating specification like 300/30 means 300 KW generator and 30 m rotor diameter.
* Specific rated capacity (SRC) is often used as a comparative index defined as:

SRC = Generator Electrical Capacity/Rotor Swept Area.

Multiple Choice Questions and answers

1. What does Heating and cooling of the atmosphere generates?
   a)Thermo line circulation
   b) Radiation currents
   c) Convection currents
   d) Conduction currents
   Answer: c
   Explanation: Wind energy can be economically used for the generation of electrical energy. Heating and cooling of the atmosphere generates convection currents. Heating is caused by the absorption of solar energy on the earth surface.
2. How much is the energy available in the winds over the earth surface is estimated to be?
   a) 2.9 X 120 MW
   b) 1.6 X 107 MW

c) 1 MW
d) 5MW
Answer: b

Explanation: The energy available in the winds over the earth surface is estimated to be 1.6 X 107 MW which is almost the same as the present day energy consumption. Wind energy can be utilized to run wind mill which in turn, is used to drive the generators.

3. How much wind power does India hold?
   a) 20,000 MW
   b) 12,000 MW
   c) 140,000 MW
   d) 5000 MW

Answer: a

Explanation: India has a potential of 20,000 MW of wind power. Wind power accounts nearly 9.87% of India's total installed power generation capacity. Generation of wind power in India mainly account from southern state of India.

4. What is the main source for the formation of wind?
   a) Uneven land
   b) Sun
   c) Vegetation
   d) Seasons

Answer: b

Explanation: Wind is free and renewable form of energy, which throughout history has been used to grind grain, power ships, and pump water. Wind is created when the sun unevenly heat the earth surface.

5. Which country created wind mills?
   a) Egypt
   b) Mongolia
   c) Iran
   d) Japan

Answer: c

Explanation: The earliest known wind mills were in Persia (Iran). These early wind mills looked like large paddle wheels. Centuries later, the people of Holland improved the basic design of wind mill. Holland is famous for its wind mills.

6. "During the day, the air above the land heats up more quickly than the air over water".
   a) True
   b) False

Answer: a

Explanation: During the day, the air above the land heats up more quickly than the air over water. The warm air over the land expands and raises, and the heavier, cooler air rushes in to take its place, creating winds.

7. What happens when the land near the earth's equator is heated?
   a) All the oceans gets heated up
   b) Small wind currents are formed
   c) Rise in tides
   d) Large atmospheric winds are created

Answer: d

Explanation: The large atmospheric winds that circle the earth are created because the land near the earth's equator is heated more by the sun than the land near the north and south poles. Wind energy is mainly used to generate electricity.

8. What type of energy is wind energy?

    a) Renewable energy

    b) Non-renewable energy

    c) Conventional energy

    d) Commercial energy

    Answer: a

    Explanation: Wind is called a renewable energy source because the wind will blow as long as the shines. Wind power, as an alternative to burning fossil fuels, is plentiful, renewable, widely distributed, clean, produces no greenhouse gas emissions during operation, consumes no water, and uses little land.

9. What are used to turn wind energy into electrical energy?

    a) Turbine

    b) Generators

    c) Yaw motor

    d) Blades

Answer: a

Explanation: Wind turbine blades capture wind energy, a form of mechanical energy, and put it to work turning a drive shaft, gearbox, and generator to produce electrical energy. Many factors affects wind turbine efficiency including turbine blade aerodynamics.

10. What is the diameter of wind turbine blades?

    a) 320 feet

    b) 220 feet

    c) 80 feet

    d) 500 feet

    Answer: b

    Explanation: Large utility-scale wind turbines can now generate more than a MW of electrical power each and deliver electricity directly in to the electric grid, these turbines are placed at 200 feet height at the rotor hub and have blades which are 220 feet or more in diameter.

11. At what range of speed is the electricity from the wind turbine is generated?

    a) 100 – 125 mph

    b) 450 – 650 mph

    c) 250 – 450 mph

    d) 30-35 mph

    Answer: d

    Explanation: Wind turbines are designed with cut-in wind speeds and cut-out speeds i.e. the wind speeds when the turbines start turning or shut off to prevent drive train damage. Typically, maximum electric generations occurs at speeds of 30-35mph.

12. When did the development of wind power in India began?

    a) 1965

    b) 1954

    c) 1990

    d) 1985

    Answer: c

    Explanation: The development of wind power in India began in 1990s. Presently India is the world's fourth largest wind power generator. The Indian energy sector has an installed capacity of 32.72 GW. Today India is a major player in the global wind energy market.

"Components of Wind Energy Conversion System".

1. How much power does the small scale wind machine generate?
a) 18 KW
b) 2 KW
c) 12 KW
d) 30 KW
View Answer

Answer: b

Explanation: These might be used on farms remote applications and other places requiring relatively low power. The generating capacity is up to 2kW. Small scale wind machines lower your electricity bills by 50% – 90%.

2. Which type of wind machines are used at several residence or local use?
a) Large size machines
b) Remote machines
c) Small size machines
d) Medium size machines
View Answer

Answer: d

Explanation: These wind turbines may be used to supply less than 100 kW rated capacity, to several residences or local use. These do not require much space they can be installed on roof tops or on some high elevated areas.

3. Which type of wind turbines produce 100 kW or greater?
a) Large machines
b) Small machines
c) Medium machines
d) Remote Machines
View Answer

Answer: a

Explanation: Large wind turbines are those of 100 kW rated capacity or greater. They are used to generate power for distribution in central power grids. They can have single generator at a single site or multiple generators sited at several places over an area.

4. Which part of the wind mill acts as a housing for the turbine?
a) Wind Vane
b) Shaft
c) Wind mill head
d) Turbine
View Answer

Answer: c

Explanation: The wind mill head supports the rotor, housing, and rotor bearings. It also has control mechanism like changing the pitch of the blades for safety devices, tail vane to orient the rotor to face the wind. Its body is the size of the mini bus.

5. A rotor installed in a fixed orientation with the swept area perpendicular to the pre dominate wind direction is called ___________
a) Nacelle
b) Yaw fixed machines
c) Blades

d) Anemometer
View Answer
Answer: b
Explanation: In the locations with the prevailing wind in one direction, the design of a turbine can be greatly simplified. The rotor can be installed in a fixed orientation with the swept area perpendicular to the pre dominate wind direction. This machine is called yaw fixed.
6. How is the action of yaw controlled in small turbines?
a) Tail vane
b) Blades
c) Shaft
d) Yaw motor
View Answer
Answer: a
Explanation: In small turbines, yaw action is controlled by a tail vane while is larger machines a servomechanism operated by a wind-direction sensor controls the yaw motor keeping the turbine properly oriented.
7. Which part of the wind turbines senses wind speed, wind direction, shaft speed and torque?
a) Turbine blade
b) Shaft
c) Rotor
d) Controller
View Answer
Answer: d
Explanation: The controller senses wind speed, wind direction, shafts speeds and torques, output power and generator temperature, Control signals are generated with the electrical output corresponding to the wind energy input.
8. Which type of wind turbine has low RPM?
a) Small wind turbine
b) Large wind turbine
c) Medium wind turbine
d) Remote wind turbine
View Answer
Answer: b
Explanation: The rate of rotation of large wind turbine generators operating at rated capacity or below is controlled by varying the pitch of the rotor blades. It has low rpm, about 40 to 50. It is necessary to increase greatly the low rotor rate of turning using transmission mechanism.
9. Why recommendation of fixed ratio gears done for top mounted equipment?
a) Because they are easy install
b) Requires less space
c) Due to its low cost
d) Because of their high efficiency
View Answer
Answer: d
Explanation: Fixed ratio gears are recommended for top mounted equipment because of their high efficiency, and minimum system risk. For bottom mounted equipment requiring a right angle drive transmission costs can be reduced on the hub by increasing rotor speed to generator.
10. Which type of generator are made use in wind turbines?
a) Recreational generators
b) Synchronous generator

c) Asynchronous generator
d) Alternator
View Answer

Answer: b
Explanation: Generators may be either constant or variable speed type. Variable speed units are expensive and/or unproved. Constant speed generator in use are synchronous induction and permanent magnet types. Synchronous unit is used for large aero generator systems. It is very versatile and has an extensive data base.

11. In which part do we find sensors and actuators?
a) Fixed gears
b) Turbines
c) Control systems
d) Blades
View Answer

Answer: c
Explanation: Control systems involves sensors and actuators. The modern large wind turbine generator requires a versatile and reliable control system. A control system is used for i) changing the orientation of the rotor into the wind. ii) Start up and cut-in of the equipment. iii) Power control of the rotor by varying the pitch of the blades.

12. How many types of supporting tower for wind mill are generally used?
a) 2
b) 4
c) 3
d) 5
View Answer

Answer: b
Explanation: Four types of generating tower are used generally:
i) The reinforced concrete tower
ii) The pole tower
iii) The built up shell tube tower
iv) The truss tower.

13. On what does the selection of supporting structure depends?
a) Length of blades
b) Rotating capacity
c) Capacity of generator
d) Transmission systems
View Answer

Answer: d
Explanation: The type of the supporting structure and its height is related to cost and the transmission system incorporated. Horizontal axis wind turbines are mounted on towers so as to be above the level of turbulence and other ground related effects.

14. At what type of location vibrations are more in the wind turbine?
a) Downwind location
b) Up wind location
c) Windward
d) Leeward
View Answer

Answer: b
Explanation: In the upwind location (i.e. the wind encounters the turbine before reaching the

tower), the wake of the passing rotor blades causes repeated changes in the wind forces on the wind forces on the tower. Due to this the tower may vibrate and may eventually be damaged.

15. At what type of location vibrations are less in the wind turbines?
a) Windward
b) Leeward
c) Downwind location
d) Upwind Location
View Answer

Answer: c
Explanation: If the turbine is downwind from the tower, vibrations are less but the blades are subjected to severe alternating forces as they pass through the tower wake. Downwind rotors are generally preferred for large aero generators.

This set of Energy Engineering Multiple Choice Questions & Answers (MCQs) focuses on "Velocity and Power from Wind".

1. Select the formula for total power p_t?
a) $P_t = 1/2gc \, \rho AV_i^3$
b) $P_t = \rho AV_i^3 D^3$
c) $P_t = 12gc \, V_i^3 D^3$
d) $P_t = 2gcVi3$
View Answer

Answer: a
Explanation:

$$P_t = \frac{1}{2gc} \rho AV_i^3$$

Where, ρ = Incoming wind density

A = Cross sectional area

g_c = conversion factor = 1.0 kg/N

V_i = incoming velocity m/s

2. Why blade velocity of wind turbine varies?
a) Due to varying wind speeds
b) Long length of blades
c) Due to the height of mount
d) Because of hotness of Sun
View Answer

Answer: b
Explanation: Wind turbine experiences change in velocity dependent upon the blade inlet angle and the blade velocity. Since the blades are long, the blade velocity varies with the radius to a greater degree than steam or gas-turbine blades and the blades are therefore twisted.

3. When was the Hall a day wind mill introduced?
a) 1920
b) 1923
c) 1854

d) 1864

View Answer

Answer: c

Explanation: Invented by Daniel Halladay in 1854, the Halladay Standard was the first commercially successful self-governing windmill in 1854 was the firms of Halladay, McCray & Co., Ellington, Conn. Partners in the company were inventor Daniel Halladay, John Burnham and Henry McCray.

4. How much ideal efficiency should practical turbine have?

a) 10 – 12%

b) 18 – 25%

c) 80 – 90%

d) 50 – 70%

View Answer

Answer: d

Explanation: As wind turbine wheel cannot be completely closed, and because of spillage and other effects, practical turbines have 50 to 70% of the ideal efficiency. The real efficiency η is the product of this and η_{max} and is the ratio of an actual to total power.

$P = \eta P_{tot}$.

5. How many types are acting on propeller type wind mill?

a) 2

b) 3

c) 4

d) 5

View Answer

Answer: a

Explanation: There are two types of forces operating on the blades of a propeller type wind turbine. They are the circumferential forces in the direction of wheel rotation that provide the torque and the axial forces in the direction of the wind stream that provide an axial thrust that must be counteracted by proper mechanical design.

6. Calculate the air density, when 10m/s wind is at 1std atmospheric pressure and 15°C?

a) 1.226 kg/m^3

b) 1.033 kg/m^3

c) 2.108 kg/m^3

d) 0.922 kg/m^3

View Answer

Answer: a

Explanation: For air, gas constant R = 287 J/kgK, 1atm = 1.01325 X 10^5 Pa
Air density, ρ = P/RT = (1.01325 ×10^5)/(287(15+273.15)) = 1.226 kg/m^3.

7. Calculate the air density when 18m/s wind is at 1std atmospheric pressure and 34°C?

a) 1.149 kg/m^3

b) 1.9 kg/m^3

c) 2.88 kg/m^3

d) 5.89 kg/m^3

View Answer

Answer: a

Explanation: For air, gas constant R = 287 J/kgK, 1atm = 1.01325 X 10^5 Pa
Air density, ρ = P/RT = (1.01325 × 10^5)/(287(34+273.15)) = 1.149 kg/m^3.

8. What is the total power produced if the turbine diameter is 120m?

a) 0.277 KW

b) 1.224 KW
c) 4.28 KW
d) 0.89 KW
View Answer

Answer: a
Explanation: Total power P,
$P = 0.245 \times (\pi D^2/4)$
$= 0.245 \times (\pi (120)^2/4)$
$= 0.277$ KW.

9. What is the total power produced if the turbine diameter is 90m?
a) 0.155KW
b) 0.982 KW
c) 1.452 KW
d) 3.12 KW
View Answer

Answer: a
Explanation: Total power P,
$P = 0.245 \times (\pi D^2/4)$
$= 0.245 \times (\pi (90)^2/4)$
$= 0.155$KW.

This set of Energy Engineering Multiple Choice Questions & Answers (MCQs) focuses on "Wind Turbine Operation".

1. What is the inherent weakness of all wind machines?
a) Their efficiencies
b) Requires powerful winds to make fan rotate
c) Their dependency on the wind speed
d) Cannot be easily repaired
View Answer

Answer: c
Explanation: An inherent weakness of all wind machines are the strong dependence of the power produced on wheel diameter and wind speed, being proportional to turbine wheel area, i.e. to the square of its diameter and to the cube of wind velocity.

2. Why severe fluctuations in power are always undesirable in windmill?
a) Because they pose power oscillations problems
b) Damage of parts due to fluctuations
c) The efficiency of the plant will be reduced
d) Results in damage to the whole plant
View Answer

Answer: a
Explanation: Severe fluctuations in power are always undesirable, because they pose power oscillation problems on the grid and severe strains on the windmill hardware. From an economic point of view, a windmill is designed to produce a rated power output corresponding to maximum, or near maximum, prevailing wind velocity at a given site would generate low powers, with full capacity of the turbine and electric generator unused much of time.

3. Maintenance of constant output at all wind speeds above rating is called __________
a) Numeric rating scale
b) Tenancy

c) Flat Rating
d) TRP
View Answer

Answer: c

Explanation: More cost-effective design to a wind mill to produce rated power at less than the maximum prevailing wind velocity, using a smaller turbine and generator and to maintain a constant output at all wind speeds above rating. This is called flat rating.

4. A wind turbine designed too to come into operation at a minimum wind speed is called __________
a) Cut in velocity
b) Windward
c) Cut out velocity
d) Upwind location
View Answer

Answer: a

Explanation: Due to several loss in efficiency and power at low wind velocities, a wind turbine is designed to come into operation at a minimum wind speed called the cut in velocity. Thus the wind turbine operates with variable load over a narrow range between cut in.

5. Why is wind turbine designed to stop operation at cut out velocity?
a) To protect wheel against damage
b) To make a quick stop in emergencies
c) To improve the efficiency
d) In order to adjust the blades to wind direction
View Answer

Answer: a

Explanation: To protect the turbine wheel against damage at very high wind velocities, it is designed to stop operation (such as feathering the blades) at cut out velocity. Thus the wind turbine operates at rated velocities and at constant power between the rated and cut out velocities and ceases the operation above the cut out velocity.

6. The fraction of time during a given period that the turbine is actually on line is called?
a) Availability factor
b) Flat rating
c) Cut in velocity
d) Cut out velocity
View Answer

Answer: a

Explanation: The availability factor is defined as the fraction of time during a given period that the turbine is actually on line. The actual wind velocity at the propeller hub that determines the turbine power is usually higher.

7. Over load factor is also called as ______________
a) availability factor
b) plant operating factor
c) flat rating
d) cut out velocity
View Answer

Answer: a

Explanation: The overall load factor, also called the plant operating factor and the plant capacity factor is the ratio of the total energy generated during a given period of time to the total rated generation capacity during the same period.

8. How many of windmills are there?
a) 2
b) 3
c) 4
d) 5
View Answer

Answer: a

Explanation: There are two classes of windmill, horizontal axis and vertical axis. The vertical axis design was popular during the early development of the windmill. However, its inefficiency of operation let to the development of numerous horizontal axis designs.

9. Name the windmill which has four blades mounted on a central post.
a) Post mill
b) Smock mill
c) Tower mill
d) Fan mill
View Answer

Answer: a

Explanation: The post mill has blades mounted on a central post. The horizontal shaft of the blade is connected to a large break wheel. The break wheel interacts with a gear system, called the wallower, which rotates a central, vertical shaft. This motion can then be used to power water pumping or grain grinding activities.

10. Name the type of windmill which consists of a sloping, horizontally weather boarded or thatched tower.
a) Post mill
b) Smock mill
c) Tower mill
d) Fan mill
View Answer

Answer: b

Explanation: The smock mill is a type of windmill that consists of a sloping, horizontally weather boarded or thatched tower, usually with six or eight sides. It is topped with a roof or cap that rotates to bring the sails into the wind. It is similar to post mill. It is named so because of its appearance.

11. Which are further improvements on smock mill?
a) Post mill
b) Smock mill
c) Tower mill
d) Fan mill
View Answer

Answer: c

Explanation: Tower mills are further improvements on smock mills. They have a rotating cap and permanent body, but this body is made of brick or stone. This fact makes it possible for the towers to be rounded. A round structure of it allows for large and taller towers.

12. Which type of windmills are been used for primary purposes?
a) Post mill
b) Smock mill
c) Tower mill
d) Fan mill
View Answer

Answer: d
Explanation: The fan type windmill is specifically made for individuals. It is much smaller and used primarily for pumping water. It consists of a fixed tower (mast), a wheel and tail assembly (fan), a head assembly, and a pump.

This set of Energy Engineering Multiple Choice Questions & Answers (MCQs) focuses on "Horizontal Axis Wind Mill".

1. In which of the following, does machine rotor drives through a step up gear box?
a) Horizontal axis with two aerodynamic blades
b) Horizontal axis propeller type wind mill
c) Horizontal axis multi bladed type wind mill
d) Sail type wind mill
View Answer

Answer: a
Explanation: In horizontal axis with two aerodynamic type windmill the machine rotor drives through a step up gear box. The blade rotor is designed to orient downwind of the tower. The components are mounted on bed plate which is attached on a pintle at the top of the tower.

2. The rotor blades are continuously flexed by unsteady aerodynamic gravitational and inertia loads.
a) True
b) False
View Answer

Answer: a
Explanation: The rotor blades are continuously flexed by unsteady aerodynamic gravitational and inertia loads, when the machine is in operation. If the blades are made using metal, flexing reduces their fatigue life.

3. Which type of the following consists of single blade?
a) Horizontal axis with two aerodynamic blades
b) Horizontal axis propeller type wind mill
c) Horizontal axis multi bladed type wind mill
d) Sail type wind mill
View Answer

Answer: b
Explanation: Horizontal axis propeller type wind mill consists of a long blade mounted on a rigid hub, induction generator and gear box. If extremely long blades are mounted on rigid hub, large blade root bending moments occur due to tower shadow, gravity and sudden shifts in wind directions.

4. Which windmill blades are made by an array of wooden slats?
a) Horizontal axis with two aerodynamic blades
b) Horizontal axis propeller type wind mill
c) Horizontal axis multi bladed type wind mill
d) Horizontal axis wind mill Dutch type
View Answer

Answer: d
Explanation: Dutch type wind mill is one of the oldest wind mills in designs. The blade surfaces are made from an array of wooden slats which rotates at high wind speeds. These types of wind mill are cheap to build since the wood is made use of to build.

5. Which type of windmill blades are made out of sheet metal or aluminum?
a) Horizontal axis with two aerodynamic blades

b) Horizontal axis propeller type wind mill
c) Horizontal axis multi bladed type wind mill
d) Sail type wind mill
View Answer

Answer: c
Explanation: Horizontal axis multi blade windmill is made from sheet metal or aluminum. The rotors have high strength to weight ratios. They have good power coefficient, high starting torque and added advantages of simplicity and low cost.

6. Which type of wind mills blade are made out of cloth?
a) Horizontal axis with two aerodynamic blades
b) Horizontal axis propeller type wind mill
c) Horizontal axis multi bladed type wind mill
d) Sail type wind mill
View Answer

Answer: d
Explanation: The blade surface of sail type wind mill is made of cloth, nylon or plastics arranged as mast and pole or sail wings. There is also variation in the number of sails used. Sails are found in different designs, from primitive common sails to the advances patent sails.

7. Which type of windmill has better performance?
a) Vertical type wind mills
b) Darrieus type machines
c) Magnus effect rotor
d) Horizontal type windmills
View Answer

Answer: d
Explanation: The horizontal axis mills generally have netter performance. They have been used for various applications including electric power generation, and pumping water. The latter introduces some complexity into the design as the mechanical energy has to be transmitted over a distance.

8. What does TSR stand for in design consideration of wind mills?
a) Tip speed ratio
b) Torque-synchronous ratio
c) Tip suspension ratio
d) Temporary speed restriction
View Answer

Answer: a
Explanation: The tip speed ratio, X, or TSR for wind turbines is the ratio between the tangential speed of the tip of a blade and the actual speed of the wind. The tip speed ratio is related to efficiency, with the optimum varying with blade design.

9. With upto how many propellers can windmills are built?
a) 4
b) 2
c) 7
d) 6
View Answer

Answer: d
Explanation: Wind turbines have been built with upto six propellers type blades but two and three bladed propellers are most common. A one bladed rotor with a balancing counter weight has some advantages, including lower weight and cost and simpler controls, over the multi-bladed type.

10. Turbines with how many propellers are used in order to avoid vibrations?
a) 1
b) 2
c) 3
d) 4
View Answer

Answer: c
Explanation: Turbines with three blades are used to avoid vibrations that occur due to the turning or yawing of the rotor in order to face in into the wind. However, this problem can be overcome by controlling the yaw rate.

11. What type of cross sections does wind turbine blades have?
a) Penta hedral cross section
b) Air foiled type cross section
c) Radar cross section
d) Turbo cross section
View Answer

Answer: b
Explanation: Wind turbine blades have an air foiled type of cross section and a variable pitch. They are slightly twisted from the outer tip to the root in order to reduce the tendency for the rotor to stall. The blades can also have constant chord length.

12. What does WECS stands for?
a) Wind energy conversion system
b) Wind engine control system
c) Wind energy combined system
d) Wind engine comparison system
View Answer

Answer: a
Explanation: A wind energy conversion system (WECS), or wind energy harvester is a machine that, powered by the energy of the wind, generates mechanical energy that can be used to directly power machinery or to power an electrical generator for making electricity.

This set of Energy Engineering Multiple Choice Questions & Answers (MCQs) focuses on "Wind Turbine Operation".

1. What is the inherent weakness of all wind machines?
a) Their efficiencies
b) Requires powerful winds to make fan rotate
c) Their dependency on the wind speed
d) Cannot be easily repaired
View Answer

Answer: c
Explanation: An inherent weakness of all wind machines are the strong dependence of the power produced on wheel diameter and wind speed, being proportional to turbine wheel area, i.e. to the square of its diameter and to the cube of wind velocity.

2. Why severe fluctuations in power are always undesirable in windmill?
a) Because they pose power oscillations problems
b) Damage of parts due to fluctuations
c) The efficiency of the plant will be reduced

d) Results in damage to the whole plant
View Answer

Answer: a

Explanation: Severe fluctuations in power are always undesirable, because they pose power oscillation problems on the grid and severe strains on the windmill hardware. From an economic point of view, a windmill is designed to produce a rated power output corresponding to maximum, or near maximum, prevailing wind velocity at a given site would generate low powers, with full capacity of the turbine and electric generator unused much of time.

3. Maintenance of constant output at all wind speeds above rating is called __________
a) Numeric rating scale
b) Tenancy
c) Flat Rating
d) TRP
View Answer

Answer: c

Explanation: More cost-effective design to a wind mill to produce rated power at less than the maximum prevailing wind velocity, using a smaller turbine and generator and to maintain a constant output at all wind speeds above rating. This is called flat rating.

4. A wind turbine designed too to come into operation at a minimum wind speed is called __________
a) Cut in velocity
b) Windward
c) Cut out velocity
d) Upwind location
View Answer

Answer: a

Explanation: Due to several loss in efficiency and power at low wind velocities, a wind turbine is designed to come into operation at a minimum wind speed called the cut in velocity. Thus the wind turbine operates with variable load over a narrow range between cut in.

5. Why is wind turbine designed to stop operation at cut out velocity?
a) To protect wheel against damage
b) To make a quick stop in emergencies
c) To improve the efficiency
d) In order to adjust the blades to wind direction
View Answer

Answer: a

Explanation: To protect the turbine wheel against damage at very high wind velocities, it is designed to stop operation (such as feathering the blades) at cut out velocity. Thus the wind turbine operates at rated velocities and at constant power between the rated and cut out velocities and ceases the operation above the cut out velocity.

6. The fraction of time during a given period that the turbine is actually on line is called?
a) Availability factor
b) Flat rating
c) Cut in velocity
d) Cut out velocity
View Answer

Answer: a

Explanation: The availability factor is defined as the fraction of time during a given period that the turbine is actually on line. The actual wind velocity at the propeller hub that determines the turbine power is usually higher.

7. Over load factor is also called as _______________
a) availability factor
b) plant operating factor
c) flat rating
d) cut out velocity
View Answer

Answer: a
Explanation: The overall load factor, also called the plant operating factor and the plant capacity factor is the ratio of the total energy generated during a given period of time to the total rated generation capacity during the same period.

8. How many of windmills are there?
a) 2
b) 3
c) 4
d) 5
View Answer

Answer: a
Explanation: There are two classes of windmill, horizontal axis and vertical axis. The vertical axis design was popular during the early development of the windmill. However, its inefficiency of operation let to the development of numerous horizontal axis designs.

9. Name the windmill which has four blades mounted on a central post.
a) Post mill
b) Smock mill
c) Tower mill
d) Fan mill
View Answer

Answer: a
Explanation: The post mill has blades mounted on a central post. The horizontal shaft of the blade is connected to a large break wheel. The break wheel interacts with a gear system, called the wallower, which rotates a central, vertical shaft. This motion can then be used to power water pumping or grain grinding activities.

10. Name the type of windmill which consists of a sloping, horizontally weather boarded or thatched tower.
a) Post mill
b) Smock mill
c) Tower mill
d) Fan mill
View Answer

Answer: b
Explanation: The smock mill is a type of windmill that consists of a sloping, horizontally weather boarded or thatched tower, usually with six or eight sides. It is topped with a roof or cap that rotates to bring the sails into the wind. It is similar to post mill. It is named so because of its appearance.

11. Which are further improvements on smock mill?
a) Post mill
b) Smock mill
c) Tower mill
d) Fan mill
View Answer

Answer: c

Explanation: Tower mills are further improvements on smock mills. They have a rotating cap and permanent body, but this body is made of brick or stone. This fact makes it possible for the towers to be rounded. A round structure of it allows for large and taller towers.

12. Which type of windmills are been used for primary purposes?
a) Post mill
b) Smock mill
c) Tower mill
d) Fan mill
View Answer

Answer: d

Explanation: The fan type windmill is specifically made for individuals. It is much smaller and used primarily for pumping water. It consists of a fixed tower (mast), a wheel and tail assembly (fan), a head assembly, and a pump.

This set of Energy Engineering Multiple Choice Questions & Answers (MCQs) focuses on "Horizontal Axis Wind Mill".

1. In which of the following, does machine rotor drives through a step up gear box?
a) Horizontal axis with two aerodynamic blades
b) Horizontal axis propeller type wind mill
c) Horizontal axis multi bladed type wind mill
d) Sail type wind mill
View Answer

Answer: a

Explanation: In horizontal axis with two aerodynamic type windmill the machine rotor drives through a step up gear box. The blade rotor is designed to orient downwind of the tower. The components are mounted on bed plate which is attached on a pintle at the top of the tower.

2. The rotor blades are continuously flexed by unsteady aerodynamic gravitational and inertia loads.
a) True
b) False
View Answer

Answer: a

Explanation: The rotor blades are continuously flexed by unsteady aerodynamic gravitational and inertia loads, when the machine is in operation. If the blades are made using metal, flexing reduces their fatigue life.

3. Which type of the following consists of single blade?
a) Horizontal axis with two aerodynamic blades
b) Horizontal axis propeller type wind mill
c) Horizontal axis multi bladed type wind mill
d) Sail type wind mill
View Answer

Answer: b

Explanation: Horizontal axis propeller type wind mill consists of a long blade mounted on a rigid hub, induction generator and gear box. If extremely long blades are mounted on rigid hub, large blade root bending moments occur due to tower shadow, gravity and sudden shifts in wind directions.

4. Which windmill blades are made by an array of wooden slats?
a) Horizontal axis with two aerodynamic blades

b) Horizontal axis propeller type wind mill
c) Horizontal axis multi bladed type wind mill
d) Horizontal axis wind mill Dutch type
View Answer

Answer: d
Explanation: Dutch type wind mill is one of the oldest wind mills in designs. The blade surfaces are made from an array of wooden slats which rotates at high wind speeds. These types of wind mill are cheap to build since the wood is made use of to build.

5. Which type of windmill blades are made out of sheet metal or aluminum?
a) Horizontal axis with two aerodynamic blades
b) Horizontal axis propeller type wind mill
c) Horizontal axis multi bladed type wind mill
d) Sail type wind mill
View Answer

Answer: c
Explanation: Horizontal axis multi blade windmill is made from sheet metal or aluminum. The rotors have high strength to weight ratios. They have good power coefficient, high starting torque and added advantages of simplicity and low cost.

6. Which type of wind mills blade are made out of cloth?
a) Horizontal axis with two aerodynamic blades
b) Horizontal axis propeller type wind mill
c) Horizontal axis multi bladed type wind mill
d) Sail type wind mill
View Answer

Answer: d
Explanation: The blade surface of sail type wind mill is made of cloth, nylon or plastics arranged as mast and pole or sail wings. There is also variation in the number of sails used. Sails are found in different designs, from primitive common sails to the advances patent sails.

7. Which type of windmill has better performance?
a) Vertical type wind mills
b) Darrieus type machines
c) Magnus effect rotor
d) Horizontal type windmills
View Answer

Answer: d
Explanation: The horizontal axis mills generally have netter performance. They have been used for various applications including electric power generation, and pumping water. The latter introduces some complexity into the design as the mechanical energy has to be transmitted over a distance.

8. What does TSR stand for in design consideration of wind mills?
a) Tip speed ratio
b) Torque-synchronous ratio
c) Tip suspension ratio
d) Temporary speed restriction
View Answer

Answer: a
Explanation: The tip speed ratio, X, or TSR for wind turbines is the ratio between the tangential speed of the tip of a blade and the actual speed of the wind. The tip speed ratio is related to efficiency, with the optimum varying with blade design.

9. With upto how many propellers can windmills are built?
a) 4
b) 2
c) 7
d) 6
View Answer

Answer: d
Explanation: Wind turbines have been built with upto six propellers type blades but two and three bladed propellers are most common. A one bladed rotor with a balancing counter weight has some advantages, including lower weight and cost and simpler controls, over the multi-bladed type.

10. Turbines with how many propellers are used in order to avoid vibrations?
a) 1
b) 2
c) 3
d) 4
View Answer

Answer: c
Explanation: Turbines with three blades are used to avoid vibrations that occur due to the turning or yawing of the rotor in order to face in into the wind. However, this problem can be overcome by controlling the yaw rate.

11. What type of cross sections does wind turbine blades have?
a) Penta hedral cross section
b) Air foiled type cross section
c) Radar cross section
d) Turbo cross section
View Answer

Answer: b
Explanation: Wind turbine blades have an air foiled type of cross section and a variable pitch. They are slightly twisted from the outer tip to the root in order to reduce the tendency for the rotor to stall. The blades can also have constant chord length.

12. What does WECS stands for?
a) Wind energy conversion system
b) Wind engine control system
c) Wind energy combined system
d) Wind engine comparison system
View Answer

Answer: a
Explanation: A wind energy conversion system (WECS), or wind energy harvester is a machine that, powered by the energy of the wind, generates mechanical energy that can be used to directly power machinery or to power an electrical generator for making electricity.

This set of Energy Engineering Multiple Choice Questions & Answers (MCQs) focuses on "Vertical Axis Wind Mill".

1. In which wind measuring device a tubular piece of thin flexible fabric hanged vertically to determine direction?
a) Wind socks
b) Weather vane
c) Pin wheels

d) Anemometers

View Answer

Answer: a

Explanation: Wind sock is a very basic device that measure wind direction and provide a rough idea of the wind's intensity. A wind sock is a tubular piece of fabric or thin, flexible fabric attached to a pole. When there is no wind, the fabric hangs vertically from the attached pole.

2. A device which is used as device for showing direction wind as well used as a decorative purpose?

a) Wind socks
b) Weather vane
c) Pin wheels
d) Anemometers

View Answer

Answer: b

Explanation: A weather vane works similarly to wind sock. Instead of a tubular sock, the weather vane is made by placing a horizontal pole at the top of vertical pole. The poles are joined together so that the horizontal pole has a flattened, vertical end that reacts to wind.

3. Which is the wind direction showing device that spins perpendicularly?

a) Wind socks
b) Weather vane
c) Pin wheels
d) Anemometers

View Answer

Answer: c

Explanation: A pinwheel is a windmill-style turbine that spins perpendicularly to the wind affecting it. Like wind socks and weather vanes, a pinwheel can be attached to a rotating base. This allows the pinwheel to change direction with the wind, and it will spin facing into the oncoming wind.

4. Which is the device that measures wind direction and its intensity?

a) Wind socks
b) Weather vane
c) Pin wheels
d) Anemometers

View Answer

Answer: d

Explanation: An anemometer is any device that measures wind direction and intensity. It may be simple, such as the devices described above, or it may be a complex, computer-aided machine that measures and records wind patterns over time. More advanced anemometer machines are used to aid in professional weather reporting and air traffic control.

5. What units does the anemometer measure in?

a) Feet per minute
b) Liters per minute
c) Centimeters per minute
d) Meter per seconds

View Answer

Answer: a

Explanation: The anemometer measures in feet per minute, or FPM. The rotation is sensed by a magnetic or optical sensor that converts the signal to FPM measurement. An arrow on the vane head identifies the direction the airflow must travel through the vane to obtain proper measurements.

6. Which of the following type of turbine or the rotor requires relatively low velocity winds for operation?
a) Cup anemometer
b) Savonius rotor
c) Darrieus type rotor
d) Magnus effect rotor
View Answer

Answer: b
Explanation: Savonius rotor is a simple WEC system which woks like a cup anemometer. This type was invented by S.J. Savonius in the year 1920. It requires relatively low velocity winds for operation. It consists of two half cylinders facing opposite directions forming as S-shaped cross section.

7. Which type of axis does a Savonius Rotor has?
a) Horizontal axis
b) Mediolateral axis
c) Vertical axis
d) Lateral Axis
View Answer

Answer: c
Explanation: A Savonius wind energy conversion system has a vertical axis and hence eliminates the expensive power transmission system from the rotor to the axis. Since it is a vertical axis machine it does not matter much about the wind direction.

8. Why is Savonius rotor not suitable for installation?
a) Because of long drive shaft
b) Because of its low capacity motor
c) Because of its typical blade design
d) Due to the light material it is made of
View Answer

Answer: a
Explanation: Savonius rotor is not useful for very high installation because of long drive shaft problems. Bracing of the topmost bearing above the rotor of a very tall vertical axis machine is difficult requiring very long guy wires.

9. When was the Darrieus type machine invented?
a) 1925
b) 1932
c) 1929
d) 1948
View Answer

Answer: a
Explanation: Darrieus type machine was invented originally and patented in 1925 by G.J.M > Darrieus, a French engineer. The Darrieus wind mill is a vertical axis machine that has the same advantage of a modern rapidly rotating propeller type windmill, by use of an efficient airfoil, effectively intercepts large area of wind with a small blade area.

10. What form of force acts on the blades of Darrieus machine?
a) Pure tension
b) Compression
c) Shear force
d) Air resistance force
View Answer

Answer: a

Explanation: Darrieus wind mill has two or three thin, curved blades with airfoil cross section and constant chord length. Both ends of blades are attached to a vertical shaft. Thus the force in the blade due to rotation is pure tension.

11. Which type of vertical wind machine has relatively low solidity and low starting torques?
a) Cup anemometer
b) Savonius rotor
c) Darrieus type rotor
d) Magnus effect rotor
View Answer

Answer: c

Explanation: Darrieus type rotors are lift devices characterized by curved blades with air foil cross sections. They have relatively low solidity and low starting torques, but high tip to wind speeds and therefore relatively high power outputs per given rotor weight and cost.

12. Which type of vertical wind machine consists of spinning cylinders?
a) Cup anemometer
b) Savonius rotor
c) Darrieus type rotor
d) Magnus effect rotor
View Answer

Answer: d

Explanation: Magnus effect rotor concept was first demonstrated by Magnus in 1912. It consists of spinning cylinders. When cylinders spun in wind stream, translational forces are produced perpendicular to the wind stream by the Magnus effect. Such a device can be used to propel ships or land vehicles.

13. Aero turbine is the fraction of power in the wind through the swept area which is converted into useful mechanical shaft power is called ______________
a) Coefficient of performance
b) Coefficient of variation
c) Coefficient of lift
d) Coefficient of spin
View Answer

Answer: a

Explanation: The coefficient of performance of an aero turbine is the fraction of power in the wind through the swept area which is converted into useful mechanical shaft power. C_p for horizontal axis wind machine has theoretical maximum value = 0.593.

1-The amount of energy available in the wind at any instant is proportional to ___ of the wind speed.
(A) Square root power of two

(B) Square root power of three

(C) Square power

(D) Cube power

2-Wind energy is harnessed as _______ energy with the help of windmill or turbine.
(A) Mechanical

(B) Solar

(C) Electrical

(D) Heat

3-Winds having following speed are suitable to operate wind turbines.
(A) 5 – 25m/s

(B) 10 – 35m/s

(C) 20 – 45m/s

(D) 30 – 55m/s

4-The following is (are) the classification of winds
(A) Global wind

(B) Local wind

(C) Both (A) and (B)

(D) None of the above

5-Global Cold wind move from
(A) Polar to equatorial region

(B) Equatorial to polar region

(C) Equatorial to oceanic region

(D) Oceanic to Equatorial region

6-Global Cold wind generated from Oceans moves to
(A) Mountains

(B) Equator

(C) Plain areas

(D) Poles
7-_____ force is responsible for forcing the global winds towards westernly direction.
(A) Coriolis

(B) Gravitational

(C) Centripetal

(D) Centrifugal

8-Global winds towards westernly direction are known as
(A) Trade winds

(B) Western winds

(C) Eastern winds

(D) None of the above

9-Uneven heating occurs on land surface and water bodies are due to _____
(A) Air Currents

(B) Solar radiation

(C) Lunar eclipse

(D) None of the above

10-The following factor(s) affects the distribution of wind energy
(A) Mountain chains

(B) The hills, trees and buildings

(C) Frictional effect of the surface

(D) All of the above

11-The wind intensity can be described by
(A) Reynolds number

(B) Mach number

(C) Beaufort number

(D) Froude number

ANSWERS:
1-(D), 2-(A), 3-(A), 4-(C), 5-(A), 6-(C), 7-(A), 8-(A), 9-(B), 10-(D), 11-(C)

12-The wind speed is measured using an instrument called
(A) Pyranometer

(B) Manometer

(C) Anemometer

(D) Wind vane

13-The rate of change of wind speed with height is called
(A) Wind shear

(B) Wind rose

(C) Wind solidity

(D) None of the above

14-At gradient height the shear force is
(A) Zero

(B) Minimum

(C) Maximum

(D) None of the above

15-The gradient height is about ______ m from the ground.
(A) 500

(B) 1000

(C) 1500

(D) 2000

16-The atmosphere with uniform wind speed is called the _____ atmosphere
(A) Plain

(B) Surface

(C) Free

(D) Shear

17-Surface layer is the air layer considered from the height of local obstruction to a height of about
(A) 50m

(B) 100m

(C) 150m

(D) 200m

18-Air layer from 100m that extends up to the gradient height is known as
(A) Surface layer

(B) Ekman layer

(C) Boundary layer

(D) None of the above

19-Low solidity rotors use which of the following force for rotation

(A) Drag

(B) Lift

(C) Centrifugal

(D) Centripetal

20-The following is the tangential velocity of the blade due to the rotation of blade.
(A) Wind velocity

(B) Incident wind velocity

(C) Blade linear velocity

(D) Relative velocity

21-Turbines blades have _____ type cross section to extract energy from wind.
(A) Aerofoil

(B) Elliptical

(C) Rectangular

(D) All of the above

22-The Nacelle of windmill houses
(A) Gearbox

(B) Brakes

(C) Generator

(D) All of the above

ANSWERS:
12-(C), 13-(A), 14-(A), 15-(D), 16-(C), 17-(B), 18-(B), 19-(B), 20-(C), 21-(A), 22-(D)

Module-III
Biomass Power

Biomass includes all the living or dead organic materials like wastes and residues. The animal and plant wastes and their residues are regarded as biomass. In addition to this the products originate from the conversion processes like paper, cellulose, organic residues for food industry and organic wastes from houses and industries are in this category.

Origin of Bio-mass: *

Animals feed on plants and plants grew up through the photosynthesis process using solar energy. Thus photosynthesis process is primarily responsible for generation of biomass energy. A small portion of solar radiation is captured and stored in plants during photosynthesis process. Therefore biomass energy is an indirect form of solar energy.

* To use biomass energy, the initial biomass may be transformed by chemical or biological processes to produce more convenient intermediate bio-fuels such as methane, producer gas, ethanol and charcoal. On combustion it reacts with oxygen to release heat.

*In nature bio-mass is formed by the process of photosynthesis of inorganic materials.

With the help of the solar radiation in the visible region (0.4-0.8 µm), the coloured material molecules (mainly chlorophyll) split water in organic cells (photolysis). The originating hydrogen along with carbon dioxide forms the biomass. During this process molecular oxygen is released into the air. The production of bio-mass can be understood by the following equation.

$$H_2O + b.\ NO_2 + c.\ SO_4 + d.\ PO_4 + CO_2 + (8\text{-}10)\ hv \xrightarrow{\text{Chlorophyl}} C_kH_mO_n + H_2O + O_2$$

(From soil of water)   (From air)   (From Sun)   Biomass   Water Vapour

+ Other material products

where b, c, d are various small quantities (ppm)

h is a Planck's constant $= 6.625 \times 10^{-34}$ JS

v is frequency $= C/\lambda$ (s-1)

C is the speed of light $= 2.99 \times 10^8$ m/sec.

$$12 \; H_2O + 6 \; CO_2 + 2.8 \; MJ \xrightarrow{\text{Chlorophyl}} C_6H_{12}O_6 + 6 \; O_2 + 6 \; H_2O$$

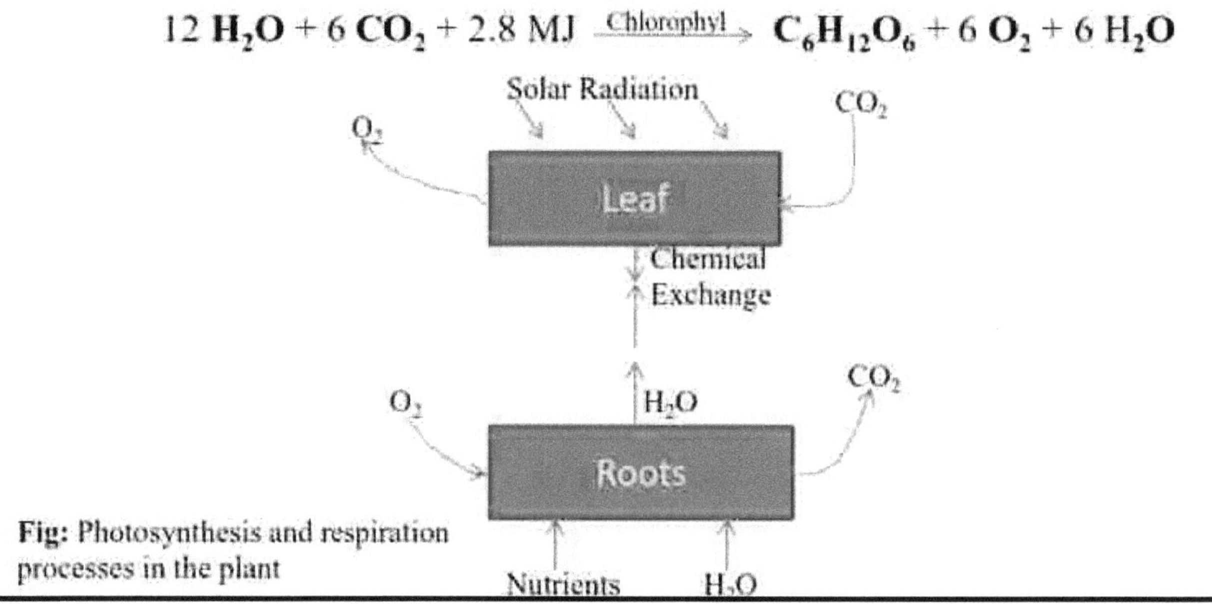

Fig: Photosynthesis and respiration processes in the plant

The energy obtained from biomass is known as biomass energy. Animals feed on plants and plants grow through photosynthesis process using solar energy. Thus, photosynthesis process is primarily responsible for generation of biomass energy.

A small portion of the solar radiation is captured and stored in the plants during photosynthesis process. Therefore, it is an indirect form of solar energy. The average efficiency of photosynthetic conversion of solar energy into biomass energy is estimated to be 0.5–1.0 per cent.

To use biomass energy, the initial biomass may be transformed by chemical or biological processes to produce more convenient intermediate bio-fuels such as methane, producer gas, ethanol and charcoal etc. On combustion it reacts with oxygen to release heat, but the elements of the material should be available for recycling in natural ecological or agricultural processes. Thus the use of industrial bio-fuels, when linked carefully to natural ecological cycle, may be nonpolluting and sustainable. For the biomass to be considered as renewable, growth must at least keep pace with its use. It is disastrous that forest and firewood consumption is significantly outpacing their growth in ever-increasing areas of the world. It is estimated that the biomass, which is 90 per cent in trees, is equivalent to the current proven extractable fossil fuel reserves in the world. The dry matter mass of biological material cycling in biosphere is about 250×10^9 tons/year. The associated energy bound in photosynthesis is

2×10^{21} J/year (equivalent to continuous flow of 0.7×10^{14} W) [49]. Biomass, mainly in the form of wood, is mankind's oldest form of energy. It has traditionally been used both in domestic as well as industrial activities, basically by direct combustion. However, it still plays a significant role in the supply of primary energy in many countries of the world.

Main advantages of biomass energy are:

- it is a renewable source;
- the energy storage is its in-built feature;
- it is indigenous source requiring little or no foreign exchange; the forestry and agricultural industries that supply feed stocks also provide substantial economic development opportunities in rural areas;
- the pollutant emissions from combustion of biomass are usually lower than those from fossil fuels;
- commercial use of biomass may avoid or reduce the problems of waste disposal in other industries, particularly municipal solid waste in urban centers;
- use of biogas plants apart from supplying clean gas, also leads to improved sanitation, better hygienic conditions in rural areas as the harmful decaying biomass gets stabilized;
- the nitrogen-rich bio-digested slurry and sludge from biogas plant serves as a very good soil conditioner and improves the fertility of the soil;
- varying capacity can be installed; any capacity can be operated, even at lower loads;
- no seasonality.

Its main disadvantages are:

- it is a dispersed and land intensive source,
- it is often of low energy density and
- it is also labor intensive and the cost of collecting large quantities for commercial application is significant. Most current commercial applications of biomass energy use material that has been collected for other reasons, such as timber and food processing residues and urban waste.
- capacity is determined by availability of biomass and not suitable for varying loads
- not feasible to set up at all locations

Manifestation of Biomass: Biomass manifests itself in various forms which are Generally present in the organism simultaneously.

These are shown in the table below.

Table: Manifestation forms of biomass and their annual Production.

Manifestation of biomass	Worldwide annual Production	
	% ge	Billion t/a
Cellulose	65	100
Hemi-cellulose	17	27
Lignin	17	27
Starch, Sugar, Fat, Protein, Chlorophyll	1	0.13
Total	100	155.28

Cellulose is the most common substance in all forms of biomass. It is polysaccharide which contains a chain of glucose molecules ($C_6H_{12}O_5$) which are held together in hydrogen bonds in the crystal bundle. Cellulose is not soluble in water and other molecule solvents but reacts with alkaline and acidic solutions to hydrate cellulose, which through formation of acids at higher temperature, can be converted to glucose.

Hemi-cellulose is a polysaccharide which made not only of a glucose molecule chain , but also of other sugars (C_5 and C_6 sugar molecules). About 20 to 40% of the lumber type plants contain in it.

Lignin is formed in the plants through the storage of lignified plant cell Membrane. It is soluble in soda lye (caustic soda solution) and calcium bisulphate but not in water. Lignin offers considerable resistance to the mechanical and enzymatic digestion of cellulose. About 30% of lumber plants contain the wood material it.

Other materials like starch, sugar, fat, protein, chlorophyll contain very little amount of contribution for biomass production.

Potential of Biomass: The worldwide existing biomass estimates to be about $2x10^{12}t = 30x10^{21}$ J = 1000billion tons of coal equivalent (land area only). Out of these estimates, about $8x10^{11} = 8x10^{11}$ t/a are used for carbon fixation. The amount of wood is estimated to be 50 to 90%. The annual growth rate of forest (storage for biomass) also decides the amount of use of biomass and this has been estimated around $1.5 x 10^{11}t = 3 x 10^{21}$ J/a = 100 billion tons COE/annum. This amount to be 10% of the total biomass estimates.

Table:12.2 Distribution of biomass Production in the Earth's Surface (Lith 1975).

Biomass Source	Area in 10^6 km^2	Net primary productivity, g/m^3 a	Net primary productivity in biom. 10^9 t/a	Calorific value in MJ/kg	Annual energy equivalent KWh/m^2 10^9 MWh		Percentage gain in solar energy in %.
Forest	50	1290	64	18.0	6.5	322	0.55
Forest land	7	600	4	16.7	3.33	23	0.30
Shrub	26	90	2.4	18.8	0.5	12	0.04
Grassland	24	600	15	17.6	2.9	70	0.30
Desert	24	1	-0	16.7	0	0	0
Culture land	14	650	9	17.2	3.1	44	0.30
Fresh water	4	1250	5	18.0	6.3	25	0.50
Total land	149	669	100	18.0	6.3	25	0.50
Ocean	361	155	55	18.8	0.8	303	0.07
Earth	510	305	155	18.4	1.6	799	0.14

The net primary production of biomass from the world's forest comprises about 7% of total production of the overall world's land area. Considering the existing land/water distribution, 60% of the total world's biomass production falls in northern hemisphere and 40% in southern hemisphere.

Forests and fresh water show a large gain from solar radiation, about 0.5% tropical forests attain a value of about 0.8%. The maximum achievable values of some of the
biomass are:
1. Sugarcane (4.8%), 2. Maize (3.2%), 3. Sugar beat (white) (5.4%).
It is always to be taken care of that only a part of the biomass energy can be harvested.
About 50% of the biomass (roots, leaves, etc) cannot be converted into energy. But it is also counted that the theoretical potential of biomass energy availability is four to six times the world's energy consumption presently.

Energy Conversion Process:-

The conversion of biomass either in the form of heat or solid, liquid or gas form of energy fuels. Using these individual elements in a particular process chain, a number of bio-conversion processes can be defined which is represented below.

Table: the elements of bio-conversion systems that may be used for a number of Bioprocesses Conversion chain (Nairobi Conference,1981).

Forms of Biomass	Method of Bio-conversion	End Product	Region of Application
1. Terrestrial Primary biomass	5. Physical conversion	8. Solid bio-fuel	14. Agriculture
2. Aquatic Primary biomass	6. Thermo-chemical methods	9. Liquid bio-fuel	15. Industry
3. Plant and animal waste	7. Biological conversion	10. Gaseous bio-fuel	16. Commercial
4. Residues		11. Electricity	17. Transport
		12. Mechanical energy	18. Domestic
		13. Heat	

Raw materials in all these processes is biomass, that is available in nature either in land or in water beds, but all is available in the form of residues or waste. Biomass waste materials cannot be used as food or for wood production like rice husk, saw dust and animal waste, etc. The biomass waste material (like straws, twigs, stem pieces may also be used for bio-conversion). These waste materials are also used for fertilizer on the earth.

From the table, it is observed that there are four forms of biomass that gets converted into useful energy forms by several processes of biomass energy conversion into useful products.

Table: Bio-conversion process, Raw material, End-product and Conversion Efficiencies.

Process	Raw material	End product	An efficiencies (%)
Physical processes			
Mechanical Compression	Wood waste, straw, saw dust	Pellets, briquettes	90
Extraction	Euphobia lathyris	Oil	20
Thermo-chemical processes			
Combustion	Wood	Steam, heat	70
Combustion	Wood	Steam, electricity	20
Gasification	Wood	Hot Producer gas	80
Gasification	Wood	Cooler producer gas	70
Gasification	Wood	Medium Joule value gas	70
Liquefaction			
1. Chemical reduction	Wood	Oil	30
2. Pyrolysis	Wood	Methanol	60
3. Synthesis	Wood	LPG	40
Biological Processes			
Fermentation (Alcohol Production)	Sugar plants, Corn Dung, algae	Ethanol	30
Fermentation (Biogas production)	Agricultural waste	Biogas	50
Composting		Heat	50

Physical Methods of Bioconversion:-

Mechanical compression of combustible materials:-

The simplest form of physical conversion of biomass is through compression of combustible material. Its density is increased by reducing the volume by compression through the processes *called briquetting, cobs or pelletization*. The end products are called *briquettes, cobs or pelletization*.

The mechanical compression of combustible materials simultaneously leads to drying of the product. There is not any uniform standardization of the end products exist. Generally the compressed biomass or pellets contain 15-18% of moisture.

Some characteristics parameters of compressed products are shown in the table below.

The whole mechanical conversion of biomass includes *collection, processing, drying etc.; which requires total energy of 10 to 15% of the respective calorific values.* So the net conversion efficiency of biomass compression process lies between 85% and 90%.

Table: Parameters of compressed biomass (Wieneke 1983)

Product	Preparation	Pressing Plant	Dia of edge length, mm	Pressing density kg/m³	Bulk density kg/m³	Specific energy requirement kWh/t
Pellets	Chopping and powdering	Grooved pressed	6 - 12	1100 - 1400	450 - 750	30 - 90
Cobs	Chopping, pressing and powdering with hammer	Grooved pressed	15 - 35	900 - 1200	403 - 600	30 - 80
Milling	Milling	Grooved and piston press	40 - 80	450 - 850	300 - 450	25 - 70

Extraction of oil from plant products:

The extraction of energy source from biomass consists of *hot press or cold press, steam extraction or acid reduction* etc. Some plants produce acid free hydrocarbons like *cellulose and lignin.* The acid free hydrocarbons can be converted into oil which can be treated as an oil. Vegetable oils are mainly edible oils along with their use in paints, soaps and cosmetic articles.

* In Europe, the main investigation on rapeseed oil have been made. The following outcomes are obtained:

(1) Rapeseed oil is a suitable power source for diesel engine and its efficiency is almost similar.

(2) A mixture of rapeseed oil and diesel fuel in the ratio 1:1, leads to resinification and carbon deposition in the engine.

(3) Emulsion of 40% oil, 40% diesel, 19% water and 1% gives good combustion in the engine and almost no deposition. However there are small problems like cold start of the engine due to higher viscosity.

* Bio-fuel development in India is the extraction of oil from Jatropha plant seeds. This bio-fuel contains 40% oil which is the quality of a rich oil. This oil has served as a replacement of bio-diesel for long decades in India. It can be used directly after extraction in generators and diesel engines. It has the potential to provide

economic benefits at the local level since with proper management, it has the potential to grow in dry marginal non-agricultural lands.

* One of the most productive oil plants in African soil is the palm oil. After simple treatment this oil has capability to produce low viscosity oil which can be used as diesel fuel. The advantages of using palm oil are: (1) it does not require any distillation, (ii) it shows small volumes (no water), (iii) continuous harvesting is possible.

* Another African extracted oil named as African milk bush which grows very fast and can be harvested several times a year.

* In the forest of South America, the famous Copaiba tree is available from which oil is extracted and used directly as fuel without any processing. The test values for the yield lie between 40 to 60 l/a per tree.

Thermo-Chemical Conversion Processes: In thermo-chemical processes, the biomass is either converted into heat through the process of oxidation or it is converted into a secondary form like producer gas by some chemical processing. One can roughly distinguish three different classes of thermochemical reactions: *(1) Combustion, (2) Gasification, and (3) Liquefaction.*

These three processes may run parallel or one after another.

A. Combustion:

One of the thermo-chemical method of bioconversion is combustion. *The main biomass which has been used over the years for combustion is wood.* Now 50% of the world are using wood for combustion. Especially in developing countries wood, dung and agricultural wastes e.g. straw, stem etc. are burned.

In the combustion process of biomass ($C_kH_mO_n$), the products produced are carbon dioxide, water vapor and ash. If it comes in contact with sulphur, then SO_2 is formed. Amount of energy (calorific value) released is equivalent to the burning of dryness fraction (x) portion of mass of fuel and rest ($1-x$) fraction is utilized for water evaporation process. The calorific value of moist biomass can therefore can be written as:

$$H_u = (1-x)H_{CDS} - x\,2441 \text{ KJ/kg}$$

where

H_{CDS} = calorific value of completely dry substance

x = dryness fraction.

About 40 to 60% moisture is present in the fresh wood. The moisture content in the fresh wood can be defined as:

$$X = \frac{m_{H_2O}}{m_{biomass}} = \frac{m_{H_2O}}{m_{H_2O} + m_{ODS}}$$

The *humidity(u) of wood* is defined as:

$$u = \frac{m_{H_2O}}{m_{CDS}} = \frac{X}{1-X}$$

Table: Calorific values of dry and moist biomasses:

Dry biomass		Moist biomass		
Material	Calorific Value, H_{CDS} (MJ/kg)	Fuel	Calorific Value, H_u (MJ/kg)	Humidity (%)
Ash Wood	18.6	Fresh Wood	6 - 8	40 - 60
Beech Wood	18.8	Air-dried Wood	14 - 16	10 - 20
Oakwood	18.3	Straw	11 - 18	15 - 18
Pine Wood	20.2	Waste	5 - 8	25 - 38
Waste Paper	17.0	Sludge	0	> 90
Sugarcane	15.0			
Algae	15.0			
Leaf Wood	18.0			
Vegetable Oils	39.0			
Heating oil	43.0			

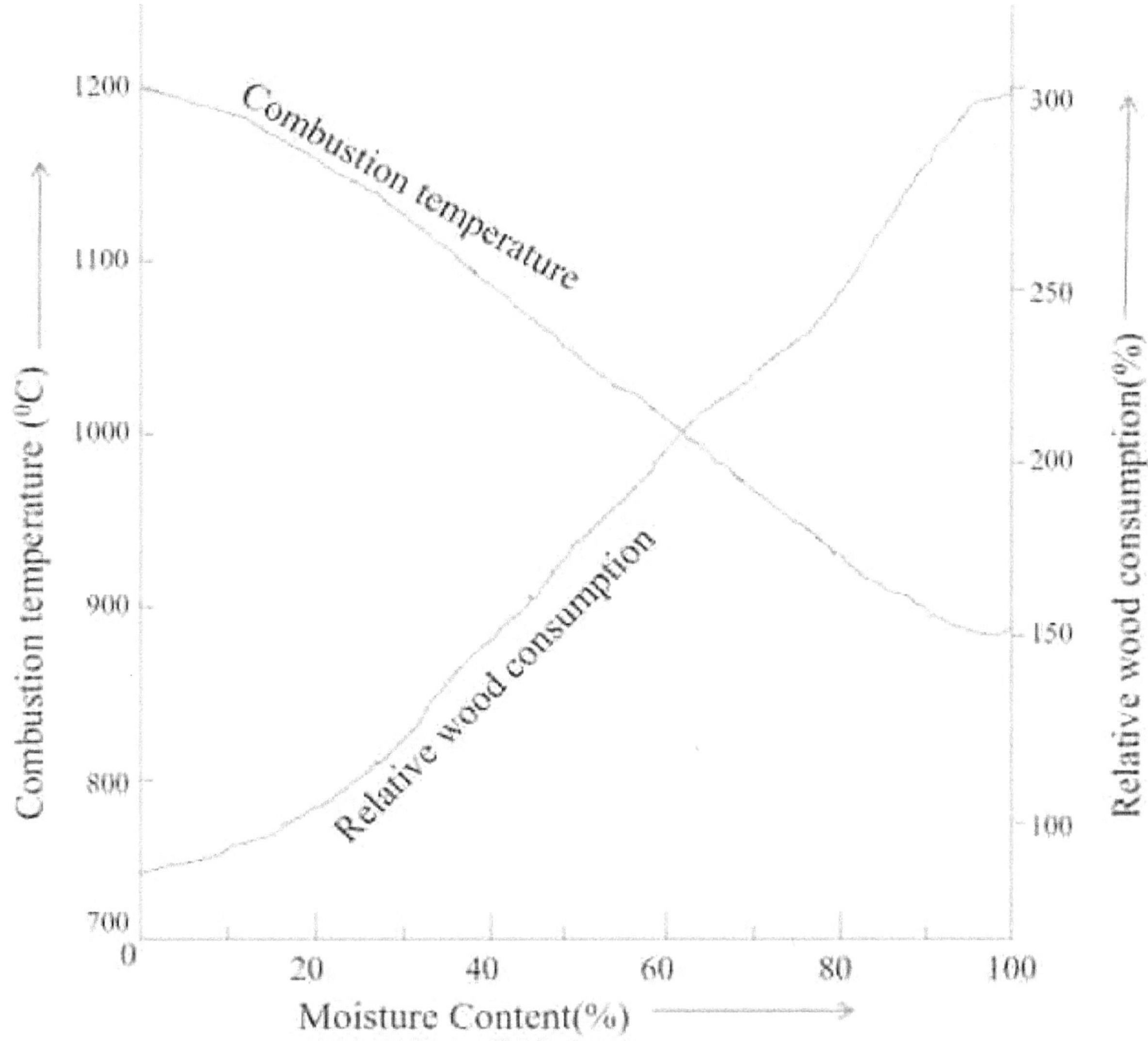

Fig: Combustion temperature and relative wood consumption as a function of moisture content (ECO 1980)

The combustion temperature decreases with increasing moisture content and the relative wood Consumption increases for generating the same amount of heat energy. For many combustion process, the wood containing moisture is heated in a *pre-combustion chamber* so that moisture is removed from the fuel. The heated fuel is burnt in *second combustion chamber*.

B. Biomass Gasification:

The complete and controlled combustion of biomass produces carbon dioxide, hydrogen, carbon monoxide and traces of methane along with dust, tar and steam vapor. *If the combustion is partial* (fuel-air supply is not as per the stochiometric), the products of combustion contains *carbon monoxide, hydrogen, and other elements is known as producer gas.* This producer gas is combustible.

The equipment used to produce producer gas through the process of biomass gasification is known as gasifier.

The steam required for gasification process is obtained from wet biomass during the first stage of combustion chamber.

Depending on the relative movement of the feedstock (biomass and air), three different kinds of gasifiers are used: (1) Updraft gasifier (the air moves upward through the biomass), (2) Downdraft gasifier (the air moves downward), and (3)Cross-draft gasifier (feed of air and biomass are perpendicular to each other).

Table: Advantage and disadvantage of various Gasifiers.

S. N.	Gasifier Type	Advantages	Disadvantages
1	Updraft (feed ↑)	1. Small Pressure drop, 2. Good thermal efficiency, 3. Little tendency towards slag formation	1. Great sensitivity to tar and moisture and moisture content of fuel, 2. Relatively long time required for start up of I.C. engine, 3. Poor reaction capability with heavy gas load.
2.	Downdraft (feed ↓)	1. Flexible adaptation of gas production to load, 2. Low sensitivity to charcoal dust and tar content of fuel.	1. Design tends to be tall, 2. Not feasible for very small particle size of fuel.
3.	Cross-draft (air → fuel)	1. Short design height, 2. Very fast response time to load, 3. Flexible gas production.	1. Very high sensitivity to slag formation, 2. High pressure drop

Almost all gasifiers fall under these three categories. The selection of gasifier depends upon the following factors:

(1) Fuel, (2) its final available form, (3) its size, (4) moisture content and (5) ash content.

(2) There are four zones in each of the gasifier. These are: (1) Drying zone, (2) Pyrolysis

(3) zone, (3) Reduction zone, and (4) Combustion zone.

(4) **Drying Zone:** Drying of wet biomass takes place.

(5) **Pyrolysis Zone:** The products like Carbon dioxide and Acetic acid are produced.

(6) **Reduction Zone:** Carbon monoxide and hydrogen are produced.

$$C + CO_2 = 2CO - 164.9 \ \text{MJ/kg mole}$$
$$C + H_2O = CO + H_2 + 42 \ \text{MJ/kg mole}$$
$$C + 2H_2 = CH_4 + 75 \ \text{MJ/kg mole}$$
$$CO_2 + H_2 = CO + H_2O - 42.3 \ \text{MJ/kg mole}$$

Combustion Zone: Steam and carbon-dioxide are formed.

$$C + O_2 = CO_2 + 393 \ \text{MJ/kg mole}$$
$$2H_2 + O_2 = 2H_2O - 242 \ \text{MJ/kg mole}$$

On an average 1 kg of biomass produces 2.5 m³ of producer gas at S.T.P. with consumption of 1.5 m³ of air (Reed *et al.*). For complete combustion of wood 4.5 m³ of air is required. For example to calculate the conversion efficiency (η_{Gas}) of wood gasifier; the calorific value of producer gas and dry wood are assumed as 5.4 MJ/m³ and 19.8MJ/kg respectively.

$$\eta_{Gas} = \frac{2.5 \times 5.4}{1 \times 19.80} = 68\%$$

Application: Producer gas can be used for many applications like:
(a) Direct heating,
(b) Shaft Power, and
(c) Chemical synthesis into methanol.

C. LIQUEFACTION OF BIOMASS

The liquefaction of gas takes place through three different processes:
1. Liquefaction through chemical reduction with the help of gasification medium.
2. Liquefaction through pyrolysis without any gasification medium.
3. Liquefaction through methanol synthesis and pre-gasification.

1. Liquefaction through Chemical Reduction:-

By introduction of carbon monoxide at high temperatures (250^0C to 400^0C) and high pressure (140-280 bar), and in the presence of an adequate alkali catalyzer, biomass can be liquefied directly. One such catalyzer is $NaHCO_3$. The cellulose in appropriate reduction to form an acidic substance and CO is reduced to CO_2. The cellulose must form a solution in 85% water. CO is obtained from the biomass in the form of producer gas (gasification) containing H_2 also. By hydrolysis, H_2 leads to hydrolysis and eventually to liquefaction.

2. Pyrolysis:-

Pyrolysis is the destructive distillation or degasification of biomass that is subjected to thermal splitting in the absence of air/oxygen. This is the reverse process of gasification where heat is supplied externally to biomass contained in

cylinders,fluidized beds or drum reactors at temperatures between 300-1000^{0}C.
The products of pyrolysis with calorific value are:
* Gas: Pyrolysis gas (10-15 MJ/m^3)
* Liquid: Pyrolysis oil   (23-30 MJ/kg)
* Solid: Coke: (20-30 MJ/kg)
The efficiency of the *pyrolysis* process depends upon the following factors:
(i)   Composition and size of the biomass
(ii) Pyrolysis temperature
(iii) Heating rate
(iv) Duration of biomass in reactor
The main product from pyrolysis is wood only. The destructive distillation of wood produces pyrolysis oil or bio oil. The properties of the pyrolysis oil are closer to the diesel oil or thermal oil.

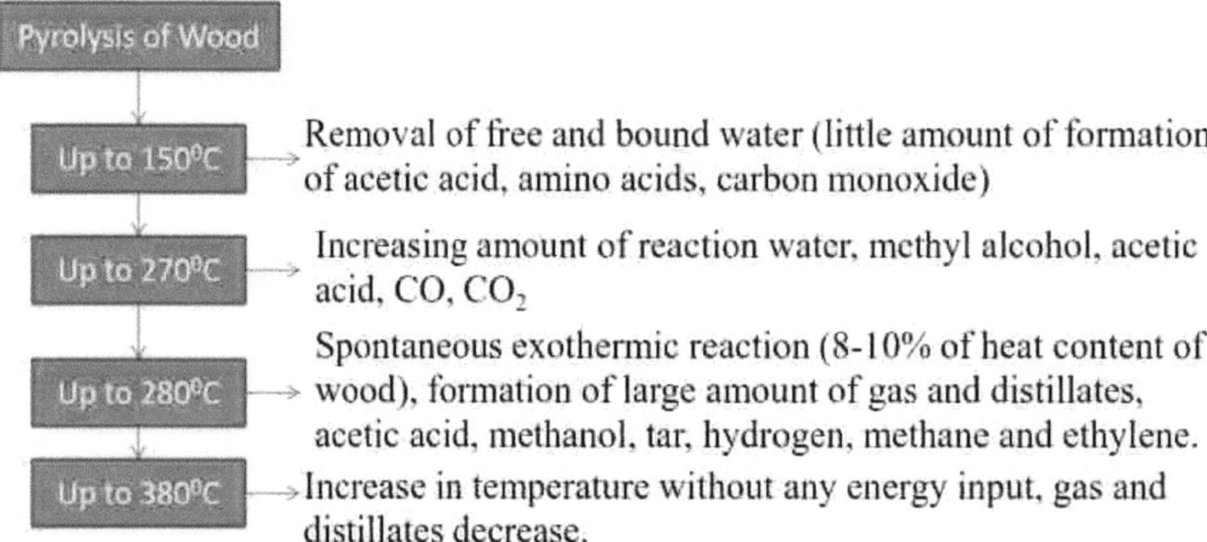

Pyrolysis of biomass, domestic or municipal waste and non-biological waste products like automobile tyres, has been of interest from the point of view of the following:
* Manufacturing of pyrolysis oil as a liquid fuel
* Production of basic raw materials.
Pyrolysis has not been a commercial success because of the following:
* Bad quality of pyrolysis oil,
* High water content
* Highly viscous fluid
* Corrosion of containers due to high acidic contents
* Partly soluble in water.
3. *Liquefaction through synthesis of Methanol:* Lowest quality of fuel, methanol is

Produced catalytically from the suitable mixture of synthetic gas (CO and H_2 mixtures). Methanol (CH_3OH) is used as a fuel in certain engines of vehicles.

$$CO + H_2 \xrightarrow{\text{Catalysis}} CH_3OH + 91 \text{ MJ/mol (heat of evolution)}$$

The various processes of methanol production can be categorized as follows:

1. Low pressure   (50 - 60 bar)   at temperature range: 230^0C to 260^0C.

2. Average pressure   (100 – 150 bar)

3. High pressure   (275 – 360 bar) ——→ at temperature of 300 and 400^0C

Catalyst used: Cu, Zn, Cr and their oxides. In comparison with petrol, methanol has the following disadvantages:

1. Low calorific value of 19.7 MJ/kg in contrast to petrol has 45.5 MJ/kg.

2. Cold start under 10^0 C is not possible.

3. Poisonous and corrosive.

Production of methanol requires H_2 and CO which can be obtained by gasification of wood. Gasification requires $H_2 : CO = 2:1$ for synthesis of methanol. Gas mixture is often reacted with steam in presence of catalyst to promote a shift to increase hydrogen content.

$$CO + H_2O \longrightarrow H_2 + CO_2$$

CO_2 and H_2S present in producer gas are removed prior to methanol reactor. Yields of methanol from woody biomass are expected to be the range 480-568 litres/ton.

Biological Methods for Biomass Conversion:-

The biological method of conversion or the biochemical method of conversion takes place at low temperature with the help of single cell micro-organisms known as microbes. For this reason these methods are called microbiological methods.

The microbiological reduction of carbon and water containing biomass usually takes place in the absence of air in an aqueous environment. The microbiological reduction of organic matter is also known as fermentation. Presently two methods are of most important from the point of view of technology and energy gain.

1. The fermentation of biomass of methane (biogas) production, and
2. The fermentation of biomass for ethanol production.
The detail discussion of these methods will be done later on this section.
Aerobic and Anaerobic Digestion: When the moist biomass comes in contact with air, it automatically decays with the help of aerobic micro-organisms. As a result C and H oxides into CO_2 and H_2O with simultaneous release of heat at temperature of 70-90^0 C. In the carbon dioxide cycle, the aerobic bacteria plays an important role. The bacteria releases CO_2 and thus mineralize the bounded carbon in the organic substance.

In anaerobic digestion the organic material is allowed to decay in absence of oxygen. The different types of bacteria make a number of exchange processes resulting the digestion of biomass and conversion into a mixture of methane and carbon dioxide.

The energy obtained is much higher than of a low temperature decaying process. There three steps in the production of methane. These are:
1. Acid production (hydrolysis) →Where the bonds are broken and acid is formed.
2. Acid reduction
3. Methane production → is formed from anaerobic bacteria

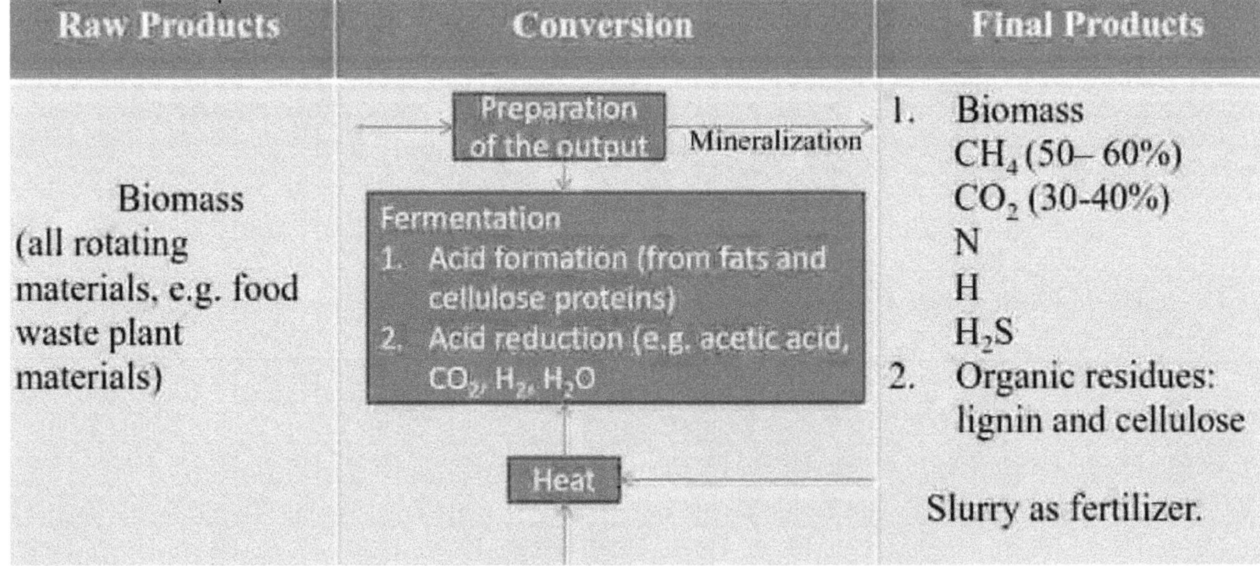

Fig: Simple scheme of an anaerobic digestion (Meinhold,980)

Step – I: (Acid production and hydrolysis):
In this hydrolysis process, the biomass like protein, fat and carbohydrates are broken through the influence of water. The polymers (large molecules) are reduced to monomers (basic molecules). The reaction is accelerated through enzymes, which are separated from bacteria. The resulting products are: Fat,

Protein, Carbohydrates, Fatty acids, Amino acids, Sugar. These products are fermented by the fermentation bacteria (bacteria which are active in this step) leading to the formation of the following products:

1. H_2, H_2O, CO_2, NH_3
2. Acetic acid (CH_3COOH)
3. Alcohol and low organic acids.

Step-II (Acid Reduction):
In the second step, the alcohol and the low organic acids are fermented into the following products through the action of acetogenic bacteria. (i) H_2O, (ii) CO_2, (iii) H, (iv) Acetic acid (CH_3COOH)
The final product of fermentation process is the acetic acid.

Step-III (Methane Production):
The acetic acid produced in the first and second step is converted into methane and CO_2 (biogas) through the effect of methanographic bacteria. At the end the residual waste is rich in nitrogen and can be used as a good fertilizer. In each step of the anaerobic digestion, a variety of bacteria are formed which cause the decaying of the organic material and which are specialized for the reduction of intermediate products.

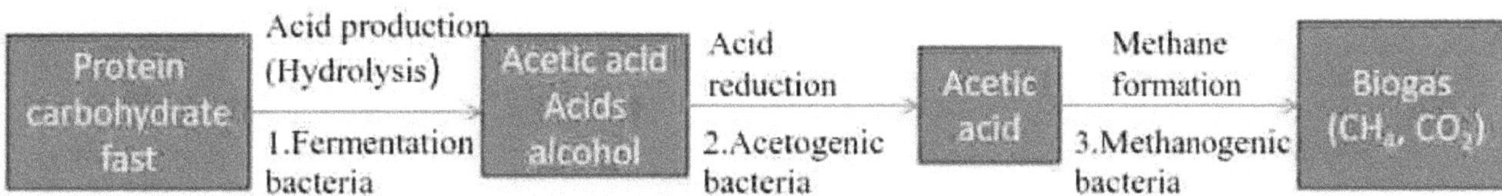

Fig: Sequence of methane production from aerobic digestion of organic waste

Influencing parameters: The amount of biogas produces through anaerobic Digestion of organic waste and also the methane content in it depends upon the following parameters:

1. Kind of substrate,   2. Dry matter content,   3. Temperature,   4. Digestion period,5. Mode of operation, 6. PH value.

Description of biogas Digesters: There are various types of digesters according to the need of the situation.

But there are two basic types of distinguishable digesters according to the loading used.

1. Batch type digester
2. Continuous flow digester.

A batch type digester is a simple digester in which organic material is filled in a closed container and allowed to be digested an aerobically over a period of two to six months time depending upon the feed material and other parameters like temperature, pressure etc.

Advantage: This type of digester is very simple to run and requires very less attention. It is easy to start and emptying out. Maximum efficiency of digestion depends upon the carefully loading and waste of biomass.

Limitation: It has the problem of handling the waste material.

A typical miniature digester with a tank of 10 liter is shown in the figure below. The batch digesters are suitable for fibrous waste and difficult to digest.According to the availability of the waste, this is more suitable for irregular availability of waste. For continuous waste supply, batch digester can be used.With increase of digestion time.

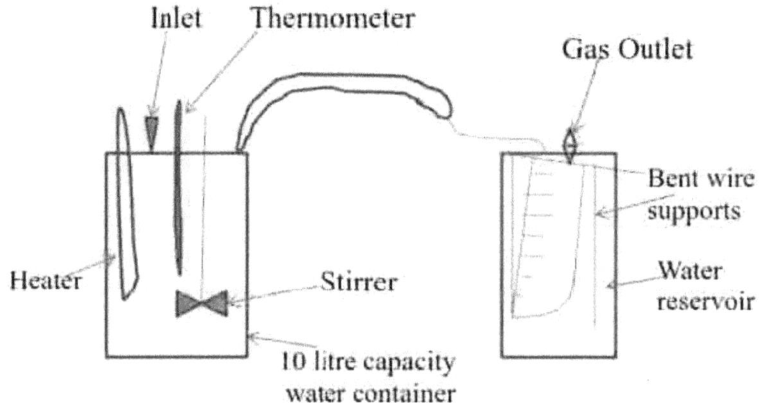

Fig: Experimental batch methane digester (Borda, 1979)

If several batch digesters are used in series, with each at a different stage in the digestion cycle, a continuous gas flow is obtained which is shown in the cycle. The digesters would be started up at regular intervals, so that the continuous gas flow is

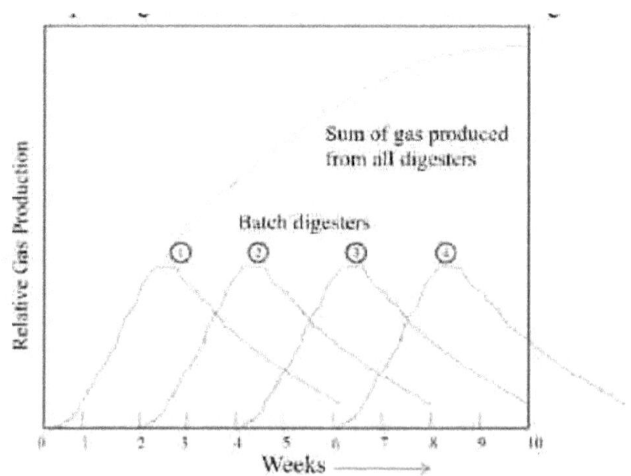

Fig: A continuous flow of biogas from four batch digesters with a staggered operation maintained

* Indian Institute of Science (IISc) Bangalore has developed a digester but that shows some heat los problem.
* Indian Institute of Technology (IIT) Delhi have made attempts to utilize solar energy systems which could be integrated with flouting or fixed dome designs for maintaining higher slurry temperature. They have produced biogas from rated value 0.3 m3 /day/m3 digester volume to 0.37-0.52 m3 /day/m3 (Bansal et al, 1985).

Biogas from agro industrial residues:

The agro-industrial residues can be conventionally converted into biomass production with suitable mixed digesters. The Commonwealth Scientific and Industrial Research Organization (CSIRO) in Australia tested various fruit processing waste in 23 m3 pilot digester. This is completely mixed through biogas recirculation.

1. Thermophilic Digestion: Most of the biogas digesters produce biogas due to action of bacteria known

As mesophilic bacteria. These type of bacteria needs 350 C but biogas can also be produced due to some of the other bacterias which need temperature around of 500 C.

The advantages of this thermophilic digestion includes:-

1. Shorter retention times,
2. Increased digestion efficiency,
3. and increased destruction of pathogens.

The disadvantages include:-

1. Greater sensitivity to temperature variation,
2. the need for better mixing,
3. and the additional energy needed for digester heating.

2. *Anaerobic Contact Reactors:* In this digester the feed enter near the top and is drawn off at the bottom. The liquid flows through a setting tank where the sludge containing methane forming micro-organisms settles out and is returned to the digester.

3. *Anaerobic Filter Reactors:* It consists of a chamber filled with a packing medium;

The methane forming bacteria form a film on the large surface and are not carried out of the digester with the effluent. For this reason, these digesters are also known as fixed film or retained film digesters. The fluid enters at the bottom and flows up through the packing medium; as the organisms in the liquid pass over the bacterial film, they are converted to biogas.

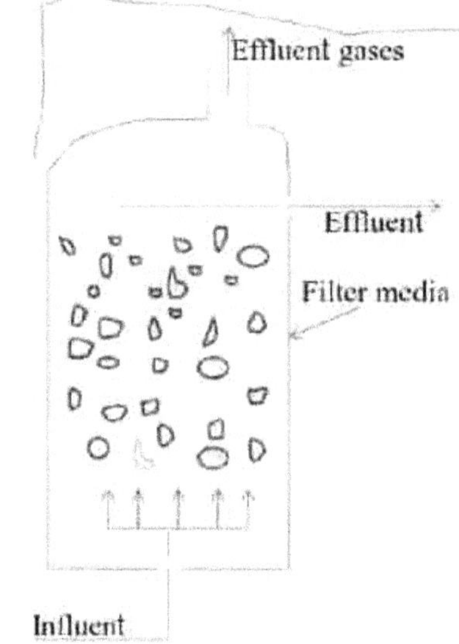

Fig: Anaerobic Filter Reactor

<u>Biogas from Human Residue:</u>

Biogas from sewage:-

In 1949's and 1950's, anaerobic digestion system were used to produce heat energy or electric power in sewage treatment in US municipalities as well as several other countries. But it was abandoned due to the cost of energy production is higher than the Govt. supply. Biogas is used in several states to fuel engines and to produce electricity. Biogas provides low pressure steam for Chicago plant and boiler fuel for a steam power plant in Los Angels. Waste heat from biogas is supplied to New York Plant for running purposes.

Biogas heat may be utilized for generation of steam which will be utilized to run the turbine to produce electricity.

* About 600,000 ft3 of biogas is produced from daily sewage treatment plant in New Delhi. About 50,000 families are using as cooking gas for their use.

Biogas from Night Soil:-

Human excreta (waste) from the human body is known as night soil. These can be used in biogas plants to produce electricity. These   type power production is quite popular in India, Nepal and China. The study has been found that night soil from 40 to 60 people are enough to produce cooking gas for one family.

Stirring Equipment: It is desirable that the digesters are thoroughly mixed to:-

1. Avoid the formation of sink layers on the floor of the fermenter,

2. Avoid the formation of scum on the uppermost surface of the substrate resulting in the cooking of the system,

3. Maintain a uniform temperature,

4. Maintain a uniform food stuff to the bacteria.

Usually mechanical stirring equipment is used for the mixing of the substrate.

Other equipments like circulation pump, gas compression, valve gear are also used for Stirring.

Production of Ethanol (C_2H_5OH):-

Ethanol production is based on the principle of anaerobic fermentation of

sugar solutions with the help of microorganism present in the yeast. This process is known as alcoholic fermentation. There are three types of biomass used for ethanol production in order of increasing complexity.

1. Sugar containing biomass,
2. Starch containing biomass,
3. Cellulose containing biomass.

Table: Inputs for Ethanol production

Sugar containing	Starch containing	Cellulose containing
Sugarcane	Maize	Wood
Sugar beat	Corn	Straw
Sugar millet	Potato	
Fodder beat (mangold)	Cassana	

Ethanol production from various crops.

Crop	Annual production tons/ha	Sugar/starch content % weight	Ethan ol %	Ethanol tons/ha	Production l/ha
Sugar beat	34 - 51	15	8	2.7 – 4.1	3375 - 5125
Wheat	3.6 – 6.3	60	32	1.2 – 2.1	1520 - 2625
Sugarcane	56 - 70	12.5	6	3.1 – 4.9	3875 - 6125
Wood	5 - 6		15	0.75 – 0.9	940 - 1125

Ethanol production from starch and cellulose biomass must be converted into sugar

before fermentation. Conversion of sugar into alcohol takes place according to the

following chemical reactions.

$$\text{Sugar} \xrightarrow{\text{Yeast}} \text{Ethanol} + CO_2$$

$$C_6H_{12}O_6 \longrightarrow 2C_2H_5OH + 2CO_2$$

$$100 \text{ kg} \longrightarrow 51 \text{ kg} + 49 \text{ kg}$$

The following types of sugars can be easily differentiated between

Glucose = grape sugar ($C_6H_{12}O_6$)

Fructose = fruit sugar ($C_6H_{12}O_6$) and

Sucrose = Beat sugar, cane sugar ($C_{12}H_{22}O_{11}$)

Starch ($C_6H_{10}O_5$) is converted to sugar through hydrolysis and then fermented to ethanol. The following chemical reaction takes place.

$$\text{Starch } (C_6H_{10}O_5) + \text{Water } (H_2O) \rightarrow \text{Glucose } (C_6H_{12}O_6)$$

$$C_6H_{12}O_6 \rightarrow 2C_2H_5OH + 2CO_2$$

Fig: Schematic of ethanol production

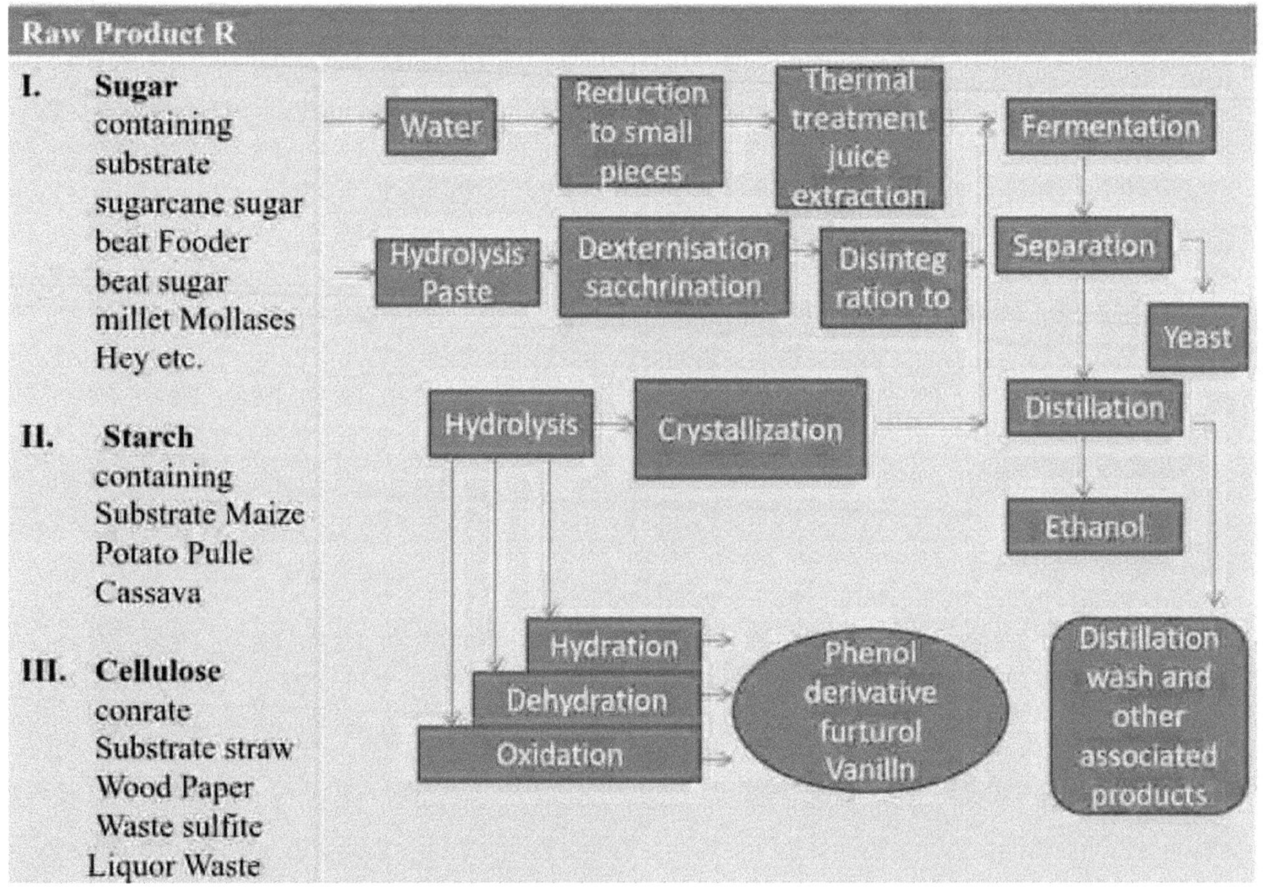

The Fermentation Process:-

The rate of alcohol production depends upon the following factors.

1. Sugar content: (generally, 10 – 18% w.r.t. mass. Higher values will slow down the fermentation process.)

2. Fermenting temperature: (30 – 400 C. The reaction being exothermic. At higher temperature, there is danger of foam formation and therefore loss of efficiency.)

3. pH value : (pH value of 4.0 or higher is required because yeast lives in the range of 3.0 to 6.0.)

4. Yeast concentration: (In stationary condition, 40 – 60 gram of yeast used for 1 litre of substrate. Aerobic process takes place. For fermentation process, air is allowed to flow through the fermenter to ensure the presence of yeast.)

5. Fermentation time: (Simple fermentation process requires 36 to 48 hours. However new technology requires 1 to 5 hours.) .

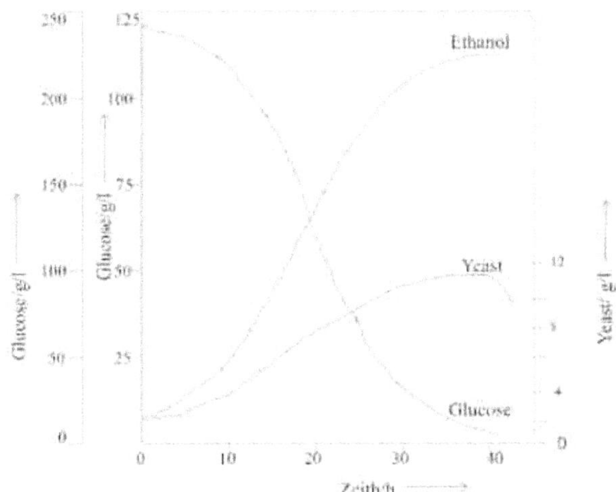

Fig: Reaction time for fermentation in a batch process (Menrad *et al.*, 1982)

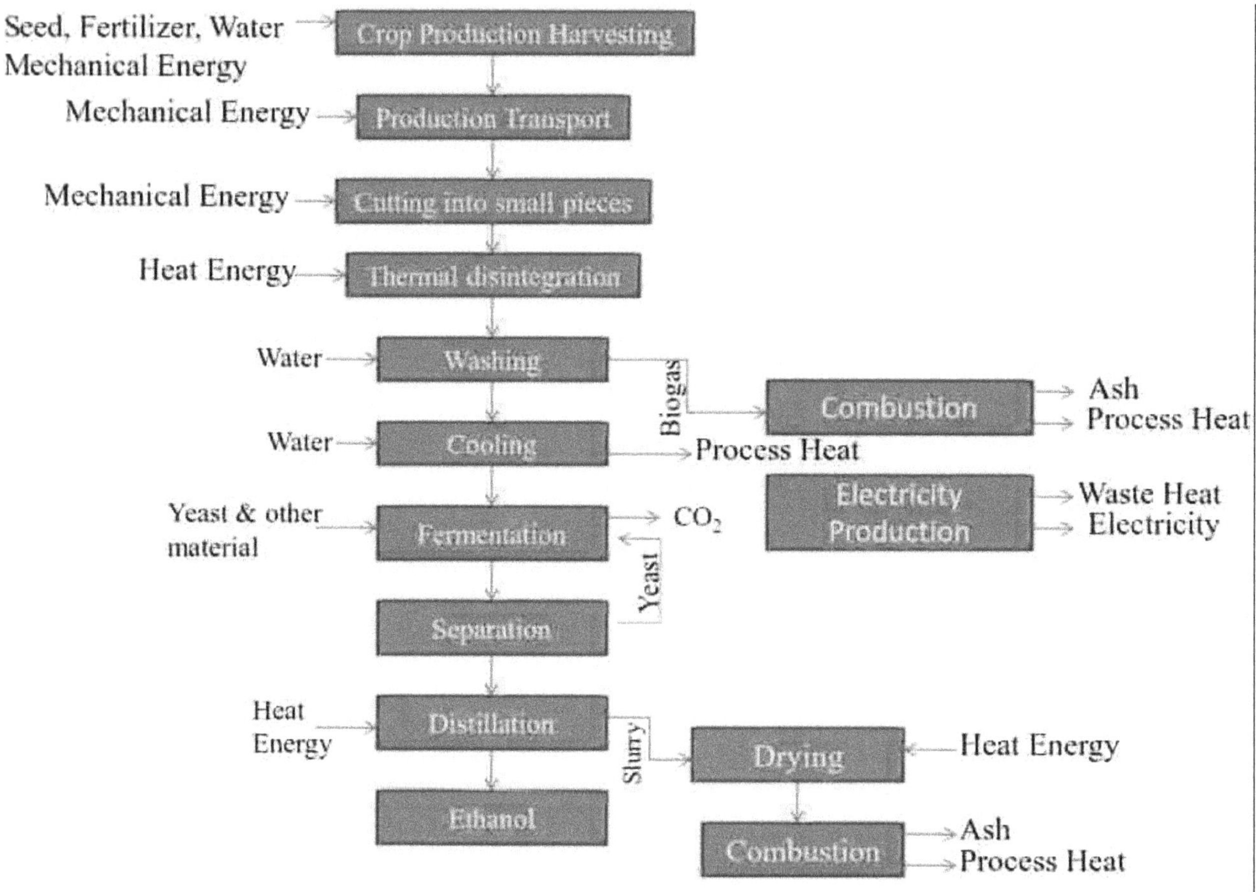

Fig: Block diagram of ethanol production from sugarcane

* At the end of the distillation, slurry remains as a waste, which is mixture of water, organic material and minerals. This slurry can be used either as fodder or as fertilizer. This slurry can also be used in biogas plants for biogas production. The slurry has been combusted and the heat produced is used for manufacturing process.

Characteristics of Ethanol:*

The calorific value of ethanol is quite lower than that of petrol.

* Since the ethanol has a lower stochiometric ratio, the calorific value of air/fuel mix is nearly same.

* The boiling point of ethanol is same as that of petrol.

* Lower volatile nature of ethanol leads to a bad engine start in cold.

Its main disadvantages are:-

(1) It is dispersed and land-intensive source.

(2) It is often low energy density.

(3) It is also labour intensive and cost of collecting large quantities for commercial application is significant.

(4) Capacity is determined by availability of bio-mass and not suitable for varying

loads.

(5) It is not feasible to set up at all locations.

Biomass Conversion Process:-

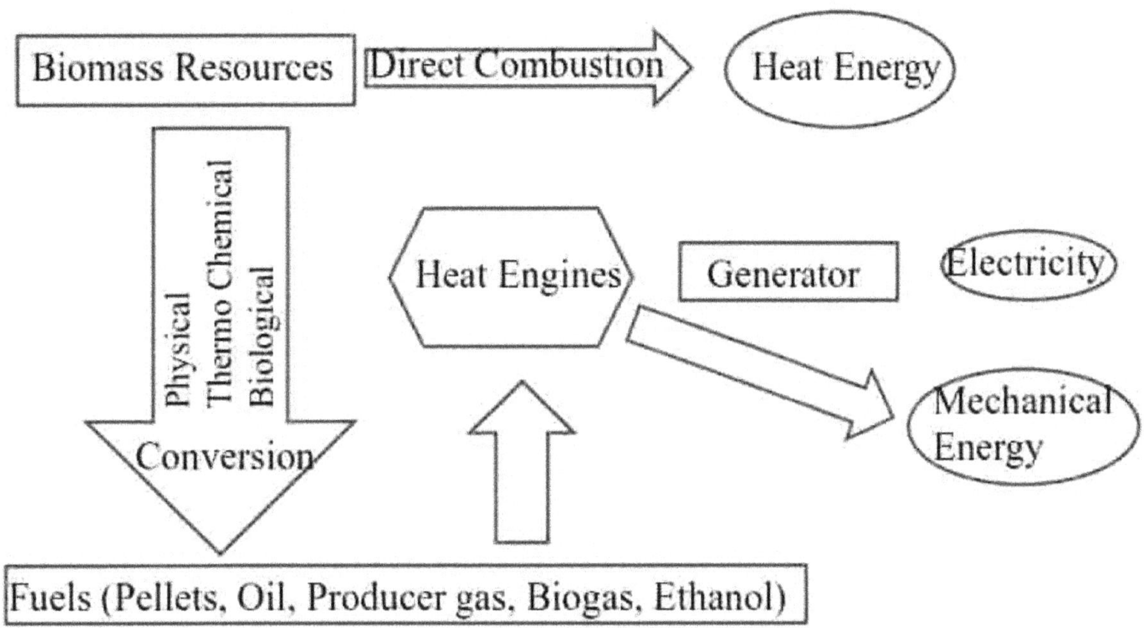

Fig: Biomass energy conversion Process

Multiple choice questions and answers

Objective tyPe Questions

1. Storage of biomass energy is:
(a) very difficult (b) inbuilt feature
(c) expensive (d) impossible

2. Biogas is predominantly:
(a) hydrogen (b) carbon monoxide
(c) carbon dioxide (d) methane

3. Heating value of producer gas is:
(a) 4–8 MJ/m3
 (b) 14–18 MJ/m3
(c) 24–28 MJ/m3
 (d) 34–38 MJ/m3

4. Fluidized bed gasifier produces:
 (a) low tar and high particulate (b) high tar and low particulate
(c) gas at low conversion efficiency (d) low exit temperature

5. The water content in anhydrous ethanol is:
(a) 20% (b) 10%
(c) 5% (d) 0.7%

6. The percentage of ethanol in blended petrol (gasohol) is:
(a) 20% (b) 30%
(c) 4% (d) 50%

7. Compared to petrol operated engine, an ethanol operated engine:
(a) produces 50% more power
(b) produces 20% more power
(c) produces comparable amount of power
(d) produces 20% less power

8. Increasing the pressure inside biogas plant:
(a) increases the gas production (b) decreases the gas production
(c) has no effect on gas production (d) causes explosion

9. When ambient temperature of biogas plant decreases below 20°C:
(a) the gas production increases
(b) the gas production first increases and then decreases
(c) the gas production decreases
(d) remains unaltered

10. The optimum solid concentration in a biogas is:
(a) 37–39 % (b) 27–29 %
(c) 17–19 % (d) 7–9 %

11. Which material should be added in the feed of biogas plant to increase nitrogen content?
(a) Lignin (b) Carbohydrate
(c) Chopped leguminous plants (d) Night soil

12. Compared to fixed dome model of biogas plant a floating drum type plant is:
(a) more efficient (b) less efficient
(c) equally efficient (d) very cheap

13. In energy farming, the plantation and harvesting is planned and managed so as to:
(a) reduce manual labour (b) insure the sustainability of the resource
(c) insure multiple harvesting per year (d) minimize the cost involved

14. Bio-diesel is:
(a) obtained from fermentation of sugars

(b) obtained from pyrolysis process
(c) exudates of plants
(d) an upgraded vegetable oil

15. Liquefaction of biomass is carried out at:
(a) high temperature and low pressure
(b) relatively low temperature and high pressure
(c) relatively low temperature and normal pressure
(d) room temperature and high pressure

16. Which of the following is a biodegradable waste?
(a) Vegetable and fruit peels (b) Silver foil
(c) Detergent (d) Rubber

17. The process in which waste material is reduced to ashes is called:
(a) biodegradation (b) composting
(c) recycling (d) incineration

18. Which of the following is not a biomass?
(a) Plants and trees (b) Wood
(c) Cattle dung (d) Water

19. Which of the following fuels can be produced by fermenting sugar cane top, sawdust, corn or wood chips?
(a) Alcohol (b) Biogas
(c) Producer gas (d) Bio-diesel

20. A small percentage of the hazardous waste is also generated in the house. Which of the following is a hazardous waste that is generated in the house?
(a) Paper (b) Leftover foodstuff
(c) Old batteries (d) Plastic bags

21. Which of the following does not have energy at all?
(a) Protein (b) Fat
(c) Carbohydrate (d) Vitamin

22. Burning of plastics, especially PVC releases which of the following harmful gases into the atmosphere:
(a) Lithium (b) Dioxins
(c) Methane (d) Nitrogen

23. The optimal pH value of slurry for biogas production ranges between:
(a) 6.8 and 7.2 (b) 5 and 5.6
(c) 8 and 9.5 (d) 0 and ± 0.5

24. The waste water from distillery can be used to produce which of the following gases
commercially?
 (a) Carbon dioxide (b) Hydrogen
 (c) Oxygen (d) Biogas

25. Gasification of biomass is which type of conversion process?
 (a) Chemical (b) Biochemical
 (c) Biological (d) Thermochemical

26. Hydrogen can be generated commercially through:
 (a) Aerobic digestion (b) Steam reforming of methane
 (c) Incineration (d) Anaerobic digestion

27. Presence of which of the following in the biogas causes corrosive effect?
 (a) Hydrogen sulfide (b) Methane
 (c) Carbon dioxide (d) Nitrogen

28. The gas generated through biomass gasification is called:
 (a) ethane (b) biogas
 (c) producer gas (d) carbon dioxide

29. Fuel reforming is a process of:
 (a) transforming of fossil fuel into hydrogen
 (b) transforming of fossil fuel into carbon monoxide
 (c) removing carbon compounds from fossil fuel
 (d) removing sulfur compounds from fossil fuel

Multiple Choice Questions and Answers

1. What is biomass?
   a) Organic materials from living organisms
   b) Inorganic materials from living organisms
   c) Inorganic materials from non-living organisms
   d) Organic materials from non-living organisms
   View Answer
Answer: a
   Explanation: Biomass is a term for all organic materials stemming from living organisms like
   plants, animals and microorganisms. Examples of biomass are – animal waste, dead plants
   and animals, sugar, fats, etc.
2. Which of the following can be classified under biomass?
   a) Steel
   b) Organic molecules containing hydrogen
   c) NaOH

d) Iron
View Answer

Answer: b

Explanation: Organic molecules containing hydrogen is a biomass. Steel is made up of inorganic materials. NaOH is a strong base which is made up of an inorganic material called sodium (Na). Iron (Fe) is another inorganic material which is used for its magnetic properties.

3. Which of the following is not used as food for humans?
    a) Sugars
    b) Glucose
    c) Cellulosic matter
    d) Fats
    View Answer

Answer: c

Explanation: Cellulosic biomass is not used as a food source for humans. It is made up of very complex sugar polymers. Sugars, glucose and fats are used in various food items.

4. ___________ is an example of cellulosic biomass.
    a) Glucose
    b) Fats
    c) Lipids
    d) Agricultural residue
    View Answer

Answer: d

Explanation: Agricultural residue is an example of cellulosic biomass. They generally include leftover material from crops like stalks and leaves. Fats, lipids and glucose are not cellulosic biomass.

5. Value of any biomass depends on ____________ properties.
    a) chemical and physical
    b) chemical and photo sensitive
    c) physical and photo sensitive
    d) the number of carbon molecules and on the number of tin molecules
    View Answer

Answer: a

Explanation: The value of any biomass depends on the chemical and physical properties. These are basically the properties of the large molecules from which it is made. It does not depend on the light and the number of molecules.

6. Which of the following are characterizes an ideal energy crop?
    a) High yield, high energy input to produce, high cost and high nutrient requirements
    b) High yield, low energy input to produce, low cost and low nutrient requirements
    c) High yield, high energy input to produce, low cost and high nutrient requirements
    d) Low yield, high energy input to produce, high cost and high nutrient requirements
    View Answer

Answer: b

Explanation: In general, the characteristics of any ideal energy crop are – high yield, low energy input to produce, low cost, consists of least contaminants and low nutrient requirements. These depend on the local climate and soil conditions.

7. Which energy forms can biomass be converted to?
   a) Electrical and light
   b) Light and chemical
   c) Electrical and heat
   d) Heat and light
   View Answer

Answer: c
   Explanation: Biomass can be converted to electrical and heat energy. It can also be used as transport fuel and chemical feedstock. It cannot be converted to light energy.

8. The heating value is expressed in BTU/kg.
   a) True
   b) False
   View Answer

Answer: a
   Explanation: The heating value is expressed in BTU/kg. BTU stands for British Thermal Unit and is used to measure thermal (heat) energy. It is the amount of energy needed to raise 1 pound of water 1 degree farad at sea level. Other commonly used units are MJ/kg and cal/g.

9. What does heat value indicate?
   a) Amount of energy consumed by biomass to produce energy
   b) Amount of energy required to process biomass to produce energy
   c) Amount of energy required as heat by the organisms
   d) Amount of energy that is available in the fuel
   View Answer

Answer: d
   Explanation: Heating value indicates the total amount of energy that is available in the fuel. It is one of the most important characteristics of a fuel. It is mostly a function of fuel's chemical composition.

10. What is higher heating value?
   a) Amount of energy available in the fuel + energy contained in water vapour in the exhaust gases
   b) Total amount of energy available in the fuel – energy contained in water vapour in the exhaust gases
   c) Total amount of energy available in the fuel * energy contained in water vapour in the exhaust gases
   d) Total amount of energy available in the fuel
   View Answer

Answer: a
   Explanation: Higher heating value is the total amount of energy available in the fuel, including energy contained in water vapour in the exhaust gases. Heating value indicates the total amount of energy available in the fuel.

11. What is lower heating value?
   a) Amount of energy available in the fuel + energy contained in water vapour in the exhaust

gases
b) Total amount of energy available in the fuel – energy contained in water vapour in the exhaust gases
c) Total amount of energy available in the fuel / energy contained in water vapour in the exhaust gases
d) Total amount of energy available in the fuel which cannot be used
View Answer

Answer: b

Explanation: Lower heating value (LHV) is total amount of energy available in the fuel – energy contained in water vapour in the exhaust gases. Generally, LHV is not an appropriate value to use for biomass combustion.

12. High moisture fuels burn readily and provide more useful heat per unit mass.
    a) True
    b) False
    View Answer

Answer: b

Explanation: High moisture content in fuels do not allow them to burn readily and provide less useful heat per unit mass. This is because water itself does not provide any energy value. In fact, much of the supplied energy is used to heat and vaporize water which leads wastage of supplied energy.

13. Moisture content can be calculated on two bases, namely ________
    a) light and heavy
    b) weighted and even
    c) wet and dry
    d) light and dry
    View Answer

Answer: c

Explanation: Moisture content can be calculated on two bases, namely, wet and dry. Weighted is generally used to calculate weighted average. Light and heavy are not related to moisture content.

14. What are the main components of cellulosic biomass?
    a) Hemicellulose and lignin
    b) Hemicellulose and sugars
    c) Cellulose, sugars and fats
    d) Cellulose, hemicellulose and lignin
    View Answer

Answer: d

Explanation: The main components of cellulosic biomass are cellulose, hemicellulose and lignin. Sugars and fats are not cellulosic biomass.

15. Biomass is seasonal.
    a) True
    b) False
    View Answer

Answer: a

Explanation: Biomass is seasonal, especially plant biomass. This is a problem because most biomass comes from agricultural feedstock. However, the energy and feedstock demands are continuous irrespective of season.

1. Which of the following can be classified under solid biomass?
   a) Agricultural residues
   b) Waste water
   c) Industrial effluents into rivers
   d) Plastic
   View Answer

Answer: a

Explanation: Agricultural residues can be classified under solid biomass resource. Waste water and polluted rivers are not solids. Plastic is not a biomass.

2. What are energy crops?
   a) Crops grown to remove insects
   b) Crops grown to be used in generating energy
   c) Crops grown to feed people
   d) Crops that produce energy
   View Answer

Answer: b

Explanation: Energy crops are crops that are grown with the specific intention to generate energy. They don't produce energy by themselves but they are used to generate energy or serve as fuel. Eg. – bioethanol.

3. Which of the following are examples of energy crops?
   a) Banyan
   b) Mango
   c) Herbaceous and woody
   d) Apple and herbaceous
   View Answer

Answer: c

Explanation: Herbaceous and woody crops are examples of energy crops. Like agricultural crops are grown to feed, energy crops are grown specifically to be used as an energy resource.

4. What are herbaceous crops?
   a) Insecticides
   b) Rice
   c) Agricultural fertilizers
   d) Agricultural byproducts
   View Answer

Answer: d

Explanation: Herbaceous crops are plants that do not have much wood and has green and soft stems. Generally, they are agricultural byproducts like columbine. Sometimes, crops like potatoes are solely grown to produce energy.

5. Which of the following are examples of woody biomass?
   a) Fallen trees due to natural disasters
   b) Mint
   c) Columbine
   d) Agricultural byproducts
   View Answer
6. Which of the following are examples of lipids?
   a) Sugar
   b) Palm oil
   c) Glucose
   d) Cellulose
   View Answer
Answer: b
   Explanation: Palm oil is an example of lipids. Other examples are soybean oil, rapeseed oil,
   wax, animal fat, etc. Glucose is an example of sugar.
7. Which of the following can be used to replenish nutrients in soil?
   a) Steel
   b) Soda
   c) Biomass ash
   d) Coal ash
   View Answer
Answer: c
   Explanation: Biomass ash can be used as a soil amendment to help replenish nutrients. Coal
   ash cannot be used for the same because it contains toxic metals. Steel and soda are not
   used to replenish soil's nutrients.
8. Which of the following is an example of short rotation coppice?
   a) Maize
   b) Wheat
   c) Corn
   d) Willow
   View Answer
Answer: d
   Explanation: Willow is an example of short rotation coppice (SRC). It is a forestry residue.
   Corn, maize and wheat are examples of herbaceous crops.
9. Algae are used as feedstocks for bioenergy.
   a) True
   b) False
   View Answer
Answer: a
   Explanation: Algae are used as feedstocks for bioenergy. They use sunlight to create biomass
   containing key components like lipids, proteins and carbohydrates. They include microalgae,
   macroalgae like seaweed and cyanobacteria or blue-green algae.
10. Which of the following found in municipal waste can be used as biomass?
   a) Agricultural residue

b) Kitchen waste
c) Residential garbage
d) Plastic covers
View Answer

Answer: b

Explanation: Kitchen waste can be used as a resource for biomass. Residential garbage and plastic covers cannot be used directly. Agricultural residue is not found in municipal waste.

11. Land fill is an example of wet waste.
   a) False
   b) True
   View Answer

Answer: b

Explanation: Land fill is an example of wet waste. It consists of residential wastes, industrial wastes and other wastes from sewage. It also consists of manure in the form of animal wastes.

12. ___________ wastes are used as methane boosters.
   a) Agricultural
   b) Forestry
   c) Industrial
   d) Municipal
   View Answer

Answer: c

Explanation: Many industrial wastes are used as methane boosters due to their extremely high methane potential. Agricultural, municipal and forestry wastes are not suitable for methane boosters.

13. ___________ biomass is used for waste water treatment.
   a) Agricultural
   b) Industrial
   c) Municipal
   d) Aquatic
   View Answer

Answer: d

Explanation: Aquatic biomass in the form of micro-organisms are used for waste water treatment. They operate in anaerobic environment during the treatment.

14. Which of the following parameters is used to define sustainability of biogas feedstock?
   a) Heating value
   b) Calorific value
   c) C:N ratio
   d) Thermal voltage
   View Answer

Answer: c

Explanation: Carbon to nitrogen (C:N) ratio is one of the most important parameters used to talk about the sustainability of the biogas feedback. Heating and calorific value are parameters to describe the available fuel in a given biomass.

15. Which of the following is not a biomass resource?
   a) Animal wastes
   b) Forestry residue
   c) Agricultural residue
   d) Sunlight
   View Answer

Answer: d

Explanation: Sunlight is not a biomass resource. Animal wastes, forestry residue and agricultural residue are biomass resources. They are used to generate energy either by combustion or bio-chemical processes.

1. Which of the following technologies are used to convert biomass into useful energy forms?
   a) Bio-chemical process
   b) Galvanization
   c) Doping
   d) Photoelectric effect
   View Answer

Answer: a

Explanation: The three main technologies used to convert biomass into useful forms of energy are bio-chemical, thermo-chemical and physio-chemical processes. Galvanization is a process used to prevent corrosion of metals. Doping and photoelectric effect are not related to biomass conversion technologies.

2. What are the four main types of thermo-chemical processes?
   a) Galvanization, photovoltaic effect, chemo-mechanical effect, pyrolysis
   b) Pyrolysis, gasification, combustion, hydrothermal processing
   c) Pyrolysis, gasification, combustion, doping
   d) Photovoltaic effect, gasification, combustion, hydrothermal processing
   View Answer

Answer: b

Explanation: The four main types of thermo-chemical processes are pyrolysis, gasification, combustion and hydrothermal processing. Photovoltaic effect, doping, chemo-mechanical effect and galvanization are not related to biomass conversion technologies.

3. What are the two primary processes under bio-chemical conversion?
   a) Photosynthesis and respiration
   b) Photosynthesis and photovoltaic
   c) Anaerobic digestion and fermentation
   d) Anaerobic digestion and photosynthesis
   View Answer

Answer: c

Explanation: Anaerobic digestion and fermentation are two primary processes under bio-chemical conversion. Photosynthesis, photovoltaic and respiration are not related to biomass conversion technologies.

4. Which of the following is an example of physio-chemical conversion technique to convert biomass into usable forms of energy?

a) Pyrolysis
b) Gasification
c) Anaerobic Digestion
d) Extraction with esterification
View Answer

Answer: d

Explanation: Physio-chemical process mainly consists of extraction with esterification. Pyrolysis and gasification are thermo-chemical conversion. Anaerobic digestion is a bio-chemical conversion process.

5. Which of the following is a product of pyrolysis of biomass?
a) Producer gas
b) Steel
c) Agricultural residue
d) Sodium
View Answer

Answer: a

Explanation: The output is producer gas. Steel and sodium are not the outputs of any pyrolysis process. Agricultural residue is a type of biomass.

6. Pyrolysis occurs in the presence of ________ oxygen.
a) large amounts of
b) absence of
c) extremely large amount of
d) low amounts of
View Answer

Answer: b

Explanation: In pyrolysis, the biomass is subjected to high temperatures in the absence of oxygen. The output of pyrolysis is producer gas which is a mixture of flammable gases (primarily CO and H2) and non-flammable gases (primarily nitrogen and carbon dioxide).

7. Which of the following best indicates the process of gasification?
a) Biomass → carbon dioxide and water → producer gas and charcoal → carbon monoxide and hydrogen
b) Biomass → carbon monoxide and hydrogen → carbon dioxide and water → producer gas and charcoal
c) Biomass → producer gas and charcoal → carbon dioxide and water → carbon monoxide and hydrogen
d) Producer gas and charcoal → carbon dioxide and water → carbon monoxide and hydrogen → biomass
View Answer

Answer: c

Explanation: Gasification basically converts all the available biomass to "gas". In the first stage, the biomass is partially combusted to form producer gas and charcoal which is then sent to the second stage. In the second stage, the carbon dioxide and water produced in the first stage is chemically reduced by charcoal to form carbon monoxide and hydrogen.

8. Which of the following is best suited for hydrothermal processing?
    a) Forestry byproducts
    b) Wheat
    c) Corn
    d) Sewage sludge
    View Answer

Answer: d

    Explanation: Feedstocks with high moisture content like sewage sludge are suitable for
    hydrothermal processing. Agricultural residue like wheat and corn and forestry byproducts
    are not best suited for hydrothermal processing.

9. What is hydrothermal processing?
    a) Heating aqueous slurries of biomass at high pressures to produce products of greater
    energy density
    b) Heating aqueous slurries of biomass at high temperatures to produce products of lower
    energy density
    c) Heating aqueous slurries of biomass at low pressures to produce products of greater
    energy density
    d) Heating aqueous slurries of biomass at low temperatures to produce products of lower
    energy density
    View Answer

Answer: a

    Explanation: Hydrothermal processing is a biomass conversion technique that involves
    heating of aqueous slurries of biomass at high pressures to produce products of greater
    energy density. Feedstocks with high moisture content like manures are best suited for this
    process.

10. What is anaerobic digestion?
    a) Produces biogas by heating the biomass
    b) Produces biogas using micro-organisms operating in anaerobic conditions
    c) Produces biogas by subjecting the biomass to high pressures
    d) Produces biogas using micro-organisms operating in aerobic conditions
    View Answer

Answer: b

    Explanation: Anaerobic digestion is a biological process of breaking down the biomass to
    produce products with high energy density – biogas. It occurs in anaerobic conditions. Waste
    water treatment plants commonly use anaerobic conditions to treat the influent.

11. Catalytic liquefaction occurs at ___________
    a) low temperature, low pressure
    b) high temperature, high pressure
    c) low temperature, high pressure
    d) high temperature, low pressure
    View Answer

Answer: c

    Explanation: Catalytic liquefaction is a thermo-chemical biomass conversion process. It requires low temperature and high pressure and the process is carried out in liquid phase under the presence of a catalyst.

12. Sugarcane is used to produce ethanol.

a) True
b) False
View Answer

Answer: a

Explanation: One of the most commonly used feedstocks to produce ethanol is sugarcane. This is very popular in developing due to the high productivity of sugarcane when supplied with sufficient water.

13. Which of the following are used to produce ethanol when water is not available in plenty?

a) Sugarcane
b) Wheat
c) Corn
d) Sorghum
View Answer

Answer: d

Explanation: Cassava or sorghum is commonly used to produce ethanol when water is not available in plenty. Sugarcane is used when there is no limitation on water content. Wheat and corn do not produce ethanol.

14. Which of the following are commonly used in fermentation process?

a) Yeast
b) Bacteria
c) Mushrooms
d) Virus
View Answer

Answer: a

Explanation: Yeast is commonly used in fermentation process. Fermentation is the process converting biomass to alcohol and carbon dioxide.

15. Fermentation is aerobic process.

a) True
b) False
View Answer

Answer: b

Explanation: Fermentation is an anaerobic process. It is another commonly used bio-chemical process of converting feedstock (biomass) to energy in the presence of micro-organisms.

1. Which of the following is a product of biomass gasification?

a) Hydrogen
b) Steel
c) Carbon (solid)
d) Iron
View Answer

Answer: a

Explanation: Biomass gasification is process that converts biomass into gases in a controlled amount of oxygen or partial combustion. Hydrogen is a product of biomass gasification. Steel, carbon (solid) and iron are not gases.

2. What is water-gas shift reaction?
   a) Carbon dioxide + water → Carbon monoxide + Hydrogen + small heat
   b) Carbon monoxide + water → Carbon dioxide + Hydrogen + small heat
   c) Carbon dioxide + water + heat → Carbon monoxide + Hydrogen
   d) Carbon monoxide + water + heat → Carbon dioxide + Hydrogen
   View Answer

Answer: b

Explanation: carbon monoxide + water → carbon dioxide + hydrogen + small heat is the water-gas shift reaction. It is an exothermic reaction as heat is released and not used.

3. Which of the following temperature ranges are suitable for biomass gasification?
   a) Above 1000 degree Celsius
   b) Between 500 and 600 degree Celsius
   c) Between 700 and 1000 degree Celsius
   d) Less than 500 degree Celsius
   View Answer

Answer: c

Explanation: The most suitable temperature range for biomass gasification is between 700 and 1000 degree Celsius. The reactant is partially oxidized to produce a mixture of gaseous products including hydrocarbons. Sometimes, steam is also used as gasification agents.

4. What are the three main types of gasifiers?
   a) Fixed bed, hydrothermal liquefaction and carbonisation
   b) Fixed bed, fluidized gasifiers and carbonisation
   c) Carbonisation, liquefaction and entrained flow gasifiers
   d) Fixed bed, fluidized gasifiers and entrained flow gasifiers
   View Answer

Answer: d

Explanation: Fixed bed, fluidized and entrained flow gasifiers are the three main types of gasifiers used in biomass gasification. Liquefaction and carbonisation are not gasifying techniques.

5. Biomass is moved at a very slow rate in fixed bed gasifier.
   a) True
   b) False
   View Answer

Answer: a

Explanation: Biomass is moved at a very slow rate in the fixed bed gasifier. Hence, it is also called as moving bed reactor and is operated around 1000 degree Celsius.

6. How is the biomass material and gasification agent fed into an updraft gasifier?
   a) Biomass from top, gasifying agent from top
   b) Biomass from top, gasifying agent from bottom
   c) Biomass from bottom, gasifying agent from top

d) Biomass from bottom, gasifying agent from bottom
View Answer

7. What is the contaminant in the product gas that is withdrawn from a low temperature zone in a fixed bed gasifier?
a) Gold
b) Platinum
c) Tar
d) Nickel
View Answer

Answer: c
Explanation: The hot gas coming from the bottom dries the biomass near the top of the vessel and provides heat for pyrolysis of the descending biomass. Along with providing heat, it also embeds tar into it. When the product gas is removed from a low temperature zone, it consists of tar which is a contaminant.

8. The product gas removed from the low temperature zone undergoes ________ before being used as fuel in combustion for electricity generator.
a) liquefaction
b) condensation
c) evaporation
d) cleaning
View Answer

Answer: d
Explanation: The product gas removed from the low temperature zone undergoes cleaning. This is to remove contaminants like tar from the gas so that it can be used as fuel in combustion engine for electricity generator.

9. How is the biomass material and gasification agent fed into a downdraft gasifier?
a) Biomass from top, gasifying agent from top
b) Biomass from top, gasifying agent from bottom
c) Biomass from bottom, gasifying agent from left side
d) Biomass from top, gasifying agent from right side
View Answer

Answer: a
Explanation: In a downdraft generator, the biomass and the gasifying agent is fed into the vessel from the top. Air or oxygen is then fed into the system homogeneously at the so called throated area.

10. The tar content of the product gas in downdraft gasifier is ________ updraft gasifier.
a) equal to
b) less than
c) greater than
d) cleaner than
View Answer

Answer: b
Explanation: The tar content of the product gas in a downdraft gasifier is lower than updraft gasifier. However, the particulate content of the gas is higher.

11. Which of the following applications is the product gas from downdraft gasifier suitable for?
    a) Fuel for combustion engine
    b) Fuel for burning wood
    c) Fuel for internal combustion engine
    d) Fuel for household purposes
    View Answer

Answer: c

Explanation: The product gas from downdraft gasifier is suitable for applications like fuel for internal combustion engine to generate electricity. This is because it consists of less amount of tar and more amount of particulate matter as compared to the product gas from an updraft gasifier.

12. Which of the following applications can the producer gas be used for?
    a) Producing nickel
    b) Producing copper
    c) Producing glucose
    d) Producing methanol
    View Answer

Answer: d

Explanation: Producer gas can be used to produce methanol in an economically viable manner. Methanol is used as fuel for heat engines as well as feedstock for industries.

13. Which of the following are keys to design a gasifier?
    a) Reducing biomass to charcoal and converting charcoal at suitable temperature to produce carbon monoxide and hydrogen
    b) Oxidizing biomass to charcoal and converting charcoal at suitable temperature to produce carbon monoxide and hydrogen
    c) Reducing biomass to charcoal and converting charcoal at suitable temperature to produce carbon dioxide and hydrogen
    d) Oxidizing biomass to charcoal and converting charcoal at suitable temperature to produce carbon dioxide and hydrogen
    View Answer

Answer: a

Explanation: The key to gasifier design is to create conditions such that biomass is reduced to charcoal and the charcoal converted to carbon monoxide and hydrogen at suitable temperatures. It is important to note that biomass is reduced and not oxidized.

14. How does air enter and exit in a cross-draft gasifier?
    a) Air enters from one of the sides and exits from the top
    b) Air enters from one side and exits from the other
    c) Air enters from one of the sides and exits from the bottom
    d) Air enters from the bottom and exits from the top
    View Answer

Answer: b

Explanation: In a cross-draft gasifier, air enters from one of the sides and exits from the other. Cross-draft gasifiers are compactly constructed and require low maintenance.

15. Ash sticks to the side in a cross-draft gasifier.
   a) True
   b) False
   View Answer

Answer: b
   Explanation: Ash falls to the bottom in a cross-draft gasifier. The ask does not interrupt the normal operation and hence the gasifier does not need a grate.

1. Which of the following is a substrate for biogas production?
   a) Municipal and residential waste
   b) E-waste
   c) Metallic waste
   d) Gaseous effluents
   View Answer

Answer: a
   Explanation: Municipal and residential waste is a good substrate for biogas production. E-waste and metallic waste do not consist of carbon compounds. Gaseous effluents are not used to produce biogas.

2. Which of the following is a preferred substrate for biogas production? Note that TS stands for total solids.
   a) Less than 1% TS
   b) 20-40% TS
   c) 1-5% TS
   d) 5-10% TS
   View Answer

Answer: b
   Explanation: 20-40% TS is a preferred substrate for biogas production. It is the solid waste in the incoming municipal and residential waste and hence is also called as solid waste.

3. What are the categories for organic dry matter on the basis of total solids (TS)?
   a) Low grade, medium grade, high grade and fixed bed
   b) Low grade, medium grade, fluidized bed and fixed bed
   c) Low grade, medium grade, high grade and solids
   d) Downdraft, circulation fluidized bed, high grade and fixed bed
   View Answer

Answer: c
   Explanation: The categorization on the basis of TS are low grade with less than 1%, medium grade with TS between 1and 5%, high grade with TS between 5 and 20% and finally solids with TS between 20 and 40%. Fixed bed and fluidized bed are types of gasifiers.

4. Which among the following is the best source for methane production?
   a) Metallic scrap
   b) E-waste
   c) Plastic waste
   d) Water hyacinth
   View Answer

Answer: d

Explanation: Water hyacinth is the best source for methane production in the given options. It is an aquatic weed with huge biomass, high C/N ratio and lignin content. Thus, yielding high amounts of methane.

5. Which of the following is used to produce biogas from biomass?
   a) Anaerobic treatment
   b) Aerobic treatment
   c) Fermentation
   d) Pyrolysis
   View Answer

Answer: a

Explanation: Anaerobic treatment of municipal and residential waste is used to produce biomass. Fermentation is used to produce ethanol and pyrolysis is used to produce gaseous products like hydrogen.

6. Which of the following best indicates the steps of anaerobic digestion?
   a) Waste water feed → biogas storage → generator → biogas
   b) Waste water feed → digester → biogas → biogas storage → generator
   c) Generator → waste water feed → digester → biogas → biogas storage
   d) Waste water feed → biogas → digester → biogas storage → generator
   View Answer

Answer: b

Explanation: Waste water feed is first sent into the anaerobic digester. The waste water is treated to produce biogas which is then stored in a special storage. The fuel is then used to produce electricity by driving a generator or for any other application.

7. Which of the following best indicates the steps inside an anaerobic digester?
   a) Hydrolysis → methanogenesis → acetogenesis → acidogenesis
   b) Hydrolysis → acidogenesis → methanogenesis → acetogenesis
   c) Hydrolysis → acidogenesis → acetogenesis → methanogenesis
   d) Methanogenesis → acidogenesis → acetogenesis → hydrolysis
   View Answer

Answer: c

Explanation: The waste is first hydrolyzed and then acidized. After acidizing, the product is then used to produce acetates which is further used to create methane in the final stage. Methanogenesis is the process of creating methane.

8. What occurs in the hydrolysis step of anaerobic digestion?
   a) Large polymers combine with water molecules
   b) Large polymers break down to form water molecules
   c) Small polymers combine to form large polymers with the help of water molecules
   d) Large polymers break down into amino acids, fatty acids and simple sugars
   View Answer

Answer: d

Explanation: Hydrolysis is used to break large polymers in the presence of an acid catalyst. Large polymers present in the waste break down into amino acids, fatty acids and simple sugars.

9. Acidogenesis further break down the molecules received from hydrolysis in anaerobic digestion.
a) True
b) False
View Answer

Answer: a
Explanation: In acidogenesis, microorganisms further break down the molecules after hydrolysis. This is because these molecules are still too large and cannot be used to generate methane. The microorganisms produce an acidic environment for the break down to occur.

10. Which of the following is produced in acetogenesis?
a) Ethanol
b) Acetate
c) Acetone
d) Ketone
View Answer

Answer: b
Explanation: In acetogenesis, a derivative of acetic acid called acetate is produced from carbon and other energy sources. This occurs in the presence of microorganisms called acetogens.

11. Which of the following is produced apart from acetates in acetogenesis step in anaerobic digestion?
a) Carbon monoxide
b) Charcoal
c) Carbon dioxide
d) Acetone
View Answer

Answer: c
Explanation: Apart from acetates, carbon dioxide and hydrogen are also produced in acetogenesis. It is important to note that acetic acid is first produced which is then converted into acetates.

12. What are the two ways to produce methane in methanogenesis step?
a) Converting carbon monoxide and carbon dioxide into methane
b) Converting carbon monoxide and acetic acid (or acetate) into methane
c) Converting methane into carbon monoxide and carbon dioxide
d) Converting carbon dioxide and acetic acid (or acetate) into methane
View Answer

Answer: d
Explanation: Methanogenesis is the process of producing methane by methanogens. In anaerobic digestion, methanogenesis occurs by converting carbon dioxide and acetic acid (or acetate) into methane.

13. Methanogens can directly use the products of hydrolysis to produce methane.
a) False
b) True
View Answer

Answer: a

Explanation: Methanogens cannot directly use the products of hydrolysis to produce methane. The molecules are still too large and need to be broken down. This occurs in the acidogenesis step.

14. What are the two main products of anaerobic digestion?
    a) Carbon monoxide and hydrogen
    b) Methane and carbon dioxide
    c) Methane and carbon monoxide
    d) Hydrogen and carbon dioxide
    View Answer

Answer: b

Explanation: The purpose of anaerobic digestion is to convert the municipal waste (biomass) into biogas. So, the two main products are methane and carbon dioxide. Carbon monoxide is not the main product.

15. Gases emitted from the digester indicates the amount of biomass left to be broken down.
    a) True
    b) False
    View Answer

Answer: a

Explanation: Gases emitted from the digester indicates the amount of biomass left to be broken down. Production levels are a good indication of production abnormalities and hence this technique is widely used in industries.

HYBRID POWER SYSTEMS-

As convention fossil fuel energy sources diminish and the world's environmental concern about acid deposition and global warming increases, renewable energy sources (solar, wind, tidal, biomass and geothermal etc) are attracting more attention as alternative energy sources. These are all pollution free and one can say eco friendly. These are available at free of cost. In India, there is severe power shortage and associated power quality problems, the quality of the grid supply in some places is characterized by large voltage and frequency fluctuations, scheduled and un scheduled power cuts and load restrictions. Load shedding in many cities in India due to power shortage and faults is a major problem for which there is no immediate remedy in the near future since the gap between the power demand and supply is increasing every year. This led to rapid usage of stand-by petrol or diesel generator sets and conventional battery inverter sets in both urban and rural areas. Shopkeepers, house owners and offices commonly use 1-5 kW fuel generators in India when utility exercises load shedding.

*In India wind and solar energy sources are available all over the year at free of cost whereas tidal and wave are costal area. Geothermal is available at specific location. To meet the demand and for the sake of continuity of power supply, storing of energy is necessary.

*Hybrid power system-The term hybrid power system is used to describe any power system combine two or more energy conversion devices, or two or more fuels for the same device, that when integrated, overcome limitations inherent in either.

*Usually one of the energy sources is a conventional one (which necessarily does not depend on renewable energy resource) powered by a diesel engine, while the other(s) would be renewable viz. solar photovoltaic, wind or hydro.

The design and structure of a hybrid energy system obviously take into account the types of renewable energy sources available locally, and the consumption the system supports. For example, the hybrid energy system presented here is a small-scale system and the consumption of power takes place during nights, so the wind energy component will make a more significant contribution in the hybrid system than solar energy.

Although the energy produced by wind during night can be used directly without storage, a battery is needed to store solar and wind energy produced during the day.

In addition to the technical considerations, cost benefit is a factor that has to be incorporated into the process of optimizing a hybrid energy system. In general, the use of wind energy is cheaper than that of solar energy. In areas where there is a limited wind source, a wind system has to be over-dimensioned in order to produce the required power, and this results in higher plant costs.

It has been demonstrated that hybrid energy systems (renewable coupled with conventional energy source) can significantly reduce the total life cycle cost of a standalone power supplies in many off-grid situations, while at the same time providing a reliable supply of electricity using a combination of energy sources. Numerous hybrid systems have been installed across the world, and expanding renewable energy industry has now developed reliable and cost competitive systems using a variety of technologies. Research in the development of hybrid systems focused on the performance analysis of demonstration systems and development of efficient power converters, such as bidirectional inverters, battery management units (storage facilities), and optimization of different sources of energy Sources, etc.

Hybrid power systems combine two or more energy conversion devices, or two or more fuels for the same device, that when integrated, overcome limitations inherent in either.

Hybrid systems can address limitations in terms of fuel flexibility, efficiency, reliability, emissions and / or economics.

Classifications

According to Wichert (1997), hybrid energy systems with or without renewables, are classified according to their configuration as series, switched hybrid, or parallel hybrid.

Series hybrid system

In this system either the renewable energy source or the diesel generator is used to maintain charge in a large battery bank. During periods of low electricity demand the diesel generator is switched off and the load can be supplied from PV together with stored energy. Power from the battery bank is converted to AC at mains voltage and frequency by a converter and is then fed to the load. Battery charging can be controlled by controlling the excitation of the alternator (Wichert, 1997). The charge controller prevents overcharging of the battery bank from PV generator when the PV power exceeds the load demand and the batteries are fully charged. The system can be operated in manual or automatic mode, with the addition of appropriate battery voltage sensing and start/stop control of the engine-driven generator.

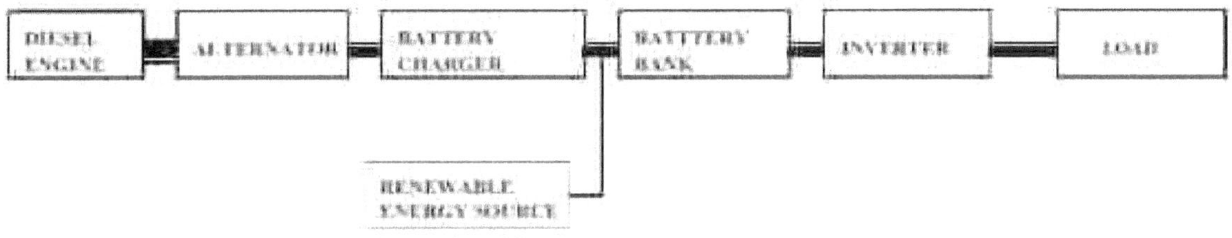

Figure 6 Series hybrid system

Advantages of this system include that the engine-driven generator can be sized to be optimally loaded while supplying the load and charging the battery bank, until the state of charge (SOC) of 70-80% is reached. No switching of AC power between the different energy sources is required thus simplifying the electrical output interface. Also the power supplied to the load is not interrupted when the diesel generator is started and the inverter can generate a sine-wave, modified square-waves, or square-wave, depending on the application.

Disadvantages are: low overall efficiency due to the series configuration of system elements; substantially larger battery capacity than the maximum peak load demand resulting in the system being more expensive component to the system; and with renewable inputs, there is limited control of diesel alternator because the system is based on level of charge in the battery rather than the site load.

A series hybrid system is characterized by low overall system efficiency since the diesel cannot supply power directly to the load; large inverter and due to the cycling profile large battery bank is required to limit the depth of discharge; and limited optimisation of diesel alternator and renewable energy sources (SOPAC Miscellaneous Report 406, 2005). The battery bank is cycled frequently, shortening its lifetime. If the inverter fails there is complete loss of power to the load, unless the load can be supplied directly from the diesel generator for emergency purposes.

Switched hybrid system

This system allows with either the engine-driven generator or the inverter as the AC source but no parallel operation of the main generation source is possible (Islam, 1999).Both the diesel generator and the PV array can charge the battery bank. The diesel alternator meets the load during the day and evening peak while the battery bank is charged by the renewables and any excess power from the diesel. Power is supplied to the load by the battery through the inverter during the low load night period. The typical layout of the system is as shown in figure .

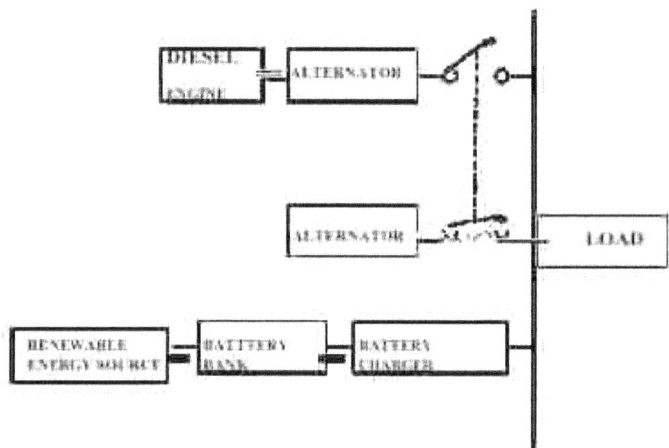

Figure Switched configuration

The main advantages of the system are quiet operation at night and partial improvements in diesel consumption. A switched hybrid system is also characterized by the fact that the diesel generator can supply the load directly, therefore improving the system efficiency and reducing the fuel consumption (SOPAC Miscellaneous Report 406, 2005). As for the series system, the diesel generator is switched off during periods of low electricity demand and the inverter can generate a sine-wave; modified square-wave, or square-wave, depending on the application. Switched hybrid energy systems can be in manual mode, although the increased complexity of the system makes it highly desirable to include an automatic controller, which can be implemented with the addition of appropriate battery voltage sensing start/stop control of the engine-driven.

Parallel hybrid System

The parallel configuration shown in figure allows all energy sources to supply the
load separately at low or medium demand, as well as supplying quick load from combined sources by synchronizing the inverter with the alternator output wave form the bi-directional inverter can charge the battery bank when access energy is available from the engine driven generator, as well as act as DC-AC converter In this case the renewables and the diesel generator supply part of the load demand directly. The diesel generator and the inverter run in parallel.

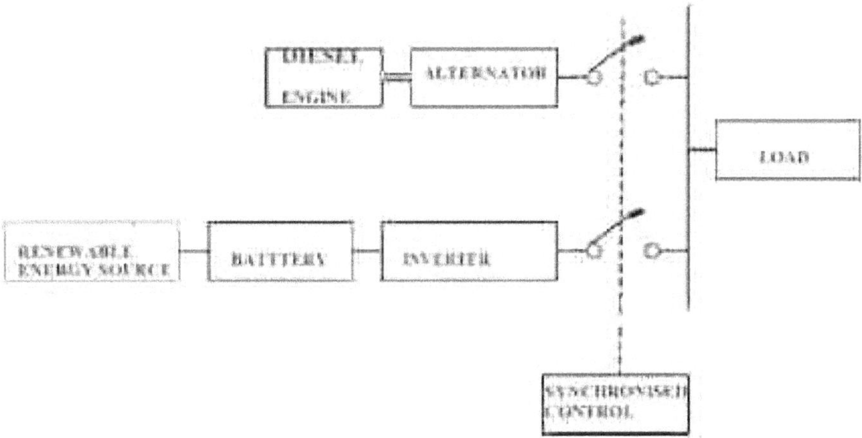

Figure : Parallel configuration

Advantages of this configuration over other system configurations are that the system load can be met in the most optimal way, diesel efficiency can be maximized, diesel generator maintenance can be minimized and there is a reduction in the capacities of diesel, battery and renewable sources while load peaks are being met. However, automatic control is essential for the reliable operation of the system and the system operation is less transparent to the untrained user of the system. Also the inverter has to
be a true sign wave inverter with the ability to synchronize with a secondary AC source.

In many regions of the world, wind generators and photovoltaic cells are combined to provide year-round renewable energy to non-grid-connected households. This is possible since variations in wind and solar power resources are usually complementary. A wind generator is thus an excellent supplement to the PV system and vice versa. Moreover, interfacing of wind generators and PV cells minimizes the battery capacity and extends the battery bank life compared to the storage requirement in solar- or wind-only systems. Figure 7.9 shows a typical wind/PV hybrid system configuration.

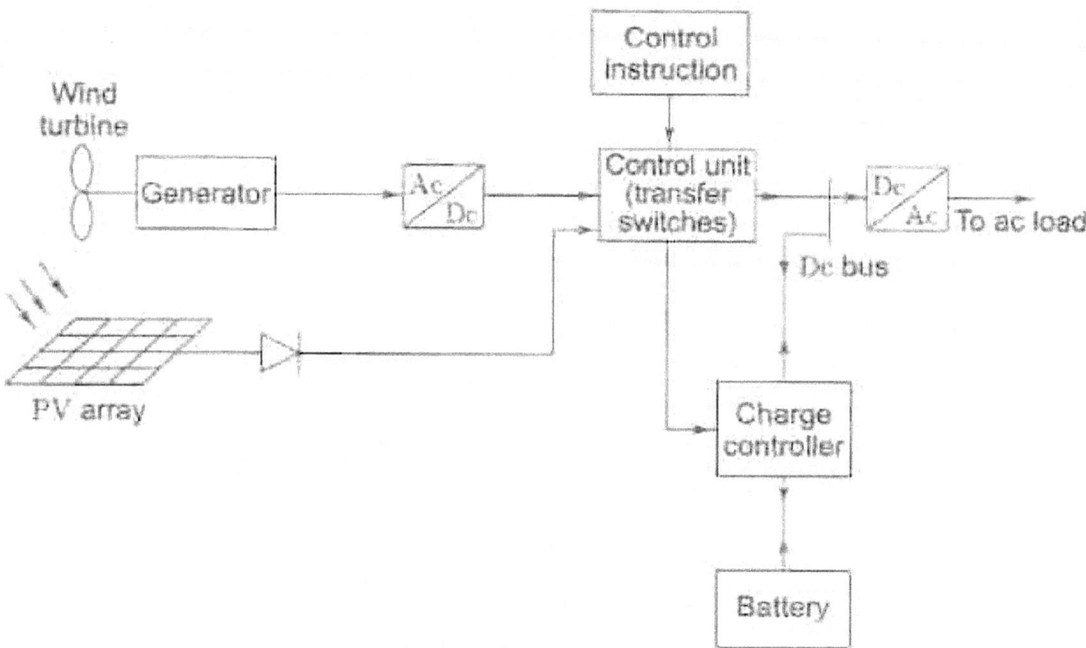

Fig. 7.9 Configuration of a typical wind–PV system

The ac output of the wind generator feeds a rectifier which is connected in parallel to the PV array through a controller to a dc bus. The dc bus also serves as a connection point for the battery through a charge controller. The blocking diode protects the PV array from voltage spikes and prevents the flow of current in the reverse direction at low irradiation. The controller decides the connection of the generating system/battery supply, or its charging, in specific situations and requirements.

<u>Multiple Choice Questions and answers</u>

1-Which of the following is (are) renewable resource(s)
(A) wind
(B) tides
(C) geothermal heat
(D) all of the above

2-Which of the following country generate all their electricity using renewable energy?
(A) Iceland
(B) England
(C) USA
(D) China

3-Renwable energy often displaces conventional fuel in which of the following area
(A) space heating
(B) transportation
(C) electricity generation
(D) all of the above

4-Which of the following is used as fuel for transportation
(A) ethanol
(B) aldehyde
(C) ketone
(D) all of the above

5-Biodiesel is produced from oils or fats using
(A) fermentation
(B) transesterification
(C) distillation
(D) none of the above

6-Photovoltaic cell converts solar energy into
(A) heat energy
(B) electric energy
(C) mechanical energy
(D) chemical energy

7-In which of the following region winds are stronger and constant
(A) deserts
(B) offshore
(C) low altitudes sites
(D) all of the above

8-Following country met more than 40% of its electricity demand from wind energy
(A) Denmark
(B) Portugal
(C) Ireland
(D) Spain

9-Concentrated solar power (CSP) systems use _____ to focus a large area of sunlight into a small beam.
(A) lenses
(B) mirrors
(C) tracking systems
(D) all of the above

10-The difference, in temperature between the core of the planet and its surface, is known as
(A) geothermal coefficient
(B) geothermal gradient
(C) geothermal constant
(D) none of the above

11-Biomass can be converted to
(A) methane gas
(B) ethanol
(C) biodiesel
(D) all of the above

12-The International Renewable Energy Agency (IRENA) was formed in
(A) 2008
(B) 2009
(C) 2010
(D) 2011

13-Which of the following was the first solar powered aircraft to complete a circumnavigation of the world?
(A) Solar impulse
(B) Solar impulse 2
(C) Solar impulse 3
(D) Solar impulse 4

14-Following is true for biomass and biofuels
(A) their contribution in reduction in CO_2 emissions is limited
(B) both emit large amount of air pollution when burned
(C) they consume large amounts of water
(D) all of the above

ANSWERS:
1-(D), 2-(A), 3-(D), 4-(A), 5-(B), 6-(B), 7-(B), 8-(A), 9-(D), 10-(B), 11-(D), 12-(B), 13-(B), 14-(D)

1. Which of the following is a nonrenewable energy resource?

    - solar
    - methane
    - hydroelectric
    - coal

2. The amount of oil that may become available for use is called oil __________.

    - reserves
    - reservoirs
    - resources
    - traps

3. A coal deposit that is not economical to mine today would be considered part of our ____________ .

    - coal reserves
    - coal resources
    - coal reservoirs
    - none of these

4. What is the leading source of energy used in the United States today?

    - coal
    - oil resources
    - natural gas
    - nuclear power

5. The first oil well was drilled in the United States in __________.

    - 1829
    - 1859
    - 1929
    - 1959

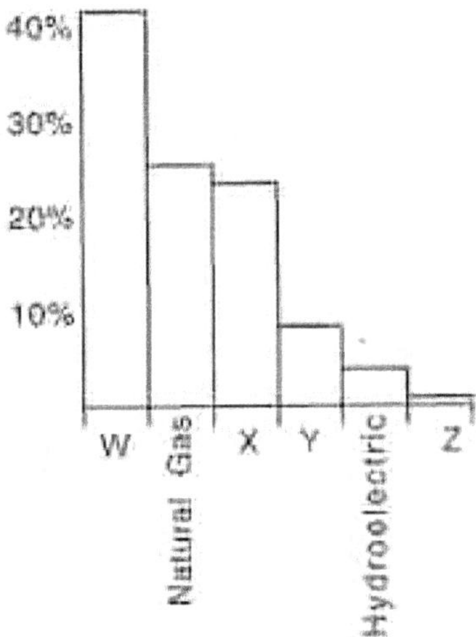

A histogram showing percentages of various types of energy used in the United States in 1997 is given above.

6. Area W represents

- coal
- solar
- nuclear
- oil

7. Area X represents

- coal
- solar
- nuclear
- oil

8. Area Y represents

- coal
- solar
- nuclear
- oil

9. Area Z represents

- coal
- solar
- nuclear
- oil

10. Oil, coal and natural gas supply approximately _________ % of the energy used in the United States

- 10
- 25
- 40
- 90

11. Of all of the energy produced in the United States, what % is lost in distribution and inefficient use?

- 10
- 25
- 40
- 50

12. Chemical reactions triggered by _________ transform organic material into hydrocarbons.

- solar energy
- hydroelectric
- elevated temperatures
- decomposition

13. Energy resources derived from natural organic materials are called _________.

- geothermal energy sources
- fossil fuels

14. A permeable rock that contains hydrocarbon fluids and gasses is called a(n)
____

15. All oil traps contain ____________.

16. Which of the following is least likely to contain an oil trap?

Cross section of an oil trap. X, Y, and Z represent three distinct fluid layers within the permeable reservoir rock.

17. The oil trap shown here is a(n) ____________

C an anticline

C fault trap

C stratigraphic trap

C salt dome trap

18. Layer X is most likely to be reservoir rock containing _________ in the pore space.

C syncrude

C water

C natural gas

C oil

19. Layer Y is most likely to be reservoir rock containing _________ in the pore space.

C syncrude

C water

C natural gas

C oil

20. Layer Z is most likely to be reservoir rock containing _________ in the pore space.

C syncrude

C water

C natural gas

C oil

21. Which of the following rock types would most likely be the best oil reservoir?.

C granite

C shale

C sandstone

C salt

22. In an oil trap formed by an anticline, __________ accumlulates on top, ______ in the middle, and __________ at the bottom.

- natural gas .... oil .... groundwater
- ground water .... oil .... natural gas
- oil .... groundwater .... natural gas
- oil .... natural gas .... ground water

23. Two-thirds of the world's known oil reserves are located in __________.

- Siberia
- Gulf of Mexico and Caribbean
- the middle East
- Indonesia

24. The world has the least amount of which of the following fuel types..

- oil
- coal
- uranium
- there are roughly equal amounts of each of these fuels

25. At the current rate of world use, the remaining oil will be depleted in approximately ______ years.

- 25
- 100
- 400
- 2000

26. Which of the following statements is true?

- in the US oil production is greater than oil consumption
- in the US oil production equals oil consumption
- in the US oil production is less than oil consumption

27. Most of the natural gas used in the United States is consumed by _________.

- industry
- residential use
- electrical utilities
- transportation

28. Burning of which of the following fuels produces the least amount of carbon dioxide per unit of energy?

- coal
- oil
- natural gas
- all of these produce the same amount of carbon dioxide.

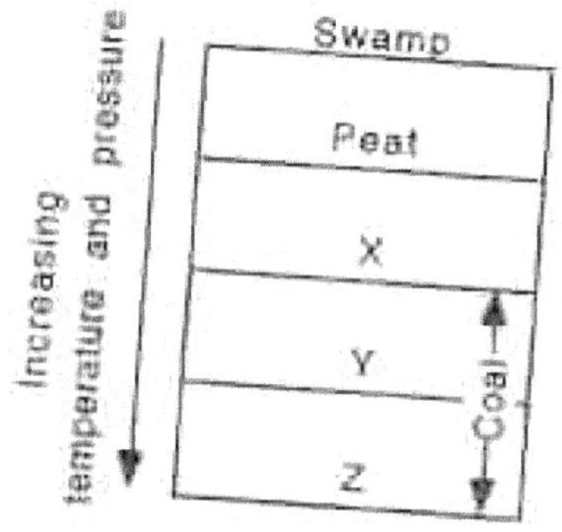

29. Layer X is _________.

- anthracite
- bituminous
- lignite
- tar

30. Layer Y is _________.

- anthracite
- bituminous

○ lignite

○ tar

31. Layer Z is __________.

○ anthracite

○ bituminous

○ lignite

○ tar

32. In addition to increasing temperature and pressure, the arrow to the left of the diagram represents increasing __________

○ metamorphism

○ heat value

○ carbon content

○ all of the above

33. Which country contains about 50% of the world's coal resources?

○ United States

○ China

○ Canada

○ the former Soviet Union

34. In the United States, coal resources should last approximately ______ years at the current rate of use.

○ 25

○ 100

○ 400

○ 2000

35. Which of the following problems is associated with the burning of coal?

○ acid rain

○ carbon dioxide emissions

○ ash with toxic metal impurities

○ all of these

36. Oil derived from coal, oil shales or tar sands is called __________.

○ natural gas

○ biomass

○ syncrude

○ none of these

37. Nuclear energy is derived by _____________.

○ combustion of atoms of U 235

○ fission of atoms of U 235

○ fusion of atoms of U 235

○ the breaking of U 235 bonds

38. Which of the following energy sources does not produce carbon dioxide?

○ oil

○ Uranium

○ coal

○ natural gas

39. About how many nuclear power plants are there in the US?

○ 10

○ 100

○ 250

○ 500

40. Which of the following statements regarding the nuclear accident at Chernobyl in the Ukraine in 1986 is false?

radioactive debris was blown into Scandinavia and western Europe

hundreds of square miles of land surrounding Chernobyl was contaminated and made uninhabitable

food supplies in many countries had to be purified in order to be consumed

excess deaths from cancer may be in the thousands over the next 40 years

41. Most of the uranium ore in the United States is located in the ______

Applachian Mountains

Basin and Range

Colorado Plateau

Great Lakes

42. The primary barrier to using solar energy in the United States is that ________

solar power is not technically feasible

solar power causes major pollution problems

solar power is not economically competitive with other energy sources

all of these

43. Hydroelectric energy provides about ________ of the energy consumed annually in the United States.

4%

12%

30%

65%

44. Solar energy stored in material such as wood, grain, sugar, and municipal waste is called __________.

fossil fuels

biomass

geothermal energy

natural gas

45. What type of energy is derived from heated groundwater?

- solar energy
- geothermal energy
- hydroelectric energy
- nuclear energy

46. The largest geothermal power plant in the United States is located near which city?

- Chicago
- Los Angeles
- New York
- San Francisco

47. The Geysers produce enough electricity to meet what portion of the needs of San Francisco?

- 10%
- 25%
- 50%
- 75%

48. The world faces an energy crisis because __________.

- world demand for energy will increase
- world oil production will peak and begin to decline
- shortages and the resulting escalation of prices can shock the economic and political order
- all of the above

Multiple Choice Questions and Answers

1. What does Heating and cooling of the atmosphere generates?
   a) Thermo line circulation
   b) Radiation currents

c) Convection currents
d) Conduction currents

Answer: c

Explanation: Wind energy can be economically used for the generation of electrical energy. Heating and cooling of the atmosphere generates convection currents. Heating is caused by the absorption of solar energy on the earth surface.

2. How much is the energy available in the winds over the earth surface is estimated to be?
   a) 2.9 X 120 MW
   b) 1.6 X 107 MW
   c) 1 MW
   d) 5MW

   Answer: b

   Explanation: The energy available in the winds over the earth surface is estimated to be 1.6 X 107 MW which is almost the same as the present day energy consumption. Wind energy can be utilized to run wind mill which in turn, is used to drive the generators.

3. How much wind power does India hold?
   a) 20,000 MW
   b) 12,000 MW
   c) 140,000 MW
   d) 5000 MW

   Answer: a

   Explanation: India has a potential of 20,000 MW of wind power. Wind power accounts nearly 9.87% of India's total installed power generation capacity. Generation of wind power in India mainly account from southern state of India.

4. What is the main source for the formation of wind?
   a) Uneven land
   b) Sun
   c) Vegetation
   d) Seasons

   Answer: b

   Explanation: Wind is free and renewable form of energy, which throughout history has been used to grind grain, power ships, and pump water. Wind is created when the sun unevenly heat the earth surface.

5. Which country created wind mills?
   a) Egypt
   b) Mongolia
   c) Iran
   d) Japan

   Answer: c

   Explanation: The earliest known wind mills were in Persia (Iran). These early wind mills looked like large paddle wheels. Centuries later, the people of Holland improved the basic design of wind mill. Holland is famous for its wind mills.

6. "During the day, the air above the land heats up more quickly than the air over water".
   a) True
   b) False

Answer: a

Explanation: During the day, the air above the land heats up more quickly than the air over water. The warm air over the land expands and raises, and the heavier, cooler air rushes in to take its place, creating winds.

7. What happens when the land near the earth's equator is heated?
   a) All the oceans gets heated up
   b) Small wind currents are formed
   c) Rise in tides
   d) Large atmospheric winds are created

   Answer: d
   Explanation: The large atmospheric winds that circle the earth are created because the land near the earth's equator is heated more by the sun than the land near the north and south poles. Wind energy is mainly used to generate electricity.
8. What type of energy is wind energy?
   a) Renewable energy
   b) Non-renewable energy
   c) Conventional energy
   d) Commercial energy
   Answer: a
   Explanation: Wind is called a renewable energy source because the wind will blow as long as the shines. Wind power, as an alternative to burning fossil fuels, is plentiful, renewable, widely distributed, clean, produces no greenhouse gas emissions during operation, consumes no water, and uses little land.
9. What are used to turn wind energy into electrical energy?
   a) Turbine
   b) Generators
   c) Yaw motor
   d) Blades
Answer: a
Explanation: Wind turbine blades capture wind energy, a form of mechanical energy, and put it to work turning a drive shaft, gearbox, and generator to produce electrical energy. Many factors affects wind turbine efficiency including turbine blade aerodynamics.
10. What is the diameter of wind turbine blades?
   a) 320 feet
   b) 220 feet
   c) 80 feet
   d) 500 feet
   Answer: b
   Explanation: Large utility-scale wind turbines can now generate more than a MW of electrical power each and deliver electricity directly in to the electric grid, these turbines are placed at 200 feet height at the rotor hub and have blades which are 220 feet or more in diameter.
11. At what range of speed is the electricity from the wind turbine is generated?
   a) 100 – 125 mph
   b) 450 – 650 mph
   c) 250 – 450 mph
   d) 30-35 mph
   Answer: d
   Explanation: Wind turbines are designed with cut-in wind speeds and cut-out speeds i.e. the wind speeds when the turbines start turning or shut off to prevent drive train damage. Typically, maximum electric generations occurs at speeds of 30-35mph.

12. When did the development of wind power in India began?
   a) 1965
   b) 1954
   c) 1990
   d) 1985
   Answer: c
   Explanation: The development of wind power in India began in 1990s. Presently India is the world's fourth largest wind power generator. The Indian energy sector has an installed capacity of 32.72 GW. Today India is a major player in the global wind energy market.

"Components of Wind Energy Conversion System".

1. How much power does the small scale wind machine generate?
a) 18 KW
b) 2 KW
c) 12 KW
d) 30 KW
View Answer
   Answer: b
   Explanation: These might be used on farms remote applications and other places requiring relatively low power. The generating capacity is up to 2kW. Small scale wind machines lower your electricity bills by 50% – 90%.
2. Which type of wind machines are used at several residence or local use?
a) Large size machines
b) Remote machines
c) Small size machines
d) Medium size machines
View Answer
   Answer: d
   Explanation: These wind turbines may be used to supply less than 100 kW rated capacity, to several residences or local use. These do not require much space they can be installed on roof tops or on some high elevated areas.
3. Which type of wind turbines produce 100 kW or greater?
a) Large machines
b) Small machines
c) Medium machines
d) Remote Machines
View Answer
   Answer: a
   Explanation: Large wind turbines are those of 100 kW rated capacity or greater. They are used to generate power for distribution in central power grids. They can have single generator at a single site or multiple generators sited at several places over an area.
4. Which part of the wind mill acts as a housing for the turbine?
a) Wind Vane
b) Shaft
c) Wind mill head
d) Turbine
View Answer

Answer: c

Explanation: The wind mill head supports the rotor, housing, and rotor bearings. It also has control mechanism like changing the pitch of the blades for safety devices, tail vane to orient the rotor to face the wind. Its body is the size of the mini bus.

5. A rotor installed in a fixed orientation with the swept area perpendicular to the pre dominate wind direction is called ____________

a) Nacelle
b) Yaw fixed machines
c) Blades
d) Anemometer

View Answer

Answer: b

Explanation: In the locations with the prevailing wind in one direction, the design of a turbine can be greatly simplified. The rotor can be installed in a fixed orientation with the swept area perpendicular to the pre dominate wind direction. This machine is called yaw fixed.

6. How is the action of yaw controlled in small turbines?

a) Tail vane
b) Blades
c) Shaft
d) Yaw motor

View Answer

Answer: a

Explanation: In small turbines, yaw action is controlled by a tail vane while is larger machines a servomechanism operated by a wind-direction sensor controls the yaw motor keeping the turbine properly oriented.

7. Which part of the wind turbines senses wind speed, wind direction, shaft speed and torque?

a) Turbine blade
b) Shaft
c) Rotor
d) Controller

View Answer

Answer: d

Explanation: The controller senses wind speed, wind direction, shafts speeds and torques, output power and generator temperature, Control signals are generated with the electrical output corresponding to the wind energy input.

8. Which type of wind turbine has low RPM?

a) Small wind turbine
b) Large wind turbine
c) Medium wind turbine
d) Remote wind turbine

View Answer

Answer: b

Explanation: The rate of rotation of large wind turbine generators operating at rated capacity or below is controlled by varying the pitch of the rotor blades. It has low rpm, about 40 to 50. It is necessary to increase greatly the low rotor rate of turning using transmission mechanism.

9. Why recommendation of fixed ratio gears done for top mounted equipment?

a) Because they are easy install
b) Requires less space
c) Due to its low cost

d) Because of their high efficiency

View Answer

Answer: d

Explanation: Fixed ratio gears are recommended for top mounted equipment because of their high efficiency, and minimum system risk. For bottom mounted equipment requiring a right angle drive transmission costs can be reduced on the hub by increasing rotor speed to generator.

10. Which type of generator are made use in wind turbines?

a) Recreational generators

b) Synchronous generator

c) Asynchronous generator

d) Alternator

View Answer

Answer: b

Explanation: Generators may be either constant or variable speed type. Variable speed units are expensive and/or unproved. Constant speed generator in use are synchronous induction and permanent magnet types. Synchronous unit is used for large aero generator systems. It is very versatile and has an extensive data base.

11. In which part do we find sensors and actuators?

a) Fixed gears

b) Turbines

c) Control systems

d) Blades

View Answer

Answer: c

Explanation: Control systems involves sensors and actuators. The modern large wind turbine generator requires a versatile and reliable control system. A control system is used for i) changing the orientation of the rotor into the wind. ii) Start up and cut-in of the equipment. iii) Power control of the rotor by varying the pitch of the blades.

12. How many types of supporting tower for wind mill are generally used?

a) 2

b) 4

c) 3

d) 5

View Answer

Answer: b

Explanation: Four types of generating tower are used generally:
i) The reinforced concrete tower
ii) The pole tower
iii) The built up shell tube tower
iv) The truss tower.

13. On what does the selection of supporting structure depends?

a) Length of blades

b) Rotating capacity

c) Capacity of generator

d) Transmission systems

View Answer

Answer: d

Explanation: The type of the supporting structure and its height is related to cost and the transmission system incorporated. Horizontal axis wind turbines are mounted on towers so as to be above the level of turbulence and other ground related effects.

14. At what type of location vibrations are more in the wind turbine?
a) Downwind location
b) Up wind location
c) Windward
d) Leeward
View Answer

Answer: b
Explanation: In the upwind location (i.e. the wind encounters the turbine before reaching the tower), the wake of the passing rotor blades causes repeated changes in the wind forces on the wind forces on the tower. Due to this the tower may vibrate and may eventually be damaged.

15. At what type of location vibrations are less in the wind turbines?
a) Windward
b) Leeward
c) Downwind location
d) Upwind Location
View Answer

Answer: c
Explanation: If the turbine is downwind from the tower, vibrations are less but the blades are subjected to severe alternating forces as they pass through the tower wake. Downwind rotors are generally preferred for large aero generators.

This set of Energy Engineering Multiple Choice Questions & Answers (MCQs) focuses on "Velocity and Power from Wind".

1. Select the formula for total power p_t?
a) $P_t = 1/2gc\ \rho A V_i{}^3$
b) $P_t = \rho A V_i{}^3 D^3$
c) $P_t = 12gc\ V_i{}^3 D^3$
d) $P_t = 2gcVi3$
View Answer

Answer: a
Explanation:

$$P_t = \frac{1}{2gc}\, \rho A V_i^3$$

Where, ρ = Incoming wind density

A = Cross sectional area

g_c = conversion factor = 1.0 kg/N

V_i = incoming velocity m/s

2. Why blade velocity of wind turbine varies?
a) Due to varying wind speeds
b) Long length of blades
c) Due to the height of mount

d) Because of hotness of Sun
View Answer

Answer: b
Explanation: Wind turbine experiences change in velocity dependent upon the blade inlet angle and the blade velocity. Since the blades are long, the blade velocity varies with the radius to a greater degree than steam or gas-turbine blades and the blades are therefore twisted.

3. When was the Hall a day wind mill introduced?
a) 1920
b) 1923
c) 1854
d) 1864
View Answer

Answer: c
Explanation: Invented by Daniel Halladay in 1854, the Halladay Standard was the first commercially successful self-governing windmill in 1854 was the firms of Halladay, McCray & Co., Ellington, Conn. Partners in the company were inventor Daniel Halladay, John Burnham and Henry McCray.

4. How much ideal efficiency should practical turbine have?
a) 10 – 12%
b) 18 – 25%
c) 80 – 90%
d) 50 – 70%
View Answer

Answer: d
Explanation: As wind turbine wheel cannot be completely closed, and because of spillage and other effects, practical turbines have 50 to 70% of the ideal efficiency. The real efficiency η is the product of this and ηmax and is the ratio of an actual to total power.
$P = \eta P_{tot}$.

5. How many types are acting on propeller type wind mill?
a) 2
b) 3
c) 4
d) 5
View Answer

Answer: a
Explanation: There are two types of forces operating on the blades of a propeller type wind turbine. They are the circumferential forces in the direction of wheel rotation that provide the torque and the axial forces in the direction of the wind stream that provide an axial thrust that must be counteracted by proper mechanical design.

6. Calculate the air density, when 10m/s wind is at 1std atmospheric pressure and 15°C?
a) 1.226 kg/m^3
b) 1.033 kg/m^3
c) 2.108 kg/m^3
d) 0.922 kg/m^3
View Answer

Answer: a
Explanation: For air, gas constant R = 287 J/kgK, 1atm = 1.01325 X 10^5 Pa
Air density, ρ = P/RT = (1.01325 ×10^5)/(287(15+273.15)) = 1.226 kg/m^3.

7. Calculate the air density when 18m/s wind is at 1std atmospheric pressure and 34°C?
a) 1.149 kg/m³
b) 1.9 kg/m³
c) 2.88 kg/m³
d) 5.89 kg/m³
View Answer

Answer: a
Explanation: For air, gas constant R = 287 J/kgK, 1atm = 1.01325 X 10⁵ Pa
Air density, ρ = P/RT = (1.01325 × 10⁵)/(287(34+273.15)) = 1.149 kg/m³.

8. What is the total power produced if the turbine diameter is 120m?
a) 0.277 KW
b) 1.224 KW
c) 4.28 KW
d) 0.89 KW
View Answer

Answer: a
Explanation: Total power P,
P = 0.245 X ($\pi D^2/4$)
= 0.245 X ($\pi (120)^2/4$)
= 0.277 KW.

9. What is the total power produced if the turbine diameter is 90m?
a) 0.155KW
b) 0.982 KW
c) 1.452 KW
d) 3.12 KW
View Answer

Answer: a
Explanation: Total power P,
P = 0.245 X ($\pi D^2/4$)
= 0.245 X ($\pi (90)^2/4$)
= 0.155KW.

This set of Energy Engineering Multiple Choice Questions & Answers (MCQs) focuses on "Wind Turbine Operation".

1. What is the inherent weakness of all wind machines?
a) Their efficiencies
b) Requires powerful winds to make fan rotate
c) Their dependency on the wind speed
d) Cannot be easily repaired
View Answer

Answer: c
Explanation: An inherent weakness of all wind machines are the strong dependence of the power produced on wheel diameter and wind speed, being proportional to turbine wheel area, i.e. to the square of its diameter and to the cube of wind velocity.

2. Why severe fluctuations in power are always undesirable in windmill?
a) Because they pose power oscillations problems
b) Damage of parts due to fluctuations
c) The efficiency of the plant will be reduced

d) Results in damage to the whole plant
View Answer

Answer: a

Explanation: Severe fluctuations in power are always undesirable, because they pose power oscillation problems on the grid and severe strains on the windmill hardware. From an economic point of view, a windmill is designed to produce a rated power output corresponding to maximum, or near maximum, prevailing wind velocity at a given site would generate low powers, with full capacity of the turbine and electric generator unused much of time.

3. Maintenance of constant output at all wind speeds above rating is called __________
a) Numeric rating scale
b) Tenancy
c) Flat Rating
d) TRP
View Answer

Answer: c

Explanation: More cost-effective design to a wind mill to produce rated power at less than the maximum prevailing wind velocity, using a smaller turbine and generator and to maintain a constant output at all wind speeds above rating. This is called flat rating.

4. A wind turbine designed too to come into operation at a minimum wind speed is called __________
a) Cut in velocity
b) Windward
c) Cut out velocity
d) Upwind location
View Answer

Answer: a

Explanation: Due to several loss in efficiency and power at low wind velocities, a wind turbine is designed to come into operation at a minimum wind speed called the cut in velocity. Thus the wind turbine operates with variable load over a narrow range between cut in.

5. Why is wind turbine designed to stop operation at cut out velocity?
a) To protect wheel against damage
b) To make a quick stop in emergencies
c) To improve the efficiency
d) In order to adjust the blades to wind direction
View Answer

Answer: a

Explanation: To protect the turbine wheel against damage at very high wind velocities, it is designed to stop operation (such as feathering the blades) at cut out velocity. Thus the wind turbine operates at rated velocities and at constant power between the rated and cut out velocities and ceases the operation above the cut out velocity.

6. The fraction of time during a given period that the turbine is actually on line is called?
a) Availability factor
b) Flat rating
c) Cut in velocity
d) Cut out velocity
View Answer

Answer: a

Explanation: The availability factor is defined as the fraction of time during a given period that the turbine is actually on line. The actual wind velocity at the propeller hub that determines the turbine power is usually higher.

7. Over load factor is also called as ______________
a) availability factor
b) plant operating factor
c) flat rating
d) cut out velocity
View Answer

Answer: a
Explanation: The overall load factor, also called the plant operating factor and the plant capacity factor is the ratio of the total energy generated during a given period of time to the total rated generation capacity during the same period.

8. How many of windmills are there?
a) 2
b) 3
c) 4
d) 5
View Answer

Answer: a
Explanation: There are two classes of windmill, horizontal axis and vertical axis. The vertical axis design was popular during the early development of the windmill. However, its inefficiency of operation let to the development of numerous horizontal axis designs.

9. Name the windmill which has four blades mounted on a central post.
a) Post mill
b) Smock mill
c) Tower mill
d) Fan mill
View Answer

Answer: a
Explanation: The post mill has blades mounted on a central post. The horizontal shaft of the blade is connected to a large break wheel. The break wheel interacts with a gear system, called the wallower, which rotates a central, vertical shaft. This motion can then be used to power water pumping or grain grinding activities.

10. Name the type of windmill which consists of a sloping, horizontally weather boarded or thatched tower.
a) Post mill
b) Smock mill
c) Tower mill
d) Fan mill
View Answer

Answer: b
Explanation: The smock mill is a type of windmill that consists of a sloping, horizontally weather boarded or thatched tower, usually with six or eight sides. It is topped with a roof or cap that rotates to bring the sails into the wind. It is similar to post mill. It is named so because of its appearance.

11. Which are further improvements on smock mill?
a) Post mill
b) Smock mill
c) Tower mill
d) Fan mill
View Answer

Answer: c

Explanation: Tower mills are further improvements on smock mills. They have a rotating cap and permanent body, but this body is made of brick or stone. This fact makes it possible for the towers to be rounded. A round structure of it allows for large and taller towers.

12. Which type of windmills are been used for primary purposes?
a) Post mill
b) Smock mill
c) Tower mill
d) Fan mill
View Answer

Answer: d

Explanation: The fan type windmill is specifically made for individuals. It is much smaller and used primarily for pumping water. It consists of a fixed tower (mast), a wheel and tail assembly (fan), a head assembly, and a pump.

This set of Energy Engineering Multiple Choice Questions & Answers (MCQs) focuses on "Horizontal Axis Wind Mill".

1. In which of the following, does machine rotor drives through a step up gear box?
a) Horizontal axis with two aerodynamic blades
b) Horizontal axis propeller type wind mill
c) Horizontal axis multi bladed type wind mill
d) Sail type wind mill
View Answer

Answer: a

Explanation: In horizontal axis with two aerodynamic type windmill the machine rotor drives through a step up gear box. The blade rotor is designed to orient downwind of the tower. The components are mounted on bed plate which is attached on a pintle at the top of the tower.

2. The rotor blades are continuously flexed by unsteady aerodynamic gravitational and inertia loads.
a) True
b) False
View Answer

Answer: a

Explanation: The rotor blades are continuously flexed by unsteady aerodynamic gravitational and inertia loads, when the machine is in operation. If the blades are made using metal, flexing reduces their fatigue life.

3. Which type of the following consists of single blade?
a) Horizontal axis with two aerodynamic blades
b) Horizontal axis propeller type wind mill
c) Horizontal axis multi bladed type wind mill
d) Sail type wind mill
View Answer

Answer: b

Explanation: Horizontal axis propeller type wind mill consists of a long blade mounted on a rigid hub, induction generator and gear box. If extremely long blades are mounted on rigid hub, large blade root bending moments occur due to tower shadow, gravity and sudden shifts in wind directions.

4. Which windmill blades are made by an array of wooden slats?
a) Horizontal axis with two aerodynamic blades

b) Horizontal axis propeller type wind mill
c) Horizontal axis multi bladed type wind mill
d) Horizontal axis wind mill Dutch type
View Answer

Answer: d
Explanation: Dutch type wind mill is one of the oldest wind mills in designs. The blade surfaces are made from an array of wooden slats which rotates at high wind speeds. These types of wind mill are cheap to build since the wood is made use of to build.

5. Which type of windmill blades are made out of sheet metal or aluminum?
a) Horizontal axis with two aerodynamic blades
b) Horizontal axis propeller type wind mill
c) Horizontal axis multi bladed type wind mill
d) Sail type wind mill
View Answer

Answer: c
Explanation: Horizontal axis multi blade windmill is made from sheet metal or aluminum. The rotors have high strength to weight ratios. They have good power coefficient, high starting torque and added advantages of simplicity and low cost.

6. Which type of wind mills blade are made out of cloth?
a) Horizontal axis with two aerodynamic blades
b) Horizontal axis propeller type wind mill
c) Horizontal axis multi bladed type wind mill
d) Sail type wind mill
View Answer

Answer: d
Explanation: The blade surface of sail type wind mill is made of cloth, nylon or plastics arranged as mast and pole or sail wings. There is also variation in the number of sails used. Sails are found in different designs, from primitive common sails to the advances patent sails.

7. Which type of windmill has better performance?
a) Vertical type wind mills
b) Darrieus type machines
c) Magnus effect rotor
d) Horizontal type windmills
View Answer

Answer: d
Explanation: The horizontal axis mills generally have netter performance. They have been used for various applications including electric power generation, and pumping water. The latter introduces some complexity into the design as the mechanical energy has to be transmitted over a distance.

8. What does TSR stand for in design consideration of wind mills?
a) Tip speed ratio
b) Torque-synchronous ratio
c) Tip suspension ratio
d) Temporary speed restriction
View Answer

Answer: a
Explanation: The tip speed ratio, X, or TSR for wind turbines is the ratio between the tangential speed of the tip of a blade and the actual speed of the wind. The tip speed ratio is related to efficiency, with the optimum varying with blade design.

9. With upto how many propellers can windmills are built?
a) 4
b) 2
c) 7
d) 6
View Answer

Answer: d
Explanation: Wind turbines have been built with upto six propellers type blades but two and three
bladed propellers are most common. A one bladed rotor with a balancing counter weight has some
advantages, including lower weight and cost and simpler controls, over the multi-bladed type.

10. Turbines with how many propellers are used in order to avoid vibrations?
a) 1
b) 2
c) 3
d) 4
View Answer

Answer: c
Explanation: Turbines with three blades are used to avoid vibrations that occur due to the turning
or yawing of the rotor in order to face in into the wind. However, this problem can be overcome by
controlling the yaw rate.

11. What type of cross sections does wind turbine blades have?
a) Penta hedral cross section
b) Air foiled type cross section
c) Radar cross section
d) Turbo cross section
View Answer

Answer: b
Explanation: Wind turbine blades have an air foiled type of cross section and a variable pitch.
They are slightly twisted from the outer tip to the root in order to reduce the tendency for the rotor
to stall. The blades can also have constant chord length.

12. What does WECS stands for?
a) Wind energy conversion system
b) Wind engine control system
c) Wind energy combined system
d) Wind engine comparison system
View Answer

Answer: a
Explanation: A wind energy conversion system (WECS), or wind energy harvester is a machine
that, powered by the energy of the wind, generates mechanical energy that can be used to directly
power machinery or to power an electrical generator for making electricity.

**This set of Energy Engineering Multiple Choice Questions & Answers
(MCQs) focuses on "Wind Turbine Operation".**

1. What is the inherent weakness of all wind machines?
a) Their efficiencies
b) Requires powerful winds to make fan rotate
c) Their dependency on the wind speed

d) Cannot be easily repaired
View Answer
Answer: c
Explanation: An inherent weakness of all wind machines are the strong dependence of the power produced on wheel diameter and wind speed, being proportional to turbine wheel area, i.e. to the square of its diameter and to the cube of wind velocity.

2. Why severe fluctuations in power are always undesirable in windmill?
a) Because they pose power oscillations problems
b) Damage of parts due to fluctuations
c) The efficiency of the plant will be reduced
d) Results in damage to the whole plant
View Answer
Answer: a
Explanation: Severe fluctuations in power are always undesirable, because they pose power oscillation problems on the grid and severe strains on the windmill hardware. From an economic point of view, a windmill is designed to produce a rated power output corresponding to maximum, or near maximum, prevailing wind velocity at a given site would generate low powers, with full capacity of the turbine and electric generator unused much of time.

3. Maintenance of constant output at all wind speeds above rating is called __________
a) Numeric rating scale
b) Tenancy
c) Flat Rating
d) TRP
View Answer
Answer: c
Explanation: More cost-effective design to a wind mill to produce rated power at less than the maximum prevailing wind velocity, using a smaller turbine and generator and to maintain a constant output at all wind speeds above rating. This is called flat rating.

4. A wind turbine designed too to come into operation at a minimum wind speed is called __________
a) Cut in velocity
b) Windward
c) Cut out velocity
d) Upwind location
View Answer
Answer: a
Explanation: Due to several loss in efficiency and power at low wind velocities, a wind turbine is designed to come into operation at a minimum wind speed called the cut in velocity. Thus the wind turbine operates with variable load over a narrow range between cut in.

5. Why is wind turbine designed to stop operation at cut out velocity?
a) To protect wheel against damage
b) To make a quick stop in emergencies
c) To improve the efficiency
d) In order to adjust the blades to wind direction
View Answer
Answer: a
Explanation: To protect the turbine wheel against damage at very high wind velocities, it is designed to stop operation (such as feathering the blades) at cut out velocity. Thus the wind turbine operates at rated velocities and at constant power between the rated and cut out velocities and ceases the operation above the cut out velocity.

6. The fraction of time during a given period that the turbine is actually on line is called?
a) Availability factor
b) Flat rating
c) Cut in velocity
d) Cut out velocity
View Answer

Answer: a
Explanation: The availability factor is defined as the fraction of time during a given period that the turbine is actually on line. The actual wind velocity at the propeller hub that determines the turbine power is usually higher.

7. Over load factor is also called as ______________
a) availability factor
b) plant operating factor
c) flat rating
d) cut out velocity
View Answer

Answer: a
Explanation: The overall load factor, also called the plant operating factor and the plant capacity factor is the ratio of the total energy generated during a given period of time to the total rated generation capacity during the same period.

8. How many of windmills are there?
a) 2
b) 3
c) 4
d) 5
View Answer

Answer: a
Explanation: There are two classes of windmill, horizontal axis and vertical axis. The vertical axis design was popular during the early development of the windmill. However, its inefficiency of operation let to the development of numerous horizontal axis designs.

9. Name the windmill which has four blades mounted on a central post.
a) Post mill
b) Smock mill
c) Tower mill
d) Fan mill
View Answer

Answer: a
Explanation: The post mill has blades mounted on a central post. The horizontal shaft of the blade is connected to a large break wheel. The break wheel interacts with a gear system, called the wallower, which rotates a central, vertical shaft. This motion can then be used to power water pumping or grain grinding activities.

10. Name the type of windmill which consists of a sloping, horizontally weather boarded or thatched tower.
a) Post mill
b) Smock mill
c) Tower mill
d) Fan mill
View Answer

Answer: b

Explanation: The smock mill is a type of windmill that consists of a sloping, horizontally weather boarded or thatched tower, usually with six or eight sides. It is topped with a roof or cap that rotates to bring the sails into the wind. It is similar to post mill. It is named so because of its appearance.

11. Which are further improvements on smock mill?
a) Post mill
b) Smock mill
c) Tower mill
d) Fan mill
View Answer

Answer: c

Explanation: Tower mills are further improvements on smock mills. They have a rotating cap and permanent body, but this body is made of brick or stone. This fact makes it possible for the towers to be rounded. A round structure of it allows for large and taller towers.

12. Which type of windmills are been used for primary purposes?
a) Post mill
b) Smock mill
c) Tower mill
d) Fan mill
View Answer

Answer: d

Explanation: The fan type windmill is specifically made for individuals. It is much smaller and used primarily for pumping water. It consists of a fixed tower (mast), a wheel and tail assembly (fan), a head assembly, and a pump.

This set of Energy Engineering Multiple Choice Questions & Answers (MCQs) focuses on "Horizontal Axis Wind Mill".

1. In which of the following, does machine rotor drives through a step up gear box?
a) Horizontal axis with two aerodynamic blades
b) Horizontal axis propeller type wind mill
c) Horizontal axis multi bladed type wind mill
d) Sail type wind mill
View Answer

Answer: a

Explanation: In horizontal axis with two aerodynamic type windmill the machine rotor drives through a step up gear box, The blade rotor is designed to orient downwind of the tower. The components are mounted on bed plate which is attached on a pintle at the top of the tower.

2. The rotor blades are continuously flexed by unsteady aerodynamic gravitational and inertia loads.
a) True
b) False
View Answer

Answer: a

Explanation: The rotor blades are continuously flexed by unsteady aerodynamic gravitational and inertia loads, when the machine is in operation. If the blades are made using metal, flexing reduces their fatigue life.

3. Which type of the following consists of single blade?
a) Horizontal axis with two aerodynamic blades

b) Horizontal axis propeller type wind mill
c) Horizontal axis multi bladed type wind mill
d) Sail type wind mill
View Answer

Answer: b
Explanation: Horizontal axis propeller type wind mill consists of a long blade mounted on a rigid hub, induction generator and gear box. If extremely long blades are mounted on rigid hub, large blade root bending moments occur due to tower shadow, gravity and sudden shifts in wind directions.

4. Which windmill blades are made by an array of wooden slats?
a) Horizontal axis with two aerodynamic blades
b) Horizontal axis propeller type wind mill
c) Horizontal axis multi bladed type wind mill
d) Horizontal axis wind mill Dutch type
View Answer

Answer: d
Explanation: Dutch type wind mill is one of the oldest wind mills in designs. The blade surfaces are made from an array of wooden slats which rotates at high wind speeds. These types of wind mill are cheap to build since the wood is made use of to build.

5. Which type of windmill blades are made out of sheet metal or aluminum?
a) Horizontal axis with two aerodynamic blades
b) Horizontal axis propeller type wind mill
c) Horizontal axis multi bladed type wind mill
d) Sail type wind mill
View Answer

Answer: c
Explanation: Horizontal axis multi blade windmill is made from sheet metal or aluminum. The rotors have high strength to weight ratios. They have good power coefficient, high starting torque and added advantages of simplicity and low cost.

6. Which type of wind mills blade are made out of cloth?
a) Horizontal axis with two aerodynamic blades
b) Horizontal axis propeller type wind mill
c) Horizontal axis multi bladed type wind mill
d) Sail type wind mill
View Answer

Answer: d
Explanation: The blade surface of sail type wind mill is made of cloth, nylon or plastics arranged as mast and pole or sail wings. There is also variation in the number of sails used. Sails are found in different designs, from primitive common sails to the advances patent sails.

7. Which type of windmill has better performance?
a) Vertical type wind mills
b) Darrieus type machines
c) Magnus effect rotor
d) Horizontal type windmills
View Answer

Answer: d
Explanation: The horizontal axis mills generally have netter performance. They have been used for various applications including electric power generation, and pumping water. The latter introduces some complexity into the design as the mechanical energy has to be transmitted over a distance.

8. What does TSR stand for in design consideration of wind mills?
a) Tip speed ratio
b) Torque-synchronous ratio
c) Tip suspension ratio
d) Temporary speed restriction
View Answer

Answer: a
Explanation: The tip speed ratio, X, or TSR for wind turbines is the ratio between the tangential speed of the tip of a blade and the actual speed of the wind. The tip speed ratio is related to efficiency, with the optimum varying with blade design.

9. With upto how many propellers can windmills are built?
a) 4
b) 2
c) 7
d) 6
View Answer

Answer: d
Explanation: Wind turbines have been built with upto six propellers type blades but two and three bladed propellers are most common. A one bladed rotor with a balancing counter weight has some advantages, including lower weight and cost and simpler controls, over the multi-bladed type.

10. Turbines with how many propellers are used in order to avoid vibrations?
a) 1
b) 2
c) 3
d) 4
View Answer

Answer: c
Explanation: Turbines with three blades are used to avoid vibrations that occur due to the turning or yawing of the rotor in order to face in into the wind. However, this problem can be overcome by controlling the yaw rate.

11. What type of cross sections does wind turbine blades have?
a) Penta hedral cross section
b) Air foiled type cross section
c) Radar cross section
d) Turbo cross section
View Answer

Answer: b
Explanation: Wind turbine blades have an air foiled type of cross section and a variable pitch. They are slightly twisted from the outer tip to the root in order to reduce the tendency for the rotor to stall. The blades can also have constant chord length.

12. What does WECS stands for?
a) Wind energy conversion system
b) Wind engine control system
c) Wind energy combined system
d) Wind engine comparison system
View Answer

Answer: a
Explanation: A wind energy conversion system (WECS), or wind energy harvester is a machine

that, powered by the energy of the wind, generates mechanical energy that can be used to directly power machinery or to power an electrical generator for making electricity.

This set of Energy Engineering Multiple Choice Questions & Answers (MCQs) focuses on "Vertical Axis Wind Mill".

1. In which wind measuring device a tubular piece of thin flexible fabric hanged vertically to determine direction?
a) Wind socks
b) Weather vane
c) Pin wheels
d) Anemometers
View Answer

Answer: a
Explanation: Wind sock is a very basic device that measure wind direction and provide a rough idea of the wind's intensity. A wind sock is a tubular piece of fabric or thin, flexible fabric attached to a pole. When there is no wind, the fabric hangs vertically from the attached pole.

2. A device which is used as device for showing direction wind as well used as a decorative purpose?
a) Wind socks
b) Weather vane
c) Pin wheels
d) Anemometers
View Answer

Answer: b
Explanation: A weather vane works similarly to wind sock. Instead of a tubular sock, the weather vane is made by placing a horizontal pole at the top of vertical pole. The poles are joined together so that the horizontal pole has a flattened, vertical end that reacts to wind.

3. Which is the wind direction showing device that spins perpendicularly?
a) Wind socks
b) Weather vane
c) Pin wheels
d) Anemometers
View Answer

Answer: c
Explanation: A pinwheel is a windmill-style turbine that spins perpendicularly to the wind affecting it. Like wind socks and weather vanes, a pinwheel can be attached to a rotating base. This allows the pinwheel to change direction with the wind, and it will spin facing into the oncoming wind.

4. Which is the device that measures wind direction and its intensity?
a) Wind socks
b) Weather vane
c) Pin wheels
d) Anemometers
View Answer

Answer: d
Explanation: An anemometer is any device that measures wind direction and intensity. It may be simple, such as the devices described above, or it may be a complex, computer-aided machine that measures and records wind patterns over time. More advanced anemometer machines are used to aid in professional weather reporting and air traffic control.

5. What units does the anemometer measure in?
a) Feet per minute
b) Liters per minute
c) Centimeters per minute
d) Meter per seconds
View Answer

Answer: a
Explanation: The anemometer measures in feet per minute, or FPM. The rotation is sensed by a magnetic or optical sensor that converts the signal to FPM measurement. An arrow on the vane head identifies the direction the airflow must travel through the vane to obtain proper measurements.

6. Which of the following type of turbine or the rotor requires relatively low velocity winds for operation?
a) Cup anemometer
b) Savonius rotor
c) Darrieus type rotor
d) Magnus effect rotor
View Answer

Answer: b
Explanation: Savonius rotor is a simple WEC system which woks like a cup anemometer. This type was invented by S.J. Savonius in the year 1920. It requires relatively low velocity winds for operation. It consists of two half cylinders facing opposite directions forming as S-shaped cross section.

7. Which type of axis does a Savonius Rotor has?
a) Horizontal axis
b) Mediolateral axis
c) Vertical axis
d) Lateral Axis
View Answer

Answer: c
Explanation: A Savonius wind energy conversion system has a vertical axis and hence eliminates the expensive power transmission system from the rotor to the axis. Since it is a vertical axis machine it does not matter much about the wind direction.

8. Why is Savonius rotor not suitable for installation?
a) Because of long drive shaft
b) Because of its low capacity motor
c) Because of its typical blade design
d) Due to the light material it is made of
View Answer

Answer: a
Explanation: Savonius rotor is not useful for very high installation because of long drive shaft problems. Bracing of the topmost bearing above the rotor of a very tall vertical axis machine is difficult requiring very long guy wires.

9. When was the Darrieus type machine invented?
a) 1925
b) 1932
c) 1929
d) 1948
View Answer

Answer: a

Explanation: Darrieus type machine was invented originally and patented in 1925 by G.J.M >
Darrieus, a French engineer. The Darrieus wind mill is a vertical axis machine that has the same
advantage of a modern rapidly rotating propeller type windmill, by use of an efficient airfoil,
effectively intercepts large area of wind with a small blade area.

10. What form of force acts on the blades of Darrieus machine?
a) Pure tension
b) Compression
c) Shear force
d) Air resistance force
View Answer

Answer: a

Explanation: Darrieus wind mill has two or three thin, curved blades with airfoil cross section and
constant chord length. Both ends of blades are attached to a vertical shaft. Thus the force in the
blade due to rotation is pure tension.

11. Which type of vertical wind machine has relatively low solidity and low starting torques?
a) Cup anemometer
b) Savonius rotor
c) Darrieus type rotor
d) Magnus effect rotor
View Answer

Answer: c

Explanation: Darrieus type rotors are lift devices characterized by curved blades with air foil cross
sections. They have relatively low solidity and low starting torques, but high tip to wind speeds
and therefore relatively high power outputs per given rotor weight and cost.

12. Which type of vertical wind machine consists of spinning cylinders?
a) Cup anemometer
b) Savonius rotor
c) Darrieus type rotor
d) Magnus effect rotor
View Answer

Answer: d

Explanation: Magnus effect rotor concept was first demonstrated by Magnus in 1912. It consists of
spinning cylinders. When cylinders spun in wind stream, translational forces are produced
perpendicular to the wind stream by the Magnus effect. Such a device can be used to propel ships
or land vehicles.

13. Aero turbine is the fraction of power in the wind through the swept area which is converted into
useful mechanical shaft power is called ______________
a) Coefficient of performance
b) Coefficient of variation
c) Coefficient of lift
d) Coefficient of spin
View Answer

Answer: a

Explanation: The coefficient of performance of an aero turbine is the fraction of power in the wind
through the swept area which is converted into useful mechanical shaft power. C_p for horizontal
axis wind machine has theoretical maximum value = 0.593.

1-The amount of energy available in the wind at any instant is proportional to ___ of the wind speed.

(A) Square root power of two

(B) Square root power of three

(C) Square power

(D) Cube power

2-Wind energy is harnessed as ______ energy with the help of windmill or turbine.
(A) Mechanical

(B) Solar

(C) Electrical

(D) Heat

3-Winds having following speed are suitable to operate wind turbines.
(A) 5 – 25m/s

(B) 10 – 35m/s

(C) 20 – 45m/s

(D) 30 – 55m/s

4-The following is (are) the classification of winds
(A) Global wind

(B) Local wind

(C) Both (A) and (B)

(D) None of the above

5-Global Cold wind move from
(A) Polar to equatorial region

(B) Equatorial to polar region

(C) Equatorial to oceanic region

(D) Oceanic to Equatorial region

6-Global Cold wind generated from Oceans moves to
(A) Mountains

(B) Equator

(C) Plain areas

(D) Poles

7-______ force is responsible for forcing the global winds towards westernly direction.
(A) Coriolis

(B) Gravitational

(C) Centripetal

(D) Centrifugal

8-Global winds towards westernly direction are known as
(A) Trade winds

(B) Western winds

(C) Eastern winds

(D) None of the above

9-Uneven heating occurs on land surface and water bodies are due to ______
(A) Air Currents

(B) Solar radiation

(C) Lunar eclipse

(D) None of the above

10-The following factor(s) affects the distribution of wind energy
(A) Mountain chains

(B) The hills, trees and buildings

(C) Frictional effect of the surface

(D) All of the above

11-The wind intensity can be described by
(A) Reynolds number

(B) Mach number

(C) Beaufort number

(D) Froude number

ANSWERS:
1-(D), 2-(A), 3-(A), 4-(C), 5-(A), 6-(C), 7-(A), 8-(A), 9-(B), 10-(D), 11-(C)

12-The wind speed is measured using an instrument called
(A) Pyranometer

(B) Manometer

(C) Anemometer

(D) Wind vane

13-The rate of change of wind speed with height is called
(A) Wind shear

(B) Wind rose

(C) Wind solidity

(D) None of the above

14-At gradient height the shear force is
(A) Zero

(B) Minimum

(C) Maximum

(D) None of the above

15-The gradient height is about _______ m from the ground.
(A) 500

(B) 1000

(C) 1500

(D) 2000

16-The atmosphere with uniform wind speed is called the _____ atmosphere
(A) Plain

(B) Surface

(C) Free

(D) Shear

17-Surface layer is the air layer considered from the height of local obstruction to a height of about
(A) 50m

(B) 100m

(C) 150m

(D) 200m

18-Air layer from 100m that extends up to the gradient height is known as
(A) Surface layer

(B) Ekman layer

(C) Boundary layer

(D) None of the above

19-Low solidity rotors use which of the following force for rotation
(A) Drag

(B) Lift

(C) Centrifugal

(D) Centripetal

20-The following is the tangential velocity of the blade due to the rotation of blade.
(A) Wind velocity

(B) Incident wind velocity

(C) Blade linear velocity

(D) Relative velocity

21-Turbines blades have _____ type cross section to extract energy from wind.
(A) Aerofoil

(B) Elliptical

(C) Rectangular

(D) All of the above

22-The Nacelle of windmill houses
(A) Gearbox

(B) Brakes

(C) Generator

(D) All of the above

ANSWERS:
12-(C), 13-(A), 14-(A), 15-(D), 16-(C), 17-(B), 18-(B), 19-(B), 20-(C), 21-(A), 22-(D)